Human Rights Interventions

Series Editors
Chiseche Mibenge
Stanford University
Stanford, CA, USA

Irene Hadiprayitno
Leiden University
Leiden, Zuid-Holland, The Netherlands

The traditional human rights frame creates a paradigm by which the duty bearer's (state) and rights holder's (civil society organizations) interests collide over the limits of enjoyment and enforcement. The series departs from the paradigm by centering peripheral yet powerful actors that agitate for intervention and influence in the (re)shaping of rights discourse in the midst of grave insecurities. The series privileges a call and response between theoretical inquiry and empirical investigation as contributors critically assess human rights interventions mediated by spatial, temporal, geopolitical and other dimensions. An interdisciplinary dialogue is key as the editors encourage multiple approaches such as law and society, political economy, historiography, legal ethnography, feminist security studies, and multi-media.

More information about this series at
http://www.palgrave.com/gp/series/15595

Jennifer K. Lobasz

Constructing Human Trafficking

Evangelicals, Feminists, and an Unexpected Alliance

Jennifer K. Lobasz
Department of Political Science
    and International Relations
University of Delaware
Wilmington, DE, USA

Human Rights Interventions
ISBN 978-3-319-91736-8   ISBN 978-3-319-91737-5   (eBook)
https://doi.org/10.1007/978-3-319-91737-5

Library of Congress Control Number: 2018948726

Cover image: M.Flynn/Alamy Stock Photo
Cover design: Laura de Grasse

This Palgrave Macmillan imprint is published by the registered company
Springer Nature Switzerland AG
The registered company address is: Gewerbestrasse 11, 6330 Cham, Switzerland

For Scott

ACKNOWLEDGEMENTS

This book represents the culmination of research I first began as a graduate student at the University of Minnesota. As such, I am grateful to the members of my doctoral examination committee, David Blaney, Lisa Disch, Ron Krebs, Joanna O'Connell, and Joan Tronto, and especially to my advisor, Raymond "Bud" Duvall. Their patience, guidance, generosity, and willingness to allow me to follow wherever the project led made a grueling intellectual journey more bearable, and brought me to a stronger and more interesting resting point for my argument than I could otherwise have discovered.

I have been blessed in my fellow travelers, and especially so with Joyce Heckman, Sheryl Lightfoot, Aaron Rapport, and Lauren Wilcox. My work and my life have been enriched by the Political Science community at the University of Minnesota as a whole, particularly the Minnesota International Relations Colloquium and the Political Theory Colloquium, as well as comrades Arjun Chowdhury, Ralitsa Donkova, Ross Edwards, Mark Hoffman, and Darrah McCracken. Without the department's administrative staff, including Judith Mitchell, Alexis Cuttance, and Beth Ethier, I would have surely drowned in paperwork. Thank you for helping me to navigate the bureaucratic jungle, lending me novels, and otherwise keeping me entertained on the fourteenth floor. I am also thankful for the assistance of Bianet Castellanos, Jude Higdon-Topaz, Dan Kelliher, Martin Sampson, David Samuels,

Dara Strolovitch, the Center for Writing, the College of Liberal Arts Office of Information Technology, and the Department of Gender, Women, and Sexuality Studies.

I am fortunate to belong to two extraordinary departments at the University of Delaware, the Department of Political Science & International Relations, and the Department of Women & Gender Studies. Both departments have been full of steadfast champions for whom I am grateful, including Neepa Acharya, Alice Ba, Gretchen Bauer, Pascha Bueno-Hansen, Bob Denemark, Kara Ellerby, Daniel Kinderman, Jennifer Naccarelli, Claire Rasmussen, David Redlawsk, Patricia Sloane-White, and Matthew Weinert. I am especially grateful to my graduate assistant, Samantha Kelley, and to Deborah Arnold, Daytonia Campbell, Lynn Corbett, Barbara Ford, and Nancy Koller for their care, diligence, and frequent assistance.

Patrick Thaddeus Jackson has my eternal gratitude for helping me to come into my own as a scholar and for lending an ear whenever I have needed one. I have learned so much from him, and appreciate everything but the introduction to Jefferson Starship.

John Picarelli deserves lengthy paragraphs of praise, but I hope that he will settle for a few heartfelt sentences. John has been my conduit to the anti-trafficking community in Washington, DC, and it is through him that I have been able to speak with Ambassador Luis CdeBaca of G/TIP, Amy O'Neill Richard of G/TIP, Barbara Stolz of GAO, and trafficking scholars too numerous to name. John and his wife Sandy have generously opened their home to me whenever I've needed a place to stay while in Washington, and John has done his utmost to keep my spirits up, my feet on the ground, a diet Pepsi or Landshark beer in my hand, and the songs of Jimmy Buffett and Bruce Springsteen in my ear. Mille grazie!

Laura Sjoberg also merits a special mention for continuing to champion my research, and for her strenuous efforts to further the feminist International Relations community. It would be impossible to pay Laura back, and so I can only promise to pay it forward. Thank you for everything, Laura.

In 2017, I was fortunate enough to be selected as the International Studies Association-Northeast's Book Circle honoree, and am grateful for the helpful feedback I received on the manuscript from Cara Daggett, Brett Ashley Leeds, Laura Sjoberg, Rosemary Skinko, and everyone who attended the Circle. I am likewise grateful to the Norwegian Institute for International Affairs and Sweden's University West for the opportunity to present and discuss selected chapters.

I have also benefited from those who have read my work, helped to sharpen my arguments, and served as sounding boards. Many thanks are due in particular to Janice Bially Mattern, Lene Hansen, Jennifer Heeg, and my cadre of writing partners: Becky Bolin Swanson, Siobhan Carroll, Emily Davis, Jennifer Moore, Ann Towns, and Kristine Węglarz. Thank you as well to Sandy Kacher, Glenn Hirsch, and Susan Epps for their wise counsel and numerous boxes of Kleenex.

Finally, and most importantly, I am grateful for the love and support of my family, and those who have become like my family. Thank you to my parents, my sisters and their families, Sherri Hubbard, the SutherlandPrice family, and especially to my husband, Scott.

CONTENTS

Acronyms

ASEAN	Association of Southeast Asian Nations
CATW	Coalition Against Trafficking in Women
CEDAW	Convention on the Elimination of All Forms of Discrimination Against Women
DHS	United States Department of Homeland Security
EU	European Union
G/TIP	Office to Monitor and Combat Trafficking in Persons
GAATW	Global Alliance Against Traffic in Women
GAO	United States Government Accountability Office
ICE	United States Immigration and Customs Enforcement
IGO	Intergovernmental organization
IHRLG	International Human Rights Law Group
IJM	International Justice Mission
ILO	International Labor Organization
INGO	International Non-governmental Organization
IOM	International Organization on Migration
NGO	Non-governmental Organization
OSCE	Organization for Security and Cooperation in Europe
TAN	Transnational Advocacy Network
THB	Trafficking in Human Beings
TIP	Trafficking in Persons
TVPA	Trafficking Victims Protection Act
UDHR	Universal Declaration of Human Rights
UN	United Nations
UNESCO	United Nations Educational, Scientific and Cultural Organization
UNICEF	United Nations Children's Fund

LIST OF TABLES

CHAPTER 1

Trafficking Is Problematic

In September of 2013, I traveled to Trollhättan, Sweden to deliver a talk on human trafficking scholarship at the University West Center for Studies of Diversity, Equality, and Integration.[1] I had planned to speak primarily about intra-feminist debates surrounding human trafficking, and how questions surrounding prostitution, or sex work, had led feminist activists down strikingly different advocacy paths. The question-and-answer period afterwards, however, didn't get that far. Instead, I was bemused to hear, the Swedes insisted I return to my opening remarks concerning the US government's definition of human trafficking. Could it really be true, they asked, that the US definition didn't privilege movement and migration? That movement was not even required?

Yes. In striking contrast to Europe, where movement and migration are considered an essential component of the meaning of human trafficking, a person in the United States can be considered a victim of trafficking without ever leaving the street on which they live.[2] While there are a number of reasons for this difference, in this book, I suggest that the

---

[1] Jennifer K. Lobasz, "Trafficking Scholarship, World-Traveling, and Loving Perception" (Trollhättan, Sweden: Center for Studies of Diversity, Equality and Integration, University West, 2013).

[2] United States Department of State, "What Is Modern Slavery?" Office to Monitor and Combat Trafficking in Persons, accessed September 29, 2009, https://www.state.gov/j/tip/what/.

© The Author(s) 2019

J. K. Lobasz, *Constructing Human Trafficking*, Human Rights Interventions, https://doi.org/10.1007/978-3-319-91737-5_1

primary explanation has to do with the political environment. In contrast to Europe, where the issue of human trafficking arose in the context of European integration and concerns about economic migration from the East,[3] trafficking gained a place on the US political agenda by virtue of feminist and faith-based activism. For these self-described "abolitionists," human trafficking is, first and foremost, about the prostitution of women and children. From this abolitionist perspective, migration might very well be a risk factor, but domestic prostitutes are no less victimized.

I open with this story to suggest that, United Nations protocols and regional agreements notwithstanding, conceptualizations of human trafficking are less clear-cut and universally accepted than commonly believed. All too often, discussions of trafficking occur in which participants rely on different, or even incompatible, definitions of the issue, but fail to recognize that they are talking about very different things. The result is poor research, poor policies, and poor outcomes for people who are abused and exploited.

In this chapter, I establish that human trafficking is a contested concept—that its meaning is neither straightforward nor unproblematic, and that constructions of trafficking reflect constellations of competing interests and values. The chapter ties the poor quality of quantitative data on human trafficking to its conceptual fluidity and contentious politics, and then goes on to explain why there is no technical or apolitical solution to this problem. Next, it provides an overview of the book's aims and arguments, and a justification for the US case. Finally, the chapter introduces my methodology and research design, and concludes with a preview of the plan for the book.

Constructing the Problems of "Human Trafficking"

Few today would dare question the existence of a global human trafficking problem.[4] Over the past two decades, human trafficking has come to be seen as a growing threat to increasingly vulnerable state borders and

---

[3] Jennifer K. Lobasz, "Beyond Border Security: Feminist Approaches to Human Trafficking," *Security Studies* 18, no. 2 (2009): 327.

[4] Or, as David Hodge puts it, "It is important to emphasize [...] that *no one* questions the existence of the problem." David R. Hodge, "Sexual Trafficking in the United States: A Domestic Problem with Transnational Dimensions," *Social Work* 53, no. 2 (2008): 144. Emphasis added.

marginalized populations. Speaking before the UN General Assembly in 2003, US President George W. Bush called attention to a humanitarian crisis in which "Each year an estimated 800,000 to 900,000 human beings are bought, sold or forced across the world's borders."[5] Bush continued,

> Those who create these victims and profit from their suffering must be severely punished. Those who patronize this industry debase themselves and deepen the misery of others. And governments that tolerate this trade are tolerating a form of slavery.[6]

The president's words echoed the position that the UN itself had taken three years prior when it approved the Protocol to Prevent, Suppress and Punish Trafficking in Persons, Especially Women and Children, Supplementing the United Nations Convention Against Transnational Organized Crime.[7] Likewise, there are at least 15 other major intergovernmental organizations (IGOs) with significant counter-trafficking efforts, including the International Labor Organization (ILO), the International Organization on Migration (IOM), the Organization for Security and Cooperation in Europe (OSCE), the European Union (EU), the Organization of American States (OAS), the Association of Southeast Asian Nations (ASEAN), and the World Bank.[8] As human trafficking "gained policy recognition and financial resources were mobilized, many more players entered the increasingly competitive field of non-governmental organizations (NGOs) and international non-governmental organizations (INGOs) activity."[9] Indeed, millions of dollars have

---

[5] George W. Bush, "Speech before the United Nations, General Assembly in New York," accessed September 29, 2009, http://www.presidentialrhetoric.com/speeches/09.23.03.html.

[6] Ibid.

[7] United Nations General Assembly, "Protocol to Prevent, Suppress and Punish Trafficking in Persons, Especially Women and Children, Supplementing the United Nations Convention against Transnational Organized Crime," accessed September 29, 2009, http://www.unhcr.org/refworld/docid/4720706c0.html.

[8] Government Accountability Office, "Human Trafficking: Better Data, Strategy, and Reporting Needed to Enhance U.S. Antitrafficking Efforts Abroad," (2006): 37–39.

[9] Liz Kelly, "'You Can Find Anything You Want': A Critical Reflection on Research on Trafficking in Persons within and into Europe," *International Migration* 43, no. 1/2 (2005): 236.

been routed through civil society by individual states and IGOs to support the "3P" framework of *prevention, protection,* and *prosecution* first articulated in 1998 by US President Bill Clinton.

Yet, despite the tremendous amount of resources that have been devoted to anti-trafficking, the very meaning of "human trafficking" remains heatedly contested. Anti-trafficking discourses link disparate practices and persons in often inconsistent or contradictory ways, and widespread disagreement remains as to the "real" nature of trafficking and how it differs from other forms of irregular migration, commercial sexual activity, exploitative labor, and slavery.[10] Given the consensus that the problem of human trafficking is significant and compels counter-trafficking action, but that there is sharp disagreement about the nature of the problem (what trafficking *is* as a problem), it is crucial that we ask how and to what effect "human trafficking" is constructed through competing anti-trafficking discourses.

Disputes over meaning are highly significant: they set the terms for how scholars, activists, legislators, and citizens conceive of the problem and its victims, perpetrators, causes, and solutions. Within the United States—a country with enormous yet under-recognized influence on counter-trafficking interventions pursued worldwide—human trafficking has largely been conceptualized in *abolitionist* terms. From an abolitionist perspective, terms such as "human trafficking" and "trafficking in persons" are euphemisms, almost offensive in their failure to convey the true problem at hand: the evil of slavery. Committed to a fight against "modern-day slavery," the neo-abolitionists represent a powerful, if unexpected, political alliance between radical feminists and evangelical Christians that has been highly successful in shaping counter-trafficking policy and practice at home and abroad. How did this alliance come to be? What made agreement between what are otherwise staunch opponents possible? What are the implications for how trafficking is conceived and acted upon, in the United States and abroad? These are the central questions of this book.

As the twenty-first century waned, "there was no comprehensive international definition of trafficking whose basic elements were

---

[10]Claudia Aradau, *Rethinking Trafficking in Women: Politics Out of Security* (New York: Palgrave Macmillan, 2008).

acceptable to State parties and key stakeholders."[11] In the words of Radhika Coomaraswamy, the UN's Special Rapporteur on Violence against Women:

> At present there is no internationally agreed definition of trafficking. The term "trafficking" is used by different actors to describe activities that range from voluntary, facilitated migration, to the exploitation of prostitution, to the movement of persons through the threat or use of force, coercion, violence, etc. for certain exploitative purposes. Increasingly, it has been recognized that historical characterizations of trafficking are outdated, ill-defined and non-responsive to the current realities of the movement of and trade in people and to the nature and extent of the abuses inherent in and incidental to trafficking.[12]

The Protocol to Prevent, Suppress and Punish Trafficking in Persons, Especially Women and Children—adopted by the UN General Assembly on November 15, 2000—was widely expected to settle vexing definitional issues.[13] The Protocol defines "trafficking in persons" as

> the recruitment, transportation, transfer, harboring or receipt of persons, by means of the threat or use of force or other forms of coercion, of abduction, of fraud, of deception, of the abuse of power or of a position of vulnerability or of the giving or receiving of payments or benefits to achieve the consent of a person having control over another person, for the purpose of exploitation. Exploitation shall include, at a minimum, the exploitation of the prostitution of others or other forms of sexual

[11] Jyoti Sanghera, "Unpacking the Trafficking Discourse," in *Trafficking and Prostitution Reconsidered: New Perspectives on Migration, Sex Work and Human Rights*, ed. Kamala Kempadoo, Jyoti Sanghera, and Bandana Pattanaik (Boulder: Paradigm Publishers, 2005), 10. See also Joel Quirk, "Trafficked into Slavery," *Journal of Human Rights* 6 (2007): 191.

[12] Radhika Coomaraswamy, "Report of the Special Rapporteur on Violence against Women: Trafficking in Women, Women's Migration and Violence against Women" (Geneva: Economic and Social Council, 2000), 8.

[13] The protocol supplements the United Nations Convention Against Transnational Organized Crime, also known as the Palermo Convention after the Italian city in which it was signed. Within the anti-trafficking community, the Protocol to Prevent, Suppress and Punish Trafficking in Persons, Especially Women and Children may be referred to as the Palermo Protocol or the Trafficking Protocol. The Trafficking Protocol entered into force on December 25, 2003.

exploitation, forced labor or services, slavery or practices similar to slavery, servitude or the removal of organs.[14]

Yet, for all of the significance attributed to the Trafficking Protocol,[15] "this new definition has not resolved the problem of what precisely is meant by the term 'trafficking,' and what should be the focus of studies on the subject."[16]

Human trafficking has been said to encompass a variety of illicit activities incorporating the loss of free will, appropriation of labor power, and violence or threat of violence. Researchers and activists are prone to reciting a laundry list of practices that may be identified as forms of trafficking, including debt bondage, forced labor, forced marriage, sexual exploitation, serfdom, and slavery. Kevin Bales—widely recognized as a leading expert on human trafficking and contemporary forms of slavery—provides a typical example:

> The types of work that trafficking victims are generally forced to do fall into several broad categories: prostitution, domestic service, agricultural work, work in small factories and workshops, mining, land clearance, selling in the market, and begging.[17]

Yet, the "several broad categories" that Bales identifies are rarely treated as problems of equal importance, nor is it self-evident that such all such practices should be linked as different manifestations of a single phenomenon. The laundry-list method of aggregating types of trafficking fails to convey the fierce disagreements surrounding efforts to fix the

---

[14] United Nations General Assembly.

[15] Quirk describes the Trafficking Protocol definition as "widely acknowledged as a fundamental benchmark." Quirk, 193. See also Asif Efrat, "Global Efforts against Human Trafficking: The Misguided Conflation of Sex, Labor, and Organ Trafficking," *International Studies Perspectives* 17, no. 1 (2016): 35.

[16] Frank Laczko, "Data and Research on Human Trafficking," *International Migration* 43, no. 1–2 (2005): 10. See also Guri Tyldum and Anette Brunovskis, "Describing the Unobserved: Methodological Challenges in Empirical Studies on Human Trafficking," ibid., no. 1/2: 20; Julia O'Connell Davidson and Bridget Anderson, "The Trouble with 'Trafficking'," in *Trafficking and Women's Rights*, ed. Christien L. van der Anker and Jeroen Doomernik (Houndsmills, Basingstoke, Hampshire: Palgrave Macmillan, 2006), 17.

[17] Kevin Bales, *Understanding Global Slavery* (Berkeley: University of California Press, 2005), 146.

meaning of what remains a contested concept.[18] I argue that decisions as to whether to categorize instances of forced begging, prostitution, the sale of human organs, or exploitative labor practices as, specifically, "human trafficking" reflect political judgments rather than objective classifications.

No Numbers Are Good Numbers

Quantitative measures of human trafficking are notoriously unreliable. Researchers complain of "slippery statistics ridden with methodological problems,"[19] "limited case studies,"[20] and data that are "fragmentary, heterogeneous, difficult to acquire, uncorrelated and often outdated."[21] Kempadoo goes as far as to argue that "many of the claims made about trafficking are unsubstantiated and undocumented, and are based on sensationalist reports, hyperbole, and conceptual confusions."[22] Declaring statistics of global trafficking flows to be "questionable,"[23] a 2006 US Government Accountability Office (GAO) report goes on to describe country-specific data as "generally not available, reliable or

---

[18] See Alisdair MacIntyre, "The Essential Contestability of Some Social Concepts," *Ethics* 84, no. 1 (1973).

[19] Elzbieta M. Gozdziak and Elizabeth A. Collett, "Research on Human Trafficking in North America: A Review of Literature," *International Migration* 43, no. 1–2 (2005): 107.

[20] Amy O'Neill Richard, "International Trafficking in Women to the United States: A Contemporary Manifestation of Slavery and Organized Crime," in *DCI Exceptional Intelligence Analyst Program* (Washington: Center for the Study of Intelligence, 2000), 3.

[21] Ernesto U. Savona and Sonia Stefanizzi, "Introduction," in *Measuring Human Trafficking: Complexities and Pitfalls*, ed. Ernesto U. Savona and Sonia Stefanizzi (New York: Springer, 2007), 2. See also Kauko Aromaa, "Trafficking in Human Beings: Uniform Definitions for Better Measuring and for Effective Counter-Measures," ibid., ed. Ernesto Savona and Sonia Stefanizzi (New York: Springer); Gillian Wylie, *The International Politics of Human Trafficking* (Basingstoke: Palgrave Macmillan, 2016).

[22] Kamala Kempadoo, "From Moral Panic to Social Justice: Changing Perspectives on Trafficking," in *Trafficking and Prostitution Reconsidered: New Perspectives on Migration, Sex Work and Human Rights*, ed. Kamala Kempadoo, Jyoti Sanghera, and Bandana Pattanaik (Boulder: Paradigm Publishers, 2005), xix.

[23] Government Accountability Office, "Human Trafficking: Better Data, Strategy, and Reporting Needed to Enhance U.S. Antitrafficking Efforts Abroad," (2006), 10.

comparable."[24] Yet even as they recognize these issues, Ernesto Savona and Sonia Stefanizzi find it "obvious that trafficking in human beings constitutes a desperate problem on a global scale."[25] They emphasize that "all experts confirm that the volume of trafficking has never been so great, nor has it ever increased at such a dizzying rate."[26]

This section will demonstrate, however, that even broad generalizations regarding the magnitude and rate of human trafficking are far from universally shared.

In 2004, the Office of HIV/AIDS and Trafficking Projects for UNESCO Bangkok released a chart to illustrate the dramatic variance among worldwide estimates of human trafficking.[27] The chart demonstrated that estimates of trafficking diverge not only in magnitude, but in the population being counted. One statistic stands out in particular. At different points in time over the past two decades, the SE Asian Women's Conference, the Protection Project, UNICEF, the IOM, Terre des Hommes, and the US government have all stated that approximately two million people are trafficked each year. Curiously, the population of two million has variously been characterized as composed of "trafficked people" (IOM 2002; US Government 1998, 2001, 2002), "trafficked women" (SE Asian Women's Conference 1991; US Government 1998), "trafficked children" (Protection Project 2001; Terres des Hommes 2001, 2002), and "trafficked women and children" (UNICEF 2001). The repetition and shifting descriptions of trafficked persons suggest that either the victimized populations are strikingly uniform, which is unlikely, or that organizations rely upon their own beliefs about what trafficking means and who is affected, and then attach quantitative measures to these categories without independent validation.

The complexities associated with the empirical study of human trafficking reflect conceptual, practical, and political quandaries. First, the

---

[24] Ibid. Laczko and Gramegna concur, noting "it is still common in many countries to mingle data relating to trafficking, smuggling, and irregular migration. Frank Laczko and Marco A. Gramegna, "Developing Better Indicators of Human Trafficking," *Brown Journal of World Affairs* 10, no. 1 (2003): 181.

[25] Savona and Stefanizzi, 2.

[26] Ibid.

[27] UNESCO Trafficking Project, "Worldwide Trafficking Estimates by Organizations," United Nations Educational, Scientific and Cultural Organization, accessed September 29, 2009, http://www.unescobkk.org/index.php?id=1963.

conflicting characterizations of trafficked persons illustrated above attest to continued conceptual confusion. Guri Tyldum and Anette Brunovskis concur that "in order to count the number of victims, or generally develop our understanding of trafficking in persons, we need to, first of all, define what constitutes trafficking and what does not." Indeed, the plethora of competing and conflicting conceptualizations of human trafficking provokes palpable anxiety among many charged with measuring and addressing the phenomenon. David Feingold voices the widespread concern that "the lack of clear agreement among the agencies of various governments and among researchers, as well as NGOs, inhibits the development of comparable data at the most basic level."[28] In a seemingly endless stream of international conferences and publications, trafficking researchers have sought to address these concerns with various proposals to establish a single, concrete definition of human trafficking amenable to deployment in readily comparable cross-national case studies. In short, "the goal of much of the literature on trafficking is to understand the 'real' nature of trafficking, thus being able to propose adequate solutions for dealing with this problem."[29]

Second, as a practical matter, attempts to actually gather trafficking data entail their own difficulties. Tyldum and Brunovskis argue that the most challenging aspect of human trafficking research is that it requires measuring a hidden population, "i.e., a group of individuals for whom the size and boundaries are unknown, and for whom no sampling frame exists."[30] In order to avoid detection, traffickers reportedly exploit victims' language and cultural barriers, mistrust of law enforcement, and fear of deportation. Trafficking victims may also face periodic relocation, furthering their isolation. Each of these factors keeping trafficked persons isolated and exploited also "limits the amount of data available on victims and makes it difficult to estimate the number of

---

[28] David A. Feingold, "Trafficking in Numbers: The Social Construction of Human Trafficking Data," in *Sex, Drugs, and Body Counts: The Politics of Numbers in Global Crime and Conflict*, ed. Peter Andreas and Kelly M. Greenhill (Ithaca, NY: Cornell University Press, 2010), 66.

[29] Aradau, 19.

[30] Tyldum and Brunovskis, 18. See also Aradau, 12; Free the Slaves and the Human Rights Center, "Hidden Slaves: Forced Labor in the US," University of California, Berkeley, accessed September 29, 2009, http://www.hrcberkeley.org/download/hidden-slaves_report.pdf; Government Accountability Office, 15; O'Neill Richard, 3.

unreported victims."[31] Laczko suggests that, given these problems, most trafficking research relies on "relatively small samples of survivors, usually identified by law enforcement agencies or persons assisted by NGOs or international organizations."[32]

Third, organizations and bureaucracies pose their own challenges for data gatherers. In a widely disseminated monograph published under the auspices of the Director of Central Intelligence, US State Department analyst Amy O'Neill Richard reports that information sharing and coordination in the United States is difficult both within and across federal, regional, state, and local agencies. "Even within the Department of Justice, information is not always shared among the concerned offices."[33] Laczko and Gramegna find an additional problem: that "existing data are frequently program-specific [...] Each agency gathers data according to its own needs, and, as a result, the same individual may appear in data produced by more than one organization."[34]

To further complicate the task of trafficking scholars, the trafficking literature is notable for muddying traditional divisions between academic and policy circles. Even putatively academic research is often funded by or conducted under the auspices of governments or IGOs.[35] For Laczko, "One of the strengths of trafficking research is its action-oriented approach, with studies often designed to prepare the ground for counter-trafficking interventions."[36] Others count the close relationship between scholarship and policy as a disadvantage, suggesting that trafficking research is unhealthily driven by the immediate policy needs and political commitments of researchers and "does not necessarily ensure a deepening of the knowledge base."[37]

---

[31] Government Accountability Office, 15.

[32] Laczko, 8.

[33] O'Neill Richard, 31.

[34] Laczko and Gramegna, 184.

[35] Aradau, 20.

[36] Laczko, 8.

[37] Liz Kelly, "'You Can Find Anything You Want': A Critical Reflection on Research on Trafficking in Persons within and into Europe," ibid., no. 1/2: 236.

Concerns regarding the politicization of trafficking research—i.e., that it may be "formulated to fit other agendas"[38]—are widely shared.[39] Some see this as the consequence of relying primarily on statistics "developed by NGOs and agencies for the purposes of advocacy, rather than the result of serious research."[40] In addition to the needs of advocacy organizations to garner public attention and support for their cause, the ideological bent of various organizations conducting and promoting trafficking research is also recognized as a factor contributing to "politicized" data. Tyldum and Brunovskis, for example, conclude that "a substantial number of publications on trafficking for sexual exploitation are influenced by political debates surrounding these topics."[41]

Certainly, it makes sense to be wary of ideologically-driven research undertaken to support a priori conclusions. I contend that the problem with the bulk of such criticism, however, lies in its reinforcement of a faulty assumption: that the subject—and subjects—of human trafficking exist independently from the political. Put differently, critics share with their targets the pervasive belief that (1) human trafficking has an essential form, even if that form has yet to be properly specified, and (2) the essence of human trafficking is or can be intelligible apart from the power relations in which it is embedded. Consider the following representative statement from an article in *Human Rights Quarterly*:

> Unfortunately, the actors responsible for putting the fight against trafficking on the public agenda—the United States, the donor/NGO community, and the media—have at the same time, wittingly or unwittingly, shaped and sometimes distorted our understandings of the problem and the efforts needed to address it.[42]

It seems natural to sympathize with complaints that the US federal government, NGOs, and the media are responsible for "distorting" the public's understanding of an issue. One might even consider it a scholar's

---

[38] Galma Jahic and James O. Finckenauer, "Representations and Misrepresentations of Human Trafficking," *Trends in Organized Crime* 8, no. 3 (2005): 25.

[39] See also Feingold; David E. Guinn, "Defining the Problem of Trafficking: The Interplay of U.S. Law, Donor, and Ngo Engagement and the Local Context in Latin America," *Human Rights Quarterly* 30, no. 1 (2008); Tyldum and Brunovskis.

[40] Feingold, 64.

[41] Tyldum and Brunovskis, 18.

[42] Guinn, 121.

duty to criticize instances of "speculation, distortion, and sometimes even outright fabrication."[43] Yet, there is an important distinction to be drawn between actors who shape "our understandings of the problem"[44] and those who fabricate or misrepresent data. While the latter may reflect unethical or inept research practices, some version of the former is inescapable. As such, my quarrel lies not with those who criticize particular representations of trafficking, but with those whose criticism implies the existence of an objective "human trafficking problem" able to be understood absent mediation or representation. Recognition of significant and potentially insurmountable weaknesses in the literature has coincided, curiously enough, with a veritable multidisciplinary boom in human trafficking research.[45] The proliferation of anti-trafficking initiatives continues likewise, conceptual ambiguity and unreliable data notwithstanding.

THE POLITICS OF MEANING

Begin with the premise, for which there is no dispute among reasonable people, that commercial sex trafficking is a horrible crime and society has an interest in protecting its victims and punishing its perpetrators.

—Glenda Holste[46]

As newspaper reporter Glenda Holste's words suggest, anti-trafficking interventions are represented as inarguably legitimate enterprises. Advocates place the justification for anti-trafficking efforts above politics, as the self-evident morally correct choice. Holste's invocation of "reasonable people" among whom "there is no dispute"[47] illustrates one effect of this strategy: critique is foreclosed through narrowing the limits of acceptable speech.[48] After all, the conventional wisdom seems to dictate, who among us would support human trafficking? Who, today, is in favor of slavery?

---

[43] Peter Andreas, "The Politics of Measuring Illicit Flows and Policy Effectiveness," in *Sex, Drugs, and Body Counts: The Politics of Numbers in Global Crime and Conflict*, ed. Peter Andreas and Kelly M. Greenhill (Ithaca, NY: Cornell University Press, 2010), 23.

[44] Guinn, 121.

[45] See Tyldum and Brunovskis, 17; Savona and Stefanizzi; Laczko.

[46] Glenda Holste, "Bipartisan Efforts Are Propelling Violence against Women Act," *The Saint Paul Pioneer Press*, October 9, 2000.

[47] Ibid.

[48] See Patrick Thaddeus Jackson, "Defending the West: Occidentalism and the Formation of Nato," *Journal of Political Philosophy* 11, no. 3 (2003): 238.

The productive power of anti-trafficking discourses continues to be rendered invisible in research, advocacy, and policy. In contrast, I argue that anti-trafficking discourses are intrinsically political—i.e., sites of power[49] that establish the conditions of possibility for subjects and practices.[50] Discourses represent subjects as embodying specific characteristics, and legitimate specific sets of practices while rendering others undesirable, unethical, or unthinkable. Anti-trafficking discourses are productive of regimes of knowledge that set boundaries for how scholars, activists, legislators, and citizens conceive of human trafficking—they establish what trafficking is and who counts as trafficked, and create narratives that explain how trafficking has become a problem and what should be done to fix it.[51] Consequently, naturalizing[52] human trafficking and its subjects leads us to miss important sites of power: the fixing and policing of conceptual boundaries; the production of subjects with given interests and identities and the concomitant production of difference; the setting of conditions of possibility on a much broader scale than is currently recognized.[53]

In claiming that anti-trafficking is inextricable from relations of power, I emphasize that this is the case regardless of whether accounts feature sensationalist representations of unwitting virgins coerced into sexual slavery or dispassionate analyses of labor migration networks and occupational safety regulations. In chapters three through five I show that

[49] By "power," I mean "the production, in and through social relations, of effects that shape the capacities of actors to determine their own circumstances and fate." Michael N. Barnett and Raymond Duvall, "Power in Global Governance," in *Power in Global Governance*, ed. Michael Barnett and Raymond Duvall (Cambridge: Cambridge University Press, 2005), 3.

[50] Michel Foucault, *The Archaeology of Knowledge and the Discourse on Language*, trans. A.M. Sheridan Smith (New York: Pantheon Books, 1972), 44–46.

[51] "The question of who should be protected, from what and why are central and necessary to the determination of how they should be protected." Ali Miller and Alison N. Stewart, "Report from the Roundtable on the Meaning of 'Trafficking in Persons': A Human Rights Perspective," *Women's Rights Law Reporter* 20, no. 1 (1998): 13.

[52] Borrowing from Weldes, et al. I hold that human trafficking and its subjects "are naturalized in the sense that they are treated as facts that…can be taken for granted." Jutta Weldes et al., "Introduction: Constructing Insecurity," in *Cultures of Insecurity: States, Communities and the Production of Danger* (Minneapolis, MN: University of Minnesota Press, 1999), 9.

[53] Jo Doezema, "Now You See Her, Now You Don't: Sex Workers at the Un Trafficking Protocol Negotiation," *Social & Legal Studies* 14, no. 1 (2005): 64.

efforts to demarcate the conceptual boundaries of human trafficking occur on terrain indelibly shaped by conflicting constellations of values. As Ethan Nadelmann recognizes, one impetus behind the creation of a global prohibition regime is "to give force and symbolic representation to the moral values, beliefs, and prejudices of those who make the laws."[54] In short, human trafficking should not be seen as simply a technical problem to be solved with an array of policies that will work if only states and civil society can properly analyze the problem and apply appropriate solutions. Rather, human trafficking is continually produced as a problem distinct from others through an array of sometimes complementary and sometimes conflicting discourses concerning gender, immigration, human rights, security, identity, sex, labor, and markets, none of which are themselves fully internally consistent.[55]

The relevance of this research goes beyond the specific issue(s) of human trafficking, encompassing the production of people and practices as "problematic" and in need of governance more generally. As Jutta Weldes has argued, "The language of policymaking [...] does not simply reflect 'real' policy issues and problems; instead, it actively produces the issues with which policymakers deal and the specific problems that they confront."[56] Drawing upon the work of critical constructivist, poststructuralist, and feminist international relations scholars, I emphasize the inescapably political nature of that which is identified as a problem to be solved, an appropriate object of governance.

Aims and Arguments

In this book, I start from the premise that human trafficking[57] is better understood as a contested concept or an unstable category than as an objectively given problem. Seen as such, the meaning of human

---

[54] Ethan A. Nadelmann, "Global Prohibition Regimes: The Evolution of Norms in International Society," *International Organization* 44, no. 4 (1990): 481.

[55] On internal tensions and the impossibility of discursive closure, see Stuart Hall, "Signification, Representation, Ideology: Althusser and the Post-Structuralist Debates," *Critical Studies in Mass Communication* 2, no. 2 (1985); Foucault, 45.

[56] Jutta Weldes, "Bureaucratic Politics: A Critical Constructivist Assessment," *Mershon International Studies Review* 42, no. 2 (1998).

[57] Human trafficking is also referred to as trafficking in persons (TIP), trafficking in human beings (THB), and modern-day slavery.

trafficking is understood to be constructed rather than inherent, and is inseparable from the political context through which it is produced. Moreover, anti-trafficking interventions are likely to be portrayed by both advocates and scholars as apolitical or nonpartisan responses to a clear and pressing problem. In contrast, I contend that efforts to demarcate the conceptual boundaries of human trafficking occur on terrain indelibly shaped by conflicting constellations of values, particularly in regard to questions of gender, racial, and economic justice. We must reject the assumption that human trafficking is a single, discrete problem or set of phenomena in favor of a focus on multiple practices linked in sometimes inconsistent or contradictory ways through anti-trafficking discourse.

Constructions of "human trafficking" emerge from the highly interconnected realms of anti-trafficking policy and human trafficking research. I investigate these realms through a discourse analysis of anti-trafficking advocacy, policy, and scholarship in the United States from the late 1970s to the passage of the Trafficking Victims Protection Act (TVPA) in 2000. This research takes the form of a genealogy of the neo-abolitionist discourses dominant within US anti-trafficking politics during this time period. Exploration of the US context is crucial for understanding the various efforts directed toward the global governance of human trafficking because of its enormous influence on global anti-trafficking interventions through NGO funding and the shaping of international and regional treaties. To date, however, scholars have focused primarily on the European Union and parts of Asia, paying relatively little attention to the United States as a case despite its disproportionate influence on the global governance of human trafficking. This study, therefore, addresses a not merely large but also highly significant empirical gap in the trafficking literature.

A number of the US-based nongovernmental actors highlighted in my research, such as the Coalition Against Trafficking in Women (CATW) and the International Justice Mission (IJM), trumpet their transnational membership and programming. Yet although anti-trafficking discourses overlap and interact at the global level, each discourse represents its own specific history that is shaped by differing political imperatives and configurations of discursive resources at the local/state level. Geopolitical concerns, the legal status of prostitution, and customary trajectories of migrant workers and refugees represent but a few examples of the factors that shape the constitution of trafficking as an issue in any given policy venue. Indeed, US anti-trafficking discourses differ from those dominant in other regions of the world in important ways. First and most notably, American abolitionism carries a distinctly evangelical Christian tone reflective of the growing influence of evangelicals within US politics at the end of the twentieth century. Chapters 3 and 5 explore the constitutive elements and productive effects of religious abolitionist discourse, showing how evangelical styles of rhetoric and invocation of specific biblical themes are used to promote anti-trafficking policies focused on the sometimes contradictory goals of eliminating prostitution and fighting "modern-day slavery." The prevalence of evangelical voices within US anti-trafficking politics occurs alongside a silencing of sex workers and sex workers' rights activists, a state of affairs that stands in marked contrast to trafficking debates in the European Union and the Asia-Pacific region. I examine the causes and effects of this silence for domestic and transnational anti-trafficking policies in Chapters 3 and 4.

My inquiry into the construction of "human trafficking" as a political problem seeks to contribute to the literature on three particular topics: human trafficking, feminism, and international norms. Regarding the former, the existence of widely disparate understandings of human trafficking is seen to prevent effective data gathering, agency collaboration, legal redress, crime enforcement, service provision, and prevention. It is unsurprising, then, that one of the primary goals of counter-trafficking efforts has been to establish a precise definition for human trafficking, clearly demarcating its boundaries as a problem.[58] My research, in contrast, suggests that an "objective" conception of trafficking is impossible, and a political consensus is unlikely given the current configuration of anti-trafficking politics.

I concur with feminists who hold that the use of sexually violated feminine innocence as the marker of those deserving protection is suggestive of a highly gendered logic of world order.[59] Yet while it has become common for feminists to criticize the manner in which trafficked persons are represented as virginal naïfs kidnapped into sex slavery, my research goes beyond criticism of specific frames to investigate how trafficking's subjects—the parties deemed worthy of protection, praise, or

---

[58] Aradau.

[59] On gendered logics of world order, see V. Spike Peterson, "A 'Gendered Global Hierarchy'?," in *Contending Images of World Politics*, ed. Greg Fry and Jacinta O'Hagan (London: Macmillan, 2000).

censure, or excluded from consideration altogether—are made intelligible as actors. Those who challenge gender and racial stereotypes within the portrayal of trafficking victims, or question the accuracy of claims regarding the relative occurrence and severity of different types of trafficking, still largely assume the unproblematic existence of a coherent and objectively real condition called "human trafficking," and a set of individuals it is possible to identify as "trafficking victims." Furthermore, feminists exemplify a related tendency to treat opposing perspectives on prostitution or sex work as both more externally dichotomous and internally stable than my research shows to be warranted. This book seeks to move beyond reiteration of the so-called "sex wars"[60] in order to complicate received portraits of feminist abolitionism and sex workers' rights perspectives.

Finally, I address what I see as essentialist tendencies within human trafficking research and the international relations (IR) literature on international norms and transnational advocacy networks more generally. IR scholars working in the liberal constructivist tradition explain the success of specific norms and transnational advocacy movements in terms of intrinsic attributes and extrinsic framing, fit, and resonance. Such explanations assume a relatively well-defined, stable norm, and indeed, accounts of the anti-trafficking norm tend to significantly overstate the conceptual coherency of human trafficking as a problem. In attempting to evaluate and explain how norms are spread, the constitution of phenomena as political problems and actors as subjects in relation to that problem are forgotten. The objective of framing analysis is to evaluate the representations of pre-constituted subjects and practices, while the objective of constitutive analysis is to understand how subjects and practices are produced, or made intelligible. Thus in contrast to scholars who examine how advocacy networks have framed human trafficking in support of anti-trafficking norms, I explore how human trafficking is produced through norms discourse.

Genealogical approaches such as my own seek to resist the impulse to read stability and unity back into history in ways that erase the inevitable moments of discursive slippage, contradiction, and incoherence. At the same time that I identify dominant discourses and central themes, this

---

[60]On the calcification of each side of the "feminist sex wars," see Ann Ferguson, "Sex War: The Debate between Radical and Libertarian Feminists," *Signs: Journal of Women in Culture and Society* 10, no. 1 (1984).

book departs from the literature to emphasize gaps, fissures and points of tension internal to individual perspectives. For example, I suggest that feminist abolitionist discourse and its construction of "human trafficking" are both less stable than conventionally depicted. In fact, the points of tension internal to feminist abolitionism help explain why its discursive boundaries are so heavily policed. Likewise, the evangelical Christian framework that undergirds religious abolitionism can be and has been drawn upon to support a variety of approaches to "human trafficking," and it may be the most likely site for a dramatic reconfiguration of anti-trafficking politics.

DISCOURSE ANALYSIS

I use discourse analysis as a tool of genealogical investigation that works to highlight the productive power of anti-trafficking discourses. Discourse refers to far more than simply what is said or written.[61] In Laura Shepherd's words, discourses are "systems of meaning-production rather than simply statements or language, systems that 'fix' meaning, however temporarily, and enable us to make sense of the world."[62] Social construction is a discursive process through which power relations are produced, reproduced, and contested. In short, "discourses are productive. They produce subjects, objects, and the relations among them."[63]

An effective genealogy requires thorough empirical investigation as much, if not more so, as it requires theoretical probing.[64] Analysis of a discursive field is necessarily analysis of discourse in action, tracing its

---

[61] Foucault, 49. See also David Campbell, *Writing Security: United States Foreign Policy and the Politics of Identity* (Minneapolis: University of Minnesota, 1992): 5; Lene Hansen, *Security as Practice: Discourse Analysis and the Bosnian War* (London: Routledge, 2006): 18–23.

[62] Laura J. Shepherd, *Gender, Violence and Security: Discourse as Practice* (London: Zed Books, 2008), 20. Shepherd goes on to caution, "In suggesting that discourses 'fix' meaning I do not want to imply that there is any transhistorical continuity or universality to meaning. Rather, the 'terms of intelligibility' are multiple, open, and fluid." Ibid.

[63] Mark Laffey and Jutta Weldes, "Methodological Reflections on Discourse Analysis," *Qualitative Methods* 2, no. 1 (2004): 28. See also Jo Doezema, "Ouch! Western Feminists' 'Wounded Attachment' to the 'Third World Prostitute'," *Feminist Review* 67, no. 1 (2001): 20.

[64] See, e.g., Moya Lloyd, "(Women's) Human Rights: Paradoxes and Possibilities," *Review of International Studies* 33 (2007): 99.

deployment by and production of specific actors in specific contexts. For Foucault:

> Discourse must not be referred to the distant presence of the origin, but treated as and when it occurs [...] we must grasp the statement in the exact specificity of its occurrence; determine its conditions of existence, fix at least its limits, establish its correlations with other statements that may be connected with it, and show what other forms of statements it excludes.[65]

My primary concern in choosing texts was to ensure coverage of dominant discourses—in this case, those associated with feminist and religious abolitionism. Immersion in abolitionist literature, news media reports, speeches, congressional hearings, and web sites allowed me to identify key texts—those frequently cross-referenced or cited, or given particular emphasis by the actors themselves—that serve as the backbones of chapters three through five. Multiple readings of these texts, seen in concert with one another, are required to account for the principle of intertextuality, or the notion that

> statements and actions are always within a broader text that give them intersubjective meaning, and this single text itself is in meaning-giving and meaning-taking relationships with other texts.[66]

Determination of texts as key is an inductive, recursive, and reflexive process; key texts were not chosen before the study but discovered as part of it through a process of reading that is ongoing, repeated, and subject to feedback and revision. I judged coverage to have been reached once key texts and basic discourses began to reappear without major changes or additions.

One of the major weaknesses of the existing literature regarding anti-human trafficking efforts lies with the failure of scholars to critically engage with trafficking discourses *on their own terms.* I specify critical engagement because these two elements are rarely found together: scholars have been quick to criticize discourses that they find morally

---

[65] Foucault, 25, 28.

[66] Ted Hopf, "The Promise of Constructivism in International Relations Theory," *International Security* 23, no. 1 (1998): 31. See also Hansen, 8.

troubling but slow to provide the generous, empirically and theoretically rich accounts of these discourses that are required for such scholarship to be found compelling to anyone not already sympathetic to the author's position. My objection is not so much that this work is "biased," but rather that scholars' moral and political commitments have shaped anti-trafficking scholarship to such an extent that even the most insightful research largely "preaches to the choir." In contrast, I begin my analysis of abolitionist networks by first engaging in what might be termed a generous or sympathetic account of the two transnational advocacy networks most central to US anti-trafficking policy. I then layer a second, critical reading upon the initial sympathetic interpretation with the intention of providing an account that simultaneously preserves the representations of each set of actors in their own terms while also showing what the various representations *do* (or do not). The final chapter revisits my contention that the meaning of human trafficking is inseparable from the moral and political judgments that animate conceptualizations of the trafficking problem.

Organization of Book

My argument in this book unfolds through the interrogation of anti-trafficking discourses in the scholarly literature, in the US federal government, and in radical feminist and evangelical Christian activism. Chapter 2 expands upon my contention that sociopolitical problems such as human trafficking should be understand instead as political problematizations. It introduces five conventional problematizations of trafficking in the scholarly and policy literature: (1) trafficking as a security problem; (2) trafficking as a human rights problem; (3) trafficking as a gender problem; (4) trafficking as a migration problem; and (5) trafficking as a labor problem. This chapter demonstrates that the distinctions drawn among the various problematizations are *political* rather than technical or empirical, and reflect competing values, interests, and worldviews. It further argues that problematizations of trafficking drive allocations of government and NGO resources, create hierarchies of victims, participate in the production of subjects (i.e., "selves" and "others") and re-entrenchment or challenging of stereotypes, and normalize exploitative practices deemed not to count as instances of human trafficking. Chapter 2 concludes with an alternative, feminist approach that seeks to denaturalize dominant constructions.

Chapter 3 sets the stage for my genealogy of anti-trafficking politics in the United States. From 1998 to 2000, members of Congress, senior officials in the Clinton administration, and a wide range of highly active members of civil society attempted to craft a comprehensive federal response to human trafficking both within the United States and abroad. I find that trafficking and anti-trafficking were constructed in gendered and racialized terms. Trafficking—understood primarily as the international transportation of women and children for forced prostitution—was characterized as a uniquely deplorable abuse of human rights, and allusions to the historic trans-Atlantic slave trade underscored demands for the United States to take leadership of global efforts to eradicate the problem. The resultant TVPA of 2000 set the parameters for the anti-trafficking initiatives of not only the next two presidential administrations, but also for the host of countries pressured by the US government and transnational civil society to improve their standing in the TVPA-mandated annual Trafficking in Persons (TIP) Report's ranking of international anti-trafficking efforts.

In Chapters 4 and 5, I undertake a genealogy of the self-described "abolitionist" discourses advanced by influential US-based radical feminist and evangelical Christian anti-trafficking advocacy networks, respectively. I situate feminist and religious abolitionism within their broader political and moral philosophies in order to understand how they *work* as discourses, or how different practices are established as instances of human trafficking and different subjects as traffickers, victims, and saviors. These two chapters explore the ways in which abolitionist TANs were responsible for establishing the conditions of possibility for the anti-trafficking debates featured in Chapter 3. I emphasize moments of discursive tension and slippage as well in order to identify avenues through which the meaning of trafficking might be reconfigured or challenged even from within particular political projects.

Chapter 6, the conclusion, returns to the importance of recognizing human trafficking as a social construct. It emphasizes that one of the reasons debates surrounding human trafficking are so contentious is the recognition—often implicit—that the manner in which trafficking and its subjects are represented has real repercussions at the level of policy and service delivery. The chapter further elaborates on the argument that attempts to deny or ignore the social construction of human trafficking, and its inextricably political nature, are themselves political acts that serve to shut down debate and delegitimate opposing viewpoints. The chapter then turns to the feminist, critical constructive theoretical perspective offered in the book, and the need for empathetic listening. Finally, the chapter concludes with a meditation on potential ways in which debates surrounding human trafficking might be reconfigured.

In this book, I have chosen not to present my own preferred mode of anti-trafficking politics insofar as such an effort encourages discursive closure rather than openness, and at this point I prefer to uncover possibilities for change as opposed to advocating on behalf of any specific program. I emphasize throughout this study that constructions of human trafficking—mine no less than that of anyone else—are political, that they reflect actors' values and interests.[67] It is not politics per se that I wish to avoid—such an effort is both misguided and futile—but rather a distraction from my central theoretical argument calling into question essentialist accounts of "the problem of human trafficking" and of a global anti-trafficking norm. In making this distinction I rely in particular on the work of feminist political theorist Wendy Brown and her call for a necessary and productive distance between the domains of politics and theory.[68] While theory-making too involves various deployments of power, the purposes of political and theoretical projects, Brown argues, are necessarily at odds with one another. Where theory is meant to question, destabilize, and open up meaning, politics is meant to create temporary and strategic stabilities.[69] Brown argues not for a theory and a politics that are completely divorced from one another, but for the maintenance of an often antagonistic conversation in which the theoretical and political spheres argue back and forth, questioning and demanding in turn:

> The questioning, the vertigo, the demand, the knowledge, and the political dislocation all incite one another, but the chain of incitation would be

[67] The words of Alisdair MacIntyre prove instructive:
Suppose someone proposed to operationalize such concepts as those of education or freedom by definitional legislation. ... Any claim about its validity would be in conflict with other categorizations and since these, as we have already seen, involve normative claims, so would the aspiring scientific theory. To operationalize would be to participate in the debate, not to escape it. MacIntyre, 8.

[68] Wendy Brown, *Politics out of History* (Princeton: Princeton University Press, 2001), 122.

[69] Ibid., 41.

aborted if the movement collapsed either through the direct politicization of knowledge or through the reduction of politics to questioning, to pure critique.[70]

Theory, in my preferred formulation, problematizes the exclusions and other effects of certain political usages while recognizing that moments of arrested meaning are necessary.[71] My hope is that both realms are shaped and invigorated from their mutual existence within the context of the other.[72]

REFERENCES

Andreas, Peter. "The Politics of Measuring Illicit Flows and Policy Effectiveness." In *Sex, Drugs, and Body Counts: The Politics of Numbers in Global Crime and Conflict*, edited by Peter Andreas and Kelly M. Greenhill, 23–45. Ithaca, NY: Cornell University Press, 2010.

Aradau, Claudia. *Rethinking Trafficking in Women: Politics Out of Security*. New York: Palgrave Macmillan, 2008.

Aromaa, Kauko. "Trafficking in Human Beings: Uniform Definitions for Better Measuring and for Effective Counter-Measures." In *Measuring Human Trafficking: Complexities and Pitfalls*, edited by Ernesto Savona and Sonia Stefanizzi, 13–26. New York: Springer, 2007.

Bales, Kevin. *Understanding Global Slavery*. Berkeley: University of California Press, 2005.

Barnett, Michael N., and Raymond Duvall, eds. *Power in Global Governance*. Cambridge: Cambridge University Press, 2005.

———. "Power in Global Governance." In *Power in Global Governance*, edited by Michael Barnett and Raymond Duvall, 1–32. Cambridge: Cambridge University Press, 2005.

Brown, Wendy. *Politics Out of History*. Princeton: Princeton University Press, 2001.

Bush, George W. "Speech before the United Nations, General Assembly in New York." Accessed September 29, 2009. http://www.presidentialrhetoric.com/speeches/09.23.03.html.

Butler, Judith. *Undoing Gender*. New York: Routledge, 2004.

Campbell, David. *Writing Security: United States Foreign Policy and the Politics of Identity*. Minneapolis: University of Minnesota, 1992.

[70] Ibid., 98.
[71] See also Judith Butler, *Undoing Gender* (New York: Routledge, 2004), 38.
[72] Brown, 43.

Chowdhry, Geeta, and Sheila Nair, eds. *Power, Postcolonialism and International Relations: Reading Race, Gender and Class.* New York and London: Routledge, 2014.

Coomaraswamy, Radhika. "Report of the Special Rapporteur on Violence against Women: Trafficking in Women, Women's Migration and Violence against Women." Geneva: Economic and Social Council, 2000.

Doezema, Jo. "Now You See Her, Now You Don't: Sex Workers at the Un Trafficking Protocol Negotiation." *Social & Legal Studies* 14, no. 1 (2005): 61–89.

———. "Ouch! Western Feminists' 'Wounded Attachment' to the 'Third World Prostitute'." *Feminist Review* 67, no. 1 (2001): 16–38.

Doty, Roxanne Lynn. "Immigration and the Politics of Security." *Security Studies* 8, no. 2/3 (1998): 71–93.

Efrat, Asif. "Global Efforts against Human Trafficking: The Misguided Conflation of Sex, Labor, and Organ Trafficking." *International Studies Perspectives* 17, no. 1 (2016): 34–54.

Feingold, David A. "Trafficking in Numbers: The Social Construction of Human Trafficking Data." In *Sex, Drugs, and Body Counts: The Politics of Numbers in Global Crime and Conflict*, edited by Peter Andreas and Kelly M. Greenhill, 46–74. Ithaca, NY: Cornell University Press, 2010.

Ferguson, Ann. "Sex War: The Debate between Radical and Libertarian Feminists." *Signs: Journal of Women in Culture and Society* 10, no. 1 (1984): 106–12.

Foucault, Michel. *The Archaeology of Knowledge and the Discourse on Language.* Translated by A. M. Sheridan Smith. New York: Pantheon Books, 1972.

Free the Slaves and the Human Rights Center. "Hidden Slaves: Forced Labor in the US." University of California, Berkeley. Accessed September 29, 2009. http://www.hrcberkeley.org/download/hiddenslaves_report.pdf.

Government Accountability Office. "Human Trafficking: Better Data, Strategy, and Reporting Needed to Enhance U.S. Antitrafficking Efforts Abroad." 2006.

Gozdziak, Elzbieta M., and Elizabeth A. Collett. "Research on Human Trafficking in North America: A Review of Literature." *International Migration* 43, no. 1–2 (2005): 99–128.

Guinn, David E. "Defining the Problem of Trafficking: The Interplay of U.S. Law, Donor, and NGO Engagement and the Local Context in Latin America." *Human Rights Quarterly* 30, no. 1 (2008): 119–45.

Hall, Stuart. "Signification, Representation, Ideology: Althusser and the Post-structuralist Debates." *Critical Studies in Mass Communication* 2, no. 2 (1985): 91–114.

Hansen, Lene. *Security as Practice: Discourse Analysis and the Bosnian War.* London: Routledge, 2006.

Hesford, Wendy S., and Wendy Kozol, eds. *Just Advocacy? Women's Human Rights, Transnational Feminisms, and the Politics of Representation*. New Brunswick, NJ: Rutgers University Press, 2005.

Hodge, David R. "Sexual Trafficking in the United States: A Domestic Problem with Transnational Dimensions." *Social Work* 53, no. 2 (April 2008): 143–52.

Holste, Glenda. "Bipartisan Efforts Are Propelling Violence against Women Act." *The Saint Paul Pioneer Press*, October 9, 2000.

Hopf, Ted. "The Promise of Constructivism in International Relations Theory." *International Security* 23, no. 1 (1998): 171–200.

Jackson, Patrick Thaddeus. *Civilizing the Enemy: German Reconstruction and the Invention of the West*. Ann Arbor: University of Michigan, 2006.

———. "Defending the West: Occidentalism and the Formation of Nato." *Journal of Political Philosophy* 11, no. 3 (2003): 223–52.

Jahic, Galma, and James O. Finckenauer. "Representations and Misrepresentations of Human Trafficking." *Trends in Organized Crime* 8, no. 3 (Spring 2005): 24–40.

Kelly, Liz. "'You Can Find Anything You Want': A Critical Reflection on Research on Trafficking in Persons within and into Europe." *International Migration* 43, no. 1/2 (January 2005): 235–65.

Kempadoo, Kamala. "From Moral Panic to Social Justice: Changing Perspectives on Trafficking." In *Trafficking and Prostitution Reconsidered: New Perspectives on Migration, Sex Work and Human Rights*, edited by Kamala Kempadoo, Jyoti Sanghera, and Bandana Pattanaik. Boulder: Paradigm Publishers, 2005.

Laczko, Frank. "Data and Research on Human Trafficking." *International Migration* 43, no. 1–2 (2005): 5–16.

Laczko, Frank, and Marco A. Gramegna. "Developing Better Indicators of Human Trafficking." *Brown Journal of World Affairs* 10, no. 1 (2003): 179–94.

Laffey, Mark, and Jutta Weldes. "Methodological Reflections on Discourse Analysis." *Qualitative Methods* 2, no. 1 (Spring 2004): 28–30.

Lloyd, Moya. "(Women's) Human Rights: Paradoxes and Possibilities." *Review of International Studies* 33 (2007): 91–103.

Lobasz, Jennifer K. "Beyond Border Security: Feminist Approaches to Human Trafficking." *Security Studies* 18, no. 2 (2009): 319–44.

———. "Trafficking Scholarship, World-Traveling, and Loving Perception." Trollhättan, Sweden: Center for Studies of Diversity, Equality and Integration, University West, 2013.

MacIntyre, Alisdair. "The Essential Contestability of Some Social Concepts." *Ethics* 84, no. 1 (1973): 1–9.

Miller, Ali, and Alison N. Stewart. "Report from the Roundtable on the Meaning of 'Trafficking in Persons': A Human Rights Perspective." *Women's Rights Law Reporter* 20, no. 1 (Fall/Winter 1998): 11–20.

Mohanty, Chandra Talpade. *Feminism without Borders: Decolonizing Theory, Practicing Solidarity.* Durham: Duke University Press, 2003.

Nadelmann, Ethan A. "Global Prohibition Regimes: The Evolution of Norms in International Society." *International Organization* 44, no. 4 (Autumn 1990): 479–526.

O'Connell Davidson, Julia, and Bridget Anderson. "The Trouble with 'Trafficking'." In *Trafficking and Women's Rights*, edited by Christien L. van der Anker and Jeroen Doomernik. Houndsmills, Basingstroke, Hampshire: Palgrave Macmillan, 2006.

O'Neill Richard, Amy. "International Trafficking in Women to the United States: A Contemporary Manifestation of Slavery and Organized Crime." In *DCI Exceptional Intelligence Analyst Program.* Washington, DC: Center for the Study of Intelligence, 2000.

Peterson, V. Spike. "A 'Gendered Global Hierarchy'?". In *Contending Images of World Politics*, edited by Greg Fry and Jacinta O'Hagan, 199–218. London: Macmillan, 2000.

Quirk, Joel. "Trafficked into Slavery." *Journal of Human Rights* 6 (2007): 181–207.

Sanghera, Jyoti. "Unpacking the Trafficking Discourse." In *Trafficking and Prostitution Reconsidered: New Perspectives on Migration, Sex Work and Human Rights*, edited by Kamala Kempadoo, Jyoti Sanghera, and Bandana Pattanaik, 3–24. Boulder: Paradigm Publishers, 2005.

Savona, Ernesto U., and Sonia Stefanizzi. "Introduction." Chap. 1 In *Measuring Human Trafficking: Complexities and Pitfalls*, edited by Ernesto U. Savona and Sonia Stefanizzi, 1–3. New York: Springer, 2007.

Shepherd, Laura J. *Gender, Violence and Security: Discourse as Practice.* London: Zed Books, 2008.

Tyldum, Guri, and Anette Brunovskis. "Describing the Unobserved: Methodological Challenges in Empirical Studies on Human Trafficking." *International Migration* 43, no. 1/2 (2005): 17–34.

UNESCO Trafficking Project. "Worldwide Trafficking Estimates by Organizations." United Nations Educational, Scientific and Cultural Organization. Accessed September 29, 2009. http://www.unescobkk.org/index.php?id=1963.

United Nations General Assembly. "Protocol to Prevent, Suppress and Punish Trafficking in Persons, Especially Women and Children, Supplementing the United Nations Convention against Transnational Organized Crime." Accessed September 29, 2009. http://www.unhcr.org/refworld/docid/4720706c0.html.

United States Department of State. "What Is Modern Slavery?" Office to Monitor and Combat Trafficking in Persons. Accessed September 29, 2009. https://www.state.gov/j/tip/what/.

Weldes, Jutta. "Bureaucratic Politics: A Critical Constructivist Assessment." *Mershon International Studies Review* 42, no. 2 (November 1998): 216–25.

Weldes, Jutta, Mark Laffey, Hugh Gusterson, and Raymond Duvall, eds. *Cultures of Insecurity: States, Communities, and the Production of Danger.* Minneapolis, MN: University of Minnesota Press, 1999.

———. "Introduction: Constructing Insecurity." In *Cultures of Insecurity: States, Communities and the Production of Danger*, 1–33. Minneapolis, MN: University of Minnesota Press, 1999.

Wylie, Gillian. *The International Politics of Human Trafficking.* Basingstoke: Palgrave Macmillan, 2016.

CHAPTER 2

Contemporary Approaches to Human Trafficking

In their review of the "methodological challenges in empirical studies on human trafficking," Tyldum and Brunovskis assert the need for

> a better understanding of the social field that constitutes trafficking, as well as it its bordering fields; i.e. is trafficking best understood as a phenomenon within the field of labor migration, international prostitution, or migration in general, or does trafficking constitute a distinct and separate phenomenon with its separate causes and mechanisms?[1]

In practice, scholars typically categorize anti-trafficking philosophies in terms of the "social fields" referred to by Tyldum and Brunovskis. Some, for example, characterize anti-trafficking research and policy initiatives as split along a law enforcement/human rights protection axis,[2] whereas

---

[1] Guri Tyldum and Anette Brunovskis, "Describing the Unobserved: Methodological Challenges in Empirical Studies on Human Trafficking," *International Migration* 43, no. 1/2 (2005): 31.

[2] Ann D. Jordan, "The Annotated Guide to the Complete UN Trafficking Protocol," (Washington, DC: International Human Rights Law Group, 2002), 4; Julie Mertus and Andrea Bertone, "Combating Trafficking: International Efforts and Their Ramifications," in *Human Traficking, Human Security, and the Balkans*, ed. H. Richard Friman and Simon Reich (Pittsburgh: University of Pittsburgh Press, 2007), 44; and Joanna Apap, Peter Cullen, and Felicita Mcdved, "Counteracting Human Trafficking: Protecting the Victims of Trafficking" (paper presented at the European Conference on Preventing and Combating Trafficking in Human Beings, Brussels, September 18–20, 2002).

© The Author(s) 2019
J. K. Lobasz, *Constructing Human Trafficking*, Human Rights Interventions, https://doi.org/10.1007/978-3-319-91737-5_2

others identify an assortment of possible social fields and then argue for their preferred categorization.[3] The problem posed by human trafficking has been represented as (1) a threat to state security, (2) a violation of human rights, (3) irregular migration, (4) prostitution, and (5) exploitative labor. For some, these problematizations[4] are seen as competing—rights activists, for example, have argued that the state security approach is wholly inappropriate for dealing with a problem more appropriately characterized as "one of the worst human rights violations of the contemporary world."[5] Others understand the different problematizations as complementary or overlapping.[6] My own account of these five problematizations is not intended to establish the superiority of any particular formulation, or to portray them as mutually exclusive. I seek instead to orient the reader in regard to contemporary trafficking debates, emphasizing that problematizations are thoroughly political discursive formations.[7]

TRAFFICKING AS A SECURITY THREAT

Formulated as a security threat, human trafficking is understood to pose a grave danger to the state insofar as it threatens the two pillars of sovereignty: control of state borders and provision of the rule of law.[8] Responding to the seemingly increased danger posed by trafficking, the

---

[3] Annuska Derks, *Combatting Trafficking in South-East Asia: A Review of Policy and Program Responses* (Geneva: International Organization for Migration, 2000).

[4] I borrow the notion of trafficking problematizations from Claudia Aradau, *Rethinking Trafficking in Women: Politics Out of Security* (New York: Palgrave Macmillan, 2008).

[5] Neil Abercrombie, "Remarks on Trafficking Victims Protection Act of 2000," (Washington, DC: U.S. House of Representatives, 2000), H2686.

[6] See Claudia Aradau, "The Perverse Politics of Four-Letter Words: Risk and Pity in the Securitization of Human Trafficking," *Millennium Journal of International Studies* 33, no. 2 (2004); Jacqueline Berman, "(Un)Popular Strangers and Crises (Un)Bounded: Discourses of Sex-trafficking, the European Political Community and the Panicked State of the Modern State," *European Journal of International Relations* 9, no. 1 (2003).

[7] See Mark Laffey and Jutta Weldes, "Beyond Belief: Ideas and Symbolic Technologies in the Study of International Relations," ibid. 3, no. 2 (1997): 218–19.

[8] Fiona B. Adamson, "Crossing Borders: International Migration and National Security," *International Security* 31, no. 1 (2006): 176. See also Apap, Cullen, and Medved, 8; Willy Bruggeman, "Illegal Immigration and Trafficking in Human Beings Seen as a Security Problem for Europe" (ibid.); Luis CdeBaca, "Question and Answer on Human Trafficking," U.S. Department of State, accessed December 1, 2010, http://www.state.gov/g/tip/rls/rm/2010/141642.htm; Government Accountability Office, "A Strategic

United Nations passed the Protocol to Prevent, Suppress and Punish Trafficking in Persons, Especially Women and Children as a supplement to the 2000 United Nations Convention Against Transnational Organized Crime.[9] The Trafficking Protocol, which came into force in 2003, calls for the criminalization of trafficking, repatriation of victims, strengthened border controls, and more secure travel and identity documents.[10] The decision to negotiate the Trafficking Protocol in the context of fighting transnational organized crime rather than protecting human rights "highlights the criminal-justice and security approach and States' interests in maintaining border integrity."[11]

Noting the centrality of the Protocol to the global governance of human trafficking, Kamala Kempadoo remarks that "anti-trafficking in this framework is synonymous with a war on international crime."[12] Indeed, the specter of transnational crime syndicates and menacing Mafiosi looms large—human trafficking is understood to represent

Framework Could Help Enhance the Interagency Collaboration Needed to Effectively Combat Trafficking Crimes," (2007), 18; Wyn Rees, "Organised Crime, Security and the European Union: Draft Paper for the ESRC Workshop, Grenoble," European Consortium for Political Research, accessed September 29, 2009, http://www.essex. ac.uk/ecpr/events/jointsessions/paperarchive/grenoble/ws8/rees.pdf; Louise I. Shelley, "Transnational Organized Crime: An Imminent Threat to the Nation-State?," *Journal of International Affairs* 48, no. 2 (1995); and White House Office of the Press Secretary, "Fact Sheet on Migrant Smuggling and Trafficking," (2000).

[9] This convention is known as the Palermo Convention after the Italian city in which it was signed. Within the anti-trafficking community, the Protocol to Prevent, Suppress and Punish Trafficking in Persons, Especially Women and Children may be referred to as the Palermo Protocol or the Trafficking Protocol.

[10] Jordan, "The Annotated Guide to the Complete UN Trafficking Protocol."

[11] Ratna Kapur, "Cross-Border Movments and the Law: Renegotiating the Boundaries of Difference," in *Trafficking and Prostitution Reconsidered: New Perspectives on Migration, Sex Work and Human Rights*, ed. Kamala Kempadoo, Jyoti Sanghera, and Bandana Pattanaik (Boulder: Paradigm Publishers, 2005), 31. See also Karen E. Bravo, "Exploring the Analogy between Modern Trafficking in Humans and the Trans-Atlantic Slave Trade," *Boston University International Law Journal* 25 (2007): 224.

[12] Kamala Kempadoo, "From Moral Panic to Social Justice: Changing Perspectives on Trafficking," in *Trafficking and Prostitution Reconsidered: New Perspectives on Migration, Sex Work and Human Rights*, ed. Kamala Kempadoo, Jyoti Sanghera, and Bandana Pattanaik (Boulder: Paradigm Publishers, 2005), xiii. See also Anne Gallagher, "Trafficking, Smuggling and Human Rights: Tricks and Treaties," *Forced Migration Review* 12 (2002): 936.

"a bonanza for organized crime."[13] In this formulation, human trafficking is seen as complimenting other activities of criminal networks "such as drug trafficking, vehicle theft, arms trafficking, and money laundering."[14] According to Louise Shelley,

> Smuggling and trafficking are undeniably part of organized crime activities. The high profits, low risk of detection, and minor penalties involved have made the human trade attractive to crime groups that previously trafficked in other commodities and to new groups which have developed recently.[15]

Shelley identifies six business models for trafficking, each of which "is an ideal type associated with a different national group and reflects deep historical influences, geographical realities, and the market forces that drive the trade."[16] Examples include the Post-Soviet Organized Crime Natural Resource Model, in which women are sold "as if they were a readily available natural resource such as timber or furs"[17] and the Chinese Traffickers' Trade and Development Model, in which "Chinese and Thai trafficking operations organize their business such that it is integrated from start to finish."[18]

Others have argued that human trafficking is more accurately characterized as "crime that is organized," as opposed to the work of traditional criminal syndicates such as the Mafia.[19] Sanghera, for example,

---

[13] Janice G. Raymond, "Prostitution as Violence against Women: NGO Stonewalling in Beijing and Elsewhere," *Women's Studies International Forum* 21, no. 1 (1998): 5.

[14] Kevin Bales, *Understanding Global Slavery* (Berkeley: University of California Press, 2005), 125. See also European Union, "Fighting Trafficking in Human Beings: An Integrated Approach and Proposals for an Action Plan," Communication from the Commission to the European Parliament and the Council, accessed September 29, 2009, http://europa.eu.int/eur-lex/lex/LexUriServ/LexUriServ.do?uri=COM:2005:0514:FIN:EN:PDF.

[15] Louise I. Shelley, "Trafficking in Women: The Business Model Approach," *Brown Journal of World Affairs* X, no. 1 (2003): 121.

[16] Ibid., 123.

[17] Ibid.

[18] Ibid., 124.

[19] James O. Finckenauer, "Russian Transnational Organized Crime and Human Trafficking," in *Global Human Smuggling: Comparative Perspectives*, ed. David Kyle and Rey Koslowski (Baltimore: Johns Hopkins University Press, 2001), 172. See also Janice G. Raymond, "Guide to the New Un Trafficking Protocol" (North Amherst, MA: Coalition Against Trafficking in Women, 2001), 2.

concedes that organized crime gangs are involved "in some instances in certain parts of the world," but goes on to claim that "it is near impossible to make a claim that trafficking is entirely or even largely a problem of organized crime."[20] Finckenauer emphasizes that "true organized crime is much more than just crime committed by organized groups."[21] He argues that the distinction between organized crime and crime that is organized is crucial for anti-traffickers to grasp:

> Use of the standard organized crime fighting tools in a false belief that the enemy is the mafia will be ineffective, inefficient, and costly—not only in dollar terms but in human terms as well. At the same time, it should be recognized that true organized crime is not vulnerable to the usual techniques used against street crime [...] For all these reasons, knowing who is the real enemy is important.[22]

Recent studies suggest that the "real enemies" to whom Finckenauer refers "are primarily small-time operators functioning mostly in an individual capacity, and are based upon personal and sometimes familial sets of relationships."[23]

Beyond the relationship between human trafficking and transnational organized crime, trafficking is represented as a security threat in terms of migration, particularly in terms of trafficked persons who are

[20] Jyoti Sanghera, "Unpacking the Trafficking Discourse," in *Trafficking and Prostitution Reconsidered: New Perspectives on Migration, Sex Work and Human Rights*, ed. Kamala Kempadoo, Jyoti Sanghera, and Bandana Pattanaik (Boulder: Paradigm Publishers, 2005), 14. See also Anthony M. DeStefano, *The War on Human Trafficking: U.S. Policy Assessed* (New Brunswick, NJ: Rutgers University Press, 2007), 20.

[21] Finckenauer, 168. According to the Palermo Convention, "'Organized criminal group' shall mean a structured group of three or more persons, existing for a period of time and acting in concert with the aim of committing one or more serious crimes or offences established in accordance with this Convention, in order to obtain, directly or indirectly, a financial or other material benefit" (Article 2). In contrast, Finckenauer defines "organized crime" in much narrower terms, stating that "if organized crime is so loosely or ambiguously defined as to encompass practically any crimes committed by, say, three or more persons, then it is a meaningless concept." Ibid., 169. See, however, Shelley, "Transnational Organized Crime: An Imminent Threat to the Nation-State?," 464.

[22] Finckenauer, 170.

[23] Sanghera, 16.

undocumented migrants.[24] Western governments in particular have emphasized changes in global labor migration as a cause of trafficking, such that "international migration has moved to the top of the international security agenda."[25]

Human trafficking emerged as a threat within the European Union in the context of three changes: the opening of internal European borders, the fall of the Soviet Union, and the intensification of globalization.[26] Following the collapse of communism in the Warsaw Pact states and the breakdown of the Soviet Union, EU officials feared an influx of economic migrants from the East and sought to balance relaxation of internal border controls with a strengthening of border controls outside the Schengen area.[27] This context facilitated the EU's securitization of migration, placing "the regulation of migration in an institutional framework that deals with the protection of internal security."[28] In the words of the European Commission, "The prevention of and the fight against human trafficking is an essential element of the EU's efforts to improve the checks and surveillance at the external borders and to enhance the fight against illegal immigration."[29]

The articulation of border insecurity to human trafficking is also present in the United States. The federal Human Smuggling and Trafficking

---

[24] See Anna M. Agathangelou, *The Global Political Economy of Sex: Desire, Violence, and Insecurity in Mediterranean Nation States* (New York: Palgrave Macmillan, 2004); Ann D. Jordan, "Human Rights or Wrongs? The Struggle for a Rights-Based Response to Trafficking in Human Beings," *Gender & Development* 10, no. 1 (2002): 30.

[25] Adamson, 165. See also International Labor Organization, "Forced Labor, Child Labor, and Human Trafficking in Europe: An ILO Perspective" (paper presented at the European Conference on Preventing and Combating Trafficking in Human Beings, Geneva, September 18–22 2002), 3–4; and Joanna Apap, Peter Cullen, and Felicita Medved, "Counteracting Human Trafficking: Protecting the Victims of Trafficking" (ibid. Brussels, September 18–20).

[26] Rees.

[27] George Katrougalos, "The Rights of Foreigners and Immigrants in Europe: Recent Trends," Web Journal of Current Legal Issues, accessed September 29, 2009, http://webjcli.ncl.ac.uk/articles5/katart5.html. The Schengen area refers to the geographical territory of the states agreeing to the Schengen conventions of 1985 and 1995, which were incorporated into EU law by the 1999 Treaty of Amsterdam. The conventions abolish internal border controls between signatories.

[28] Jeff Huysmans, "The European Union and the Securitization of Migration," *Journal of Common Market Studies* 38, no. 5 (2000).

[29] European Union.

Center (HSTC), for example, was established in 2004 as a joint project of the Departments of State, Homeland Security, and Justice in order "to meet three inextricably intertwined international threats[30] to national security or human rights, all of which tend to have the common denominator of illicit or fraudulent travel."[31] A government fact sheet points to the role of border control—under the purview of ICE—in this effort:

> U.S. Immigration and Customs Enforcement (ICE), the largest investigative agency in the Department of Homeland Security (DHS), has responsibility for enforcing laws related to human smuggling and trafficking. As a result, ICE plays a leading role in the Human Smuggling and Trafficking Center (HSTC).[32]

I further discuss formulations of trafficking as a problem of border security and related debates concerning special visas for trafficking victims in Chapter 3.

Trafficking as an Abuse of Human Rights

The meaning of security began to evolve during the 1980s. Security scholars have broadened conceptions of security beyond the military realm to incorporate issue areas such as economics, the environment, and health, while also deepening approaches to security through additional levels of analysis.[33] Alternative security frameworks employ "a broad

---

[30] The three threats refer to "human smuggling, trafficking in persons, and criminal support of clandestine terrorist travel." "Report to Congress on the Establishment of the Human Smuggling and Trafficking Center" (Washington, DC, 2005), 11.

[31] Ibid. The HSTC was authorized under Section 7202 of the Intelligence Reform and Terrorism Prevention Act of 2004 (IRTPA), a bill that was itself written to implement recommendations of the National Commission on Terrorist Attacks upon the United States (the 9/11 Commission).

[32] U.S. Immigration and Customs Enforcement, "Fact Sheet: Human Smuggling and Trafficking Center," accessed September 29, 2009, http://www.ice.gov/news/library/factsheets/hstc.htm.

[33] See, e.g., Keith Krause and Michael C. Williams, "Broadening the Agenda of Security Studies: Politics and Methods," *Mershon International Studies Review* 40, no. 2 (1996); Jessica Tuchman Mathews, "Redefining Security," *Foreign Affairs* 68, no. 2 (1989). A small number of notable calls to rethink the concept of security preceded the end of the Cold War, notably Arnold Wolfers, "'National Security' as an Ambiguous Symbol," *Political Science Quarterly* 67, no. 4 (1952); and Richard H. Ullman, "Redefining Security," *International Security* 8, no. 1 (1983).

definition of security that takes the individual, situated in broader social structures, as its starting point."[34] Rather than emphasizing threats to the state, human rights-based conceptualizations of human trafficking consider instead the security of trafficked persons. From this perspective, security threats arise not only from traffickers but from the state itself.[35] Feminist activists and scholars were among the first to widely insist that trafficking is first and foremost a violation of human rights, a problem best understood by paying attention to the experiences of trafficked persons.[36]

Feminists and other human rights advocates oppose the security approach to human trafficking on ethical and practical grounds. The ethical argument has three components: (1) human trafficking is characterized by the violation of victims' human rights, (2) states are required under international law to prevent human rights abuses, and (3) state efforts to address human trafficking are unsatisfactory in protecting human rights and indeed may contribute to the violation of those rights. According to the Global Alliance Against Traffic in Women (GAATW) human trafficking entails the routine violation of rights enumerated in the Universal Declaration of Human Rights (UDHR). These include:

- the right to be free from physical violence, including rape, sexual assault, domestic violence, forced prostitution, and trafficking (Article 3)
- freedom from slavery (Article 4)

[34] J. Ann Tickner, *Gendering World Politics* (New York: Columbia University Press, 2001), 48.

[35] The two problematizations need not be mutually exclusive. Aradau and Berman each call into question the extent to which human rights/humanitarian approaches to trafficking challenge rather than supplement or strengthen state security approaches and governmental apparatuses. Berman; Aradau, "The Perverse Politics of Four-Letter Words: Risk and Pity in the Securitization of Human Trafficking."; *Rethinking Trafficking in Women: Politics out of Security*. Likewise, according to Bravo, "Both the international and the U.S. domestic instruments evidence a mix of law enforcement and human rights concerns." Bravo, 230.

[36] See Kathleen Barry, *Female Sexual Slavery* (New York: New York University Press, 1979). This is not to say that human rights problematizations of trafficking are necessarily feminist. Feminists are unique in their insistence upon the necessity of gender as a category of analysis. Further, they not only establish women as a referent of security and focus on gender-related human rights abuses but also, and perhaps more significantly, study the manner in which gender stereotypes are used to establish and reproduce categories of practices, perpetrators, and victims.

- the right not to be tortured or submitted to cruel or degrading treatment (Article 5)
- the right to personal autonomy (Article 12)
- freedom of choosing residence and moving within own country (Article 13.1)
- the right to safe and healthy working conditions (Article 23.1)
- the right to equal pay for equal work (Article 23.2)
- the right to just and favorable remuneration (Article 23.3)
- the right to enjoy psychological, physical and sexual health (Article 25)[37]

It is both rhetorically and legally significant that human trafficking involves not simply elements that most people would find undesirable or even morally repugnant but abuses that specifically contravene the UDHR.[38] The ability of activists to forcefully connect the plight of trafficked persons to a document that "has been endorsed, regularly and repeatedly, by virtually all states"[39] has been essential in the international effort to shift states away from the security approach exemplified in the Trafficking Protocol and early EU initiatives to a victim-centered approach that demands trafficked individuals be viewed as vulnerable humans rather than dangerous threats.[40]

From a human rights perspective, the security approach further errs by treating trafficked persons as criminals as opposed to victims.[41]

---

[37] Elaine Pearson, *Human Rights and Trafficking in Persons: A Handbook* (Bangkok: Global Alliance Against Traffic in Women, 2000), 42–43.

[38] Harold Koh, Subcommittee on International Operations and Human Rights of the Committee on International Relations, *Hearing on Trafficking of Women and Children in the International Sex Trade*, 106th Cong. 1st session, September 14, 1999, 9.

[39] Jack Donnelly, *Universal Human Rights in Theory and Practice*, 2nd ed. (Ithaca: Cornell University Press, 2002), 22. See also Margaret E. Keck and Kathryn Sikkink, *Activists Beyond Borders: Advocacy Networks in International Politics* (Ithaca, NY: Cornell University Press, 1998).

[40] Aradau, "The Perverse Politics of Four-Letter Words: Risk and Pity in the Securitization of Human Trafficking," 253; Janie Chuang, "The United States as Global Sheriff: Using Unilateral Sanctions to Combat Human Trafficking," *Michigan Journal of International Law* 27 (2005/2006): 446; and Mertus and Bertone, 44.

[41] Janice G. Raymond and Donna M. Hughes, "Sex Trafficking of Women in the United States: International and Domestic Trends" (New York: Coalition Against Trafficking in Women, 2001).

DeStefano cites this issue as a major concern for US negotiators in crafting the Trafficking Protocol:

> Experience, even in the United States, showed that trafficked persons were often treated like criminals, particularly in prostitution cases, when women sex workers frequently ended up in jail or were held as material witnesses with little concern for their well-being.[42]

The problem is especially apparent in cases of migrants. While the Trafficking Protocol and the Migrant Smuggling Protocol were intended to differentiate between coercive and voluntary migration, in practice trafficked persons who have crossed borders are still frequently seen as "illegal immigrants" instead of trafficking victims.[43] Various states and international organizations have responded to such criticism by introducing measures for victim protection. The UN, for example, has introduced a Special Rapporteur on the human rights of trafficking victims.[44] Likewise, the Trafficking Protocol contains multiple stipulations concerning the human rights of trafficked persons, including provisions for legal assistance, medical and psychological services, housing, and training.[45] Rights advocates note, however, that the human rights requirements are noticeably less forceful than the security obligations. As Jordan points out, "the law enforcement provisions in the Trafficking Protocol contain mandatory language, such as 'state parties shall,' while the protections and assistance provisions (see Protocol Articles 6 and 7 and Convention Articles 24 and 25) contain weaker terms, such as 'in appropriate cases' and 'to the extent possible.'"[46]

---

[42] DeStefano, 21. See also Christopher H. Smith, "Remarks on Trafficking Victims Protection Act of 2000" (Washington, DC: U.S. House of Representatives, 2000), H2684.

[43] Berman; Jo Goodey, "Sex Trafficking in Women from Central and East European Countries: Promoting a 'Victimcentered' and 'Womancentered' Approach to Criminal Justice Intervention," *Feminist Review* 2006 (2004).

[44] United Nations, "Special Rapporteur on trafficking in persons, especially women and children," accessed June 6, 2018, http://www.ohchr.org/EN/Issues/Trafficking/Pages/TraffickingIndex.aspx.

[45] United Nations General Assembly, "Protocol to Prevent, Suppress and Punish Trafficking in Persons, Especially Women and Children, Supplementing the United Nations Convention against Transnational Organized Crime," accessed September 29, 2009, http://www.unhcr.org/refworld/docid/4720706c0.html.

[46] Jordan, "The Annotated Guide to the Complete UN Trafficking Protocol."

Human rights advocates argue that treating trafficking victims like criminals is both wrong and counterproductive, multiplying rather than ameliorating the harms of trafficking.[47] A focus on strengthened border controls, for instance, may actually increase an individual's vulnerability to trafficking insofar as migrants become more likely to contract with professional human smugglers for assistance crossing the border.[48] Moreover, when migrants who have been trafficked are deported, they risk being trafficked once again by the same individuals who originally exploited them.[49]

TRAFFICKING AS MIGRATION

One persistent issue anti-traffickers face is whether "trafficking" necessarily entails movement or transport, or whether the illicit buying and selling of goods—in this case, persons—can be considered trafficking regardless of how or whether the commodity is transported. The former construction—trafficking as necessarily a subset of migration—has traditionally prevailed.[50] The articulation of human trafficking to movement and transportation is readily apparent in even a casual review of scholarly articles, policy documents, and media reports.[51] The Trafficking Protocol, for example, includes "transit" among its three categories of qualifying conditions for an act to be classified as trafficking in persons.[52]

---

[47] Jennifer K. Lobasz, "Beyond Border Security: Feminist Approaches to Human Trafficking," *Security Studies* 18, no. 2 (2009).

[48] Berman, 37. See also Jordan, "The Annotated Guide to the Complete UN Trafficking Protocol," 4.

[49] United States Department of State, "Victims of Trafficking and Violence Protection Act of 2000: Trafficking in Persons Report," accessed September 29, 2009, http://www.state.gov/g/tip/rls/tiprpt/2004/.

[50] Ali Miller and Alison N. Stewart, "Report from the Roundtable on the Meaning of 'Trafficking in Persons': A Human Rights Perspective," *Women's Rights Law Reporter* 20, no. 1 (1998): 13.

[51] Md. Shahidul Haque, "Ambiguities and Confusions in Migration-Trafficking Nexus: A Development Challenge," in *Trafficking and the Global Sex Industry*, ed. Delika Amir and Karen Beeks (Lanham, MD: Lexington Books, 2006), 6; Quirk, 191.

[52] Quirk identifies (1) transit, (2) technique, and (3) terms of exploitation as the Trafficking Protocol's three categories of qualifying conditions, noting that "one condition from each of these categories is required." 192–93.

Etymology provides little guidance in settling the question. *Oxford English Dictionary* entries for the noun and verb forms of "traffic" show that the term has historically been used to signify both "the *transportation* of merchandise for the purpose of trade" and trade—i.e., commerce—itself.[53] Moreover, "to traffic" has also been used to mean "to interact," albeit with the implication that such interaction is undertaken for nefarious or sinful purposes.[54] Miller and Stewart's report of a 1998 meeting of anti-trafficking human rights activists, scholars and professionals organized by the Women's Rights Advocacy Program (WRAP) of the International Human Rights Law Group (IHRLG) speaks to the significance of word choice in this matter.[55] In their account of the Roundtable on the Meaning of "Trafficking in Persons," Miller and Stewart report:

> First, the crossing of borders requirement was rejected. The discussion of this element turned on the meaning of 'traffic.' It was agreed that some sort of physical movement or transport was required but that the crossing of borders of any kind—international, national, state, intra-state—was not a necessary element to the crime of trafficking because the harm to victims can be the same whether they are moved two miles across a national border or 1,000 miles across national boundaries.[56]

The participants' focus on physical movement or transportation reportedly stemmed from their recognition that physical, emotional, cultural, and linguistic isolation play a central role in victimization of trafficked persons.[57]

Formulations of human trafficking as a migration problem face the challenge of distinguishing between human trafficking and human smuggling. As late as 1994 the International Organization for Migration

---

[53]"Traffic, N.," *OED Online* (Oxford University Press, 2011), accessed September 29, 2009, http://www.oed.com/view/Entry/204333?rskey=QD1HFv&result=1&isAdvanced=false. Emphasis added. The entry goes on to note that connotations range from neutral to highly negative.

[54]"Traffic, V.," *OED Online* (Oxford University Press, 2011), accessed September 29, 2009, http://www.oed.com/view/Entry/204333?rskey=QD1HFv&result=1&isAdvanced=false.

[55]Miller and Stewart.

[56]Ibid., 14.

[57]Ibid., 15.

(IOM) still defined human trafficking in terms of smuggling willing migrants across borders.[58] In fact, it was not until the adoption of two separate protocols to the 2000 Palermo Convention that one found an international legal effort to distinguish between the two phenomena. In contrast to the Trafficking Protocol's emphasis on coercion and exploitation, the Protocol against the Smuggling of Migrants by Land, Sea and Air defines migrant smuggling as "the procurement, in order to obtain, directly or indirectly, a financial or other material benefit, of the illegal entry of a person into a State Party of which the person is not a national or a permanent resident."[59]

Yet the distinction between human trafficking and human smuggling can be difficult to maintain. Some argue that trafficking and smuggling are better thought of as two ends of a continuum.[60] Adam Graycar notes, "It is frequently difficult to establish whether there were elements of deception and/or coercion, and whether these were sufficient to elevate the situation from one of voluntary undocumented migration, to trafficking."[61] Many trafficking victims consent to being smuggled across borders but do not consent to the exploitation that occurs in the host country.[62] Likewise, smuggled migrants often experience exploitation and abuse, sometimes sexual, while in transit.[63] Furthermore, the identification of trafficking with migration is increasingly challenged by those who argue that the *means* (force, fraud, or coercion) and the *ends* (exploitation) are together sufficient to establish an incident as trafficking. From this perspective, transit is the primary but not the only means of isolating and gaining control over victims.

---

[58] Aradau, *Rethinking Trafficking in Women: Politics Out of Security*, 21; Frank Laczko, "Data and Research on Human Trafficking," *International Migration* 43, no. 1–2 (2005): 10.

[59] United Nations, "Protocol against the Smuggling of Migrants by Land, Sea and Air, Supplementing the United Nations Convention against Transnational Crime," (G.A. Res. 55/25, annex III, U.N. GAOR, 55th Sess., Supp. No. 49, at 65, U.N. Doc. A/45/49, 2001).

[60] Moisés Naím, *Illicit: How Smugglers, Traffickers, and Copycats Are Hijacking the Global Economy* (Doubleday, 2005), 89.

[61] Adam Graycar, "Trafficking in Human Beings" (paper presented at the International Conference on Migration, Culture and Crime, Israel, 1999), 2. See also Haque.

[62] Quirk, 101.

[63] Apap, Cullen, and Medved.

TRAFFICKING AS PROSTITUTION

Sina is Vietnamese but was kidnapped at the age of 13 and taken to Cambodia, where she was drugged. She said she woke up naked and bloody on a bed with a white man — she doesn't know his nationality — who had purchased her virginity.

After that, she was locked on the upper floors of a nice hotel and offered to Western men and wealthy Cambodians. She said she was beaten ferociously to force her to smile and act seductive [...]

Sina mostly followed instructions and smiled alluringly at men because she would have been beaten if men didn't choose her. But sometimes she was in such pain that she resisted, and then she said she would be dragged down to a torture chamber in the basement.

"Many of the brothels have these torture chambers," she said. "They are underground because then the girls' screams are muffled."

—Nicholas D. Kristof[64]

Sina's account of being kidnapped, raped, and tortured by a Cambodian sex trafficking ring appeared in a 2009 *New York Times* column written by Nicholas D. Kristof, a Pulitzer Prize-winning journalist who has increasingly chosen to focus his reportage on sex trafficking and other issues related to the oppression of women.[65] Stories such as these have played no small role in the popular conflation of human trafficking and forced prostitution.

The singular focus on trafficking in women for sexual exploitation is due in part to media sensationalism of a "sexy" topic.[66] Journalist Anthony DeStefano writes:

Since the mid-1990s the news media had related numerous stories about enslaved women who were forced into sexual servitude. Despite publicized

---

[64]Nicholas D. Kristof, "The Evil Behind the Smiles," *The New York Times*, January 1, 2009.

[65]"Raiding a Brothel in India," *The New York Times*, May 25, 2011.

[66]H. Richard Friman and Simon Reich, "Human Trafficking and the Balkans," in *Human Trafficking, Human Security, and the Balkans*, ed. H. Richard Friman and Simon Reich (Pittsburgh: University of Pittsburgh Press, 2007), 8. See also DeStefano on his three-year series in *Newsday*, "Smuggled for Sex." DeStefano, xvii.

cases of other kinds of trafficking and forced labor situations, these stories of sex slaves became emblematic of the issue and were sure to catch readers' attention.[67]

DeStefano goes on to note the resemblance between contemporary accounts of trafficking and reportage from the Progressive Era, echoing those who see parallels between current problematizations of human trafficking and the previous century's uproar regarding "white slavery."[68] Meanwhile, leading feminist abolitionists Donna Hughes and Janice Raymond cite national and local media stories regarding sex trafficking in the United States as evidence that "trafficking for commercial sexual exploitation is a national problem, one that is increasing in scope and magnitude.[69]

It is no coincidence that the most lurid and sensationalist contemporary accounts of trafficking evoke fin-de-siècle tales of damsels in distress. Although contemporary accounts of human trafficking make frequent use of terms such as "slavery" and "abolition,"[70] anti-trafficking discourses today share more in common with nineteenth- and early twentieth-century opposition to "white slavery" than with opposition to the earlier trans-Atlantic black slave trade.[71] According to Miller and Stewart, "The historical understanding of trafficking in international law has been primarily the movement (often implicitly) across borders for the purpose of prostitution."[72]

"White slavery" refers primarily to migratory prostitution occurring from the late 1890s to World War I, the demand for which was fueled by mass migration of single men.[73] Much like today, concerns about "migratory prostitution engaged the era's full spectrum of activists, academics,

---

[67] DeStefano, 37.

[68] Ibid., 37–38.

[69] Raymond and Hughes, 2.

[70] See, e.g., Bales; John R. Miller, "Call It Slavery," *Wilson Quarterly* 32, no. 3 (2008); E. Benjamin Skinner, *A Crime So Monstrous: Face-to-Face with Modern-Day Slavery* (New York: Free Press, 2009).

[71] Quirk, 186; Bravo, 121.

[72] Miller and Stewart, 14.

[73] Eileen Scully, "Pre-Cold War Traffic in Sexual Labor and Its Foes: Some Contemporary Lessons," in *Global Human Smuggling: Comparative Perspectives*, ed. David Kyle and Rey Koslowski (Baltimore: Johns Hopkins University, 2001), 75. According to Scully, "The pre-Cold War history of forced migratory prostitution comprised three

philanthropists, officials, professionals, and social tinkerers."[74] Victorians and their counterparts on the European continent and later the United States publicized dire stories of innocent young white women seduced or abducted, sexually violated, and forced into a brutal life of prostitution.[75]

By the end of the nineteenth century, Scully writes, "public discourse beheld domestic and migratory prostitution as an integrated, international problem to be dealt with multilaterally."[76] In 1904, the International Agreement for the Suppression of the 'White Slave Traffic' was signed by the United Kingdom (including the British Empire), Germany, Belgium, Denmark, Spain, France, Italy, the Netherlands, Portugal, Russia, Sweden, Norway, and Switzerland.[77] The 1904 law was not an abolitionist document, and thus while it condemned "the procuring of women or girls for immoral purposes abroad," the treaty was restricted to women "who have suffered abuse or compulsion," and to underage girls.[78] Only the title signified an exclusive application to white women.[79] The 1904 Agreement was supplanted by the

---

distinct periods: (1) the 1840s to about 1895; (2) the late 1890s to World War I; (3) 1919 through World War II." Ibid.

[74] Ibid., 84.

[75] Margit Stange, *Personal Property: Wives, White Slaves, and the Market in Women* (Baltimore: Johns Hopkins University Press, 2002); Gretchen Soderlund, "Covering Urban Vice: The New York Times, "White Slavery," and the Construction of Journalistic Knowledge," *Critical Studies in Media Communication* 19, no. 4 (2002).

[76] Scully, 84. See also Kempadoo, x–xi.

[77] *The Cultivation of Resentment: Treaty Rights and the New Right* (Stanford: Stanford University Press).

[78] Ibid. On the non-abolitionist character of the 1904 and 1910 legislation see Jo Doezema, "Who Gets to Choose? Coercion, Consent, and the UN Trafficking Protocol," *Gender and Development* 10, no. 1 (2002): 23.

[79] See also "Loose Women or Lost Women? The Re-emergence of the Myth of 'White Slavery' in Contemporary Discourses of 'Trafficking in Women'," *Gender Issues* 18, no. 1 (2000); Frederick Grittner, "Prostitutes in History: From Parables in Pornography to Metaphors of Modernity," *The American Historical Review* 140 (1990); Mary Ann Irwin, "'White Slavery' as Metaphor: Anatomy of a Moral Panic," *Ex Post Facto: The History Journal* 5 (1996), accessed September 29, 2009, http://userwww.sfsu.edu/~epf/1996/wslavery.html; Stephanie A. Limoncelli, *The Politics of Trafficking: The First International Movement to Combat the Sexual Exploitation of Women* (Palo Alto: Stanford University

1910 International Convention for the Suppression of the 'White Slave Traffic,' known as the Paris Convention.[80] The Paris Convention expanded upon the original treaty's definition of trafficking, specifying that its target was "whoever, in order to gratify the passions of another person, has, by fraud, or by means of violence, threats, abuse of authority, or any other method of compulsion, procured, enticed, or led away a woman or girl over age, for immoral purposes."[81] 1910 was also the year that the United States passed the White Slave Traffic Act (later referred to as the Mann Act after its sponsor, Representative James R. Mann of Illinois). The Mann Act specifically addressed the transportation of women and girls across state lines by those who would "induce, entice, or compel such woman or girl to become a prostitute or to give herself up to debauchery, or to engage in any other immoral practice."[82]

Later anti-trafficking treaties expanded their definitions of trafficking to encompass a wider range of victims. The 1921 International Convention for the Suppression of the Traffic in Women and Children, for example, applied to all prostituted adult women, and to male as well as female minors.[83] The 1949 Convention for the Suppression of the Traffic in Persons and of the Exploitation of the Prostitution of Others went even further in describing *all* prostitutes as victims of trafficking, irrespective of the presence of consent or coercion, and notably included adult male prostitutes in its category of individuals to be protected.[84] The 1949 Convention still, however, conceptualized trafficking strictly in terms of prostitution.[85]

Press, 2010); and Soderlund; Judith R. Walkowitz, *Prostitution and Victorian Society: Women, Class, and the State* (Cambridge University Press, 1982); Irwin.

[80] *Dudgeon V. United Kingdom*, Council of Europe. See also Emek M. Uçarer, "Trafficking in Women: Alternate Migration or Modern Slave Trade," in *Gender Politics in Global Governance*, ed. Mary K. Meyer and Elisabeth Prügl (Lanham, MD: Rowman & Littlefield, 1999).

[81] *Dudgeon V. United Kingdom*.

[82] *Kentucky V. Wasson*, 842 Kentucky 487 (1992).

[83] *The Rules of Sociological Method* (New York: The Free Press).

[84] "Human Rights and the Triumph of the Individual in World Culture," *Cultural Sociology* 1, no. 3. See also Andrea M. Bertone, "Transnational Activism to Combat Trafficking in Persons," *Brown Journal of World Affairs* 10, no. 2 (2004): 10.

[85] Kevin Bales, "The Social Psychology of Modern Slavery," *Scientific American* 286, no. 4 (2002): 126

Public interest in problems of human trafficking waned following the passage of the convention only to be stoked again amidst late twentieth-century anxieties regarding globalization.[86] Present-day feminist and faith-based self-described "abolitionists" participating in the Vienna negotiations argued for a Trafficking Protocol that would reflect the 1949 Convention's ban on prostitution.[87] As I discuss at length in Chapters 4 and 5, abolitionists maintain that prostitution is antithetical to women's human rights, and therefore all prostitutes are victims of trafficking.[88]

TRAFFICKING AS COERCED AND EXPLOITED LABOR

Critics of abolitionism take issue with both the traditional security approach to trafficking and with claims that the prostitution of women and children is exhaustive of or represents the most significant form of human trafficking. For those who problematize trafficking in terms of labor coercion and exploitation, trafficking is a subset of a larger problem: abusive treatment of migrants and low-wage laborers,[89] including, but not limited to, sex workers.[90] Insofar as not all trafficked

---

[86] Aradau, *Rethinking Trafficking in Women: Politics Out of Security*, 12.

[87] Raymond, "Guide to the New Un Trafficking Protocol"; Melissa Ditmore and Marjan Wijers, "The Negotiations on the UN Protocol on Trafficking in Persons," *Nemesis* 4 (2003); Jo Doezema, "Now You See Her, Now You Don't: Sex Workers at the UN Trafficking Protocol Negotiation," *Social & Legal Studies* 14, no. 1 (2005); and Jordan, "The Annotated Guide to the Complete UN Trafficking Protocol," 8.

[88] See, e.g., Barry; Sheila Jeffreys, "Trafficking in Women Versus Prostitution: A False Distinction," in *Townsville International Women's Conference* (Australia, 2002); Dorchen A. Leidholdt, "Prostitution: A Modern Form of Slavery," in *Making the Harm Visible: Global Sexual Exploitation of Women and Girls*, ed. Donna M. Hughes and Claire M. Roche (Kingston, RI: Coalition Against Trafficking in Women, 1999); and Raymond, "Prostitution as Violence against Women: Ngo Stonewalling in Beijing and Elsewhere."

[89] In the quoted excerpt, Kempadoo specifically refers to poor women of color. While acknowledging that men and boys are also trafficked, she states that critical "reformulations of the concept of trafficking—to encompass a gendered quality of labor migration, exploitation, and oppression—combine with the knowledge that women are disproportionately represented among the poor, the undocumented, the debt-bonded, and the international migrant workforce, which leads to a continual foregrounding of women's lives and experiences." ix.

[90] Critics of abolitionism generally prefer the terminology of "sex work" and "sex workers" to "prostitution" and "prostitutes" or "prostituted women." "[Sex worker] is a term that suggests we view prostitution not as an identity—a social or psychological

persons are sex workers, and not all human trafficking occurs in sex industries, coercion and exploitation rather than prostitution are seen as the problem. Formulated as a labor exploitation problem, human trafficking is produced by and productive of not only the oppression of women, but global economic inequalities and systems of domination more broadly.[91]

In comparison to the traffic of women and children for sexual exploitation, significantly less attention has been paid to the traffic of women and men for non-sex labor.[92] Media reports, legislative hearings, social service programs, academic research, and transnational advocacy organizations putatively oriented around human trafficking are frequently restricted to sex trafficking.[93] Media coverage is particularly notable for its overwhelming focus on titillating reports of "sex slavery" instead of enslaved domestic staff or abused farm workers.[94]

Scholars connect the labor exploitation problematization of human trafficking to a number of loosely-linked and sometimes overlapping groups, advocacy networks, and social movements including sex workers and proponents of sex workers' rights, libertarian and sex-positive feminists, labor unions, civil rights organizations, and anti-sweatshop activists. Sex workers' rights activists and other feminists have largely taken

characteristic of women, often indicated by "whore"—but as an income-generating activity or form of labor for women and men. The definition stresses the social location of those engaged in sex industries as working people." Kamala Kempadoo, "Introduction: Globalizing Sex Workers' Rights," in *Global Sex Workers: Rights, Resistance, and Redefinition*, ed. Kamala Kempadoo and Jo Doezema (New York: Routledge, 1998), 3.

[91] Bravo, 236.

[92] Elzbieta M. Gozdziak and Elizabeth A. Collett, "Research on Human Trafficking in North America: A Review of Literature," *International Migration* 43, no. 1–2 (2005): 117.

[93] Government Accountability Office, "Human Trafficking: Better Data, Strategy, and Reporting Needed to Enhance U.S. Antitrafficking Efforts Abroad," (2006), 15.

[94] Liz Kelly, "'You Can Find Anything You Want': A Critical Reflection on Research on Trafficking in Persons within and into Europe," *International Migration* 43, no. 1/2 (2005). See, e.g., Finnegan; Kristof, "The Evil Behind the Smiles."; Peter Landesman, "The Girls Next Door," ibid., 25 January 2004; Kathryn Jean Lopez, "Sexual Gulags: Facing and Fighting Sex Trafficking," National Review Online; Michael Specter, "Traffickers' New Cargo: Naïve Slavic Women," *The New York Times*, January 11, 1998. For one notable exception, see Christine Evans et al., "Modern Day Slavery: A Palm Beach Post Special Report," *The Palm Beach Post* 2003.

the lead in rejecting the abolitionist position that sex work is synonymous with human trafficking.[95] Sex workers allied with GAATW during the Trafficking Protocol negotiations in Vienna, for example, were instrumental in rejecting the conflation of trafficking and prostitution per se.[96]

Recognizing that sex work is often abusive and exploitative, rights activists emphasize that these problems are neither inherent nor unique to the sex industries, particularly in comparison to other low-status and low-wage jobs. Whereas feminist abolitionists draw connections between sex trafficked women and all women on the grounds that women as a class are subjected to sexual slavery, proponents of sex workers' rights draw connections between sex workers and workers of all genders in low-paying, low-prestige, and frequently dangerous occupations. Jo Bindman contends that a focus on sex trafficking to the exclusion of

[95] On sex-positive feminism and sex workers' rights organizations, see Wendy Chapkis, *Live Sex Acts: Women Performing Erotic Labor* (New York: Routledge, 1997); Jill Nagle, ed. *Whores and Other Feminists* (New York: Routledge, 1997); and Carol Vance, ed. *Pleasure and Danger: Exploring Female Sexuality* (New York: Pandora Press, 1989). Prominent sex worker advocacy groups and unions include COYOTE (Call Off Your Old Tired Ethics) in the United States, the Scarlet Alliance in Australia, the Red Thread in the Netherlands, Hydra and Hookers United (HGW) in Germany, the Durbar Mahila Samanwaya Committee (DMSC) in India, the Association of Women Prostitutes of Argentina (ANMAR), the Democratic Coalition of Sex Workers in Korea, the International Committee for the Rights of Sex Workers in Europe, the Asia Pacific Network of Sex Workers, the Network of Sex Work Projects, the International Union of Sex Workers, the International Committee for Prostitutes' Rights, and The International Prostitutes' Collective. Gregor Gall, *Sex Worker Union Organizing: An International Study* (Houndsmills, Basingstroke, Hampshire: Palgrave Macmillan, 2006).

[96] Alison Murray, "Debt Bondage and Trafficking: Don't Believe the Hype," in *Global Sex Workers: Rights, Resistance, and Redefinition*, ed. Kamala Kempadoo and Jo Doezema (New York: Routledge, 1998), 98. It should be noted, however, that sex workers' rights proponents are divided on the question of whether "trafficking" is or has the potential to be a politically useful category for addressing worker exploitation. Rights activists disagree about the trade-offs entailed in connecting their political projects to anti-trafficking efforts; Soderlund identifies a split between "those who believed forced sex trafficking was a worthy object of political intervention and those who felt intensive campaigns against trafficking necessarily undermined efforts to secure sex worker rights." Gretchen Soderlund, "Running from the Rescuers: New U.S. Crusades against Sex Trafficking and the Rhetoric of Abolition," *NWSA Journal* 17, no. 3 (2005): 70. See also Jo Doezema, "Forced to Choose: Beyond the Voluntary v. Forced Prostitution Dichotomy," in *Global Sex Workers: Rights, Resistance, and Redefinition*, ed. Kamala Kempadoo and Jo Doezema (New York: Routledge, 1998).

other forms of trafficking unfairly stigmatizes women in the sex industry and places them in a disempowered position.

> The designation of prostitution as a special human rights issue emphasizes the distinction between sex work and other forms of female, dangerous and low-status labor, such as domestic or food service work, or work in factories and on the land. It hides the commonality, the shared experience of exploitation, which links people in all such work.[97]

Sex workers' rights activists argue that stereotypical representations of sex trafficking reproduce the identification of women with sex, suggesting that this dimension of women's experience outweighs all others. They note as well that singling out forced sex work as wholly distinct from forced agricultural, domestic, and factory work leads to a troubling paradox insofar as sexual violence outside of prostitution is overlooked. Insofar as sex work is concerned, rights activists argue that legal or decriminalized prostitution allows sex workers to protest abusive conditions while remaining in the industry should they choose to do so.[98]

At the same time sex workers' rights advocates were pressing for a more expansive understanding of human trafficking, organizations such as the International Labor Organization (ILO) and the US Department of Labor and Department of Justice were engaged in parallel efforts to address and publicize labor trafficking. Two incidents in particular caught the attention of the US federal government: (1) the 1995 El Monte, California case[99] in which the Justice Department discovered 71

---

[97] Jo Bindman, "An International Perspective on Slavery in the Sex Industry," ibid., 65. See also Jo Doezema, "Forced to Choose: Beyond the Voluntary v. Forced Prostitution Dichotomy," ibid., 42.

[98] Priscilla Alexander, "Feminism, Sex Workers, and Human Rights," in *Whores and Other Feminists*, ed. Jill Nagle (New York: Routledge, 1997). On the controversial issue of "choice," Sharon Bell clarifies, "Prostitutes' rights groups do not claim that prostitution is a free choice; they claim that it is as free a choice as other choices make in a capitalist, patriarchal, and racist system." Shannon Bell, *Reading, Writing, and Rewriting the Prostitute Body* (Bloomington and Indianapolis: Indiana University Press, 1994), 111. See also Chapkis, 49.

[99] According to Batstone, the nascent anti-trafficking community in California was horrified by the U.S. government's treatment of the El Monte victims: "After the intervention at El Monte, Secretary of Labor Robert Reich called it 'the worst case of slavery in America's recent history.' Nevertheless, the multiagency strike force that raided the compound treated the victims like illegal aliens. Having survived seven years of enslavement, the women now had to endure another form of captivity—behind bars and forced to wear

Thai men and women who had been held captive and forced to work in a sweatshop; and (2) the 1997 discovery that "dozens of hearing-impaired Mexican nationals were enslaved and forced to peddle trinkets on the streets of New York, Los Angeles and Chicago. Their captors held them through beatings, physical restraint and torture."[100] According to William Yeomans, Chief of Staff for the Civil Rights Division of the Department of Justice, "In 1998, concerned that these cases suggested a bigger problem, the Department of Justice took the lead in forming the Worker Exploitation Task Force."[101]

At the international level, the ILO emphasizes that the gendering of most conceptualizations of human trafficking excludes cases of trafficking for purposes other than sex, including men trafficked for forced labor. A 2008 report specifies:

> Designing anti-trafficking programs requires gender mainstreaming in the reverse sense. Initially, international instruments and programs focused primarily on women and children, however, there is growing consensus that human trafficking can affect men as well. The superficial distinction between women who are trafficked and men who are smuggled (and thus excluded as victims) does not hold in reality. The ILO, through its research and advocacy, has highlighted these conceptual gaps by focusing on labor trafficking into sectors that traditionally involve male migrant workers.[102]

---

prison uniforms. Their treatment sent a horrible message to slaves held anywhere in the United States, supporting the slaveholders' warning: 'Report us to the authorities, and you will be the ones thrown in jail.'" *Not for Sale: The Return of the Global Slave Trade—and How We Can Fight It* (San Francisco: Harper Collins, 2007), 237.

[100] Subcommittee on Near Eastern and South Asian Affairs of the Committee on Foreign Relations, *Hearings on International Trafficking in Women and Children: Prosecution, Testimonies, and Prevention*, 106th Cong. 2nd session, February 22 and April 4, 2000, 76–77. Regarding the California case, see also Bill Wallace, "70 Immigrants Found in Raid on Sweatshop: Thai Workers Tell Horror Stories of Captivity," *The San Francisco Chronicle*, August 4, 1995. Regarding the New York case, see also DeStefano, 6; Deborah Sontag, "Deaf Mexicans Are Found in Forced Labor," *The New York Times*, June 20, 1997.

[101] *Hearings on International Trafficking in Women and Children: Prosecution, Testimonies, and Prevention*, 76–77. See also Amy Driscoll, "Federal Task Force Seeks to Root out Involuntary Servitude," *The Miami Herald*, July 11, 1999.

[102] International Labor Organization, *ILO Action against Trafficking in Human Beings* (Geneva: International Labor Office, 2008), 29.

At the same time, the organization recognizes that "current evidence suggests that women and children make up the majority of victims and tend to be more vulnerable to abusive practices than men."[103]

TRAFFICKING IN INTERNATIONAL RELATIONS

As undertaken by scholars of international relations (IR), trafficking research is not markedly different from that produced within the disciplines of criminology, sociology, and other social sciences. It is in the study of anti-trafficking norms and transnational advocacy networks (TANs)[104] that IR scholars have made the most identifiable contributions to the literature.[105] At the same time, their focus on norm emergence, adoption, and implementation naturalizes the existence of a specific human trafficking "problem" and pays insufficient attention to the power relations that pervade such processes.

The central argument of norms and networks literature on trafficking is that TANs have been responsible for the widespread institutionalization of a norm against human trafficking over the past two decades.[106] Andrea Bertone, for instance, draws upon extensive participant-observation to explore the interplay of state and non-state actors in anti-trafficking campaigns.[107] She finds that global efforts to end trafficking "reflect a

---

[103] Ibid.

[104] I borrow the term from Keck and Sikkink. ibid. Others refer to similar groups of actors as "transnational civil society." See Richard Price, "Transnational Civil Society and Advocacy in World Politics," *World Politics* 55 (2003).

[105] By no means should this claim be read as dismissive of earlier IR feminist research on global sex industries and forced prostitution such as Cynthia Enloe, *Bananas, Beaches & Bases: Making Feminist Sense of International Politics* (Berkeley: University of California Press, 1990); Christine B. N. Chin, *In Service and Servitude: Foreign Female Domestic Workers and the Malaysian 'Modernity' Project* (New York: Columbia University Press, 1988); Katharine H. S. Moon, *Sex among Allies: Military Prostitution in U.S.-Korea Relations* (New York: Columbia University Press, 1997); and Agathangelou. I am making a rather narrower claim about the self-described "human trafficking literature."

[106] See, e.g. Laura Gómez-Mera, "Regime Complexity and Global Governance: The Case of Trafficking in Persons," *European Journal of International Relations* 22, no. 3 (2016); Hannah E. Britton and Laura A. Dean, "Policy Responses to Human Trafficking in Southern Africa: Domesticating International Norms," *Human Rights Review* (2014); and Gillian Wylie, *The International Politics of Human Trafficking* (Palgrave Macmillan, 2016).

[107] Andrea M. Bertone, "Sexual Trafficking in Women: International Political Economy and the Politics of Sex," *Gender Issues* 18, no. 1 (2000); "Transnational Activism to

fairly classic boomerang pattern,"[108] referring to Keck and Sikkink's term for situations in which "domestic NGOs bypass their state and directly search out international allies to try to bring pressure on their states from outside."[109] Similarly, Birgit Locher presents a conventional constructivist account of TAN success in promoting an international norm against human trafficking with an in-depth case study of EU policies targeting trafficking in women.[110] Drawing upon Finnemore and Sikkink's model of a "norm life-cycle,"[111] Locher identifies three intervening variables— actors, frames, and political opportunity structures—as responsible for the dramatic increase in EU efforts during the late 1990s to implement a "revitalized"[112] norm against trafficking. For Locher, and others working in a similar vein, the rhetorical force of human rights and violence against women frames plays a central role in moving human trafficking to the top of the international agenda.[113]

   In their analysis of UN General Assembly resolutions concerning human trafficking, Volha Charnysh, Paulette Lloyd, and Beth Simmons find that the growing international determination to address trafficking is the result of efforts to frame the issue as a common threat linked to transnational crime.[114] Like Bertone and Locher, Charnysh, Lloyd, and Simmons focus on policies intended to address international

---

Combat Trafficking in Persons"; "Human Trafficking on the International and Domestic Agendas: Examining the Role of Transnational Advocacy Networks between Thailand and United States" (University of Maryland, 2008).

[108] "Transnational Activism to Combat Trafficking in Persons," 13.

[109] Keck and Sikkink, 12.

[110] Birgit Locher, *Trafficking in Women in the European Union: Norms, Advocacy-Networks and Policy-Change*, 1. Aufl. ed. (Wiesbaden: VS Verlag für Sozialwissenschaften, 2007), Thesis (doctoral) - Universität Bremen, 2002.

[111] Martha Finnemore and Kathryn Sikkink, "International Norm Dynamics and Political Change," *International Organization* 52, no. 4 (1998).

[112] Locher, 27.

[113] See also Alison Brysk, "Beyond Framing and Shaming," *Journal of Human Security* 5, no. 3 (2009); Alison Brysk and Austin Choi-Fitzpatrick, eds., *From Human Trafficking to Human Rights: Reframing Contemporary Slavery* (Philadelphia: University of Pennsylvania Press, 2012).

[114] Volha Charnysh, Paulette Lloyd, and Beth Simmons, "Frames and Consensus Formation in International Relations: The Case of Trafficking in Persons," *European Journal of International Relations* 21, no. 2 (2014).

sex trafficking of women and girls, as opposed to more expansive conceptualizations of the problem.

A second strand of IR research on human trafficking is more attentive to the manner in which the problem is not just framed, but conceptualized.[115] Yet Efrat[116] illustrates how even scholars who wish to challenge the conflation of different types of trafficking can nonetheless fail to appreciate the ways in which their own conceptual apparatus naturalizes specific groupings of practices and participants. Working from the UN Trafficking Protocol definition, Efrat identifies three purposes of human trafficking—sexual exploitation, labor exploitation, and the removal of organs—and argues that scholars and policymakers "[overlook] fundamental differences between the three forms of human trafficking."[117] Of course, the sex/labor/organ removal trinity is not the only way to divide the practices associated with human trafficking, even if we restrict ourselves to the narrower UN definition of the problem. Efrat, for example, groups "forced labor or services," "slavery or practices similar to slavery," and "servitude" under the category of "labor trafficking," and then criticizes studies that "examine two forms of sex and labor trafficking together as two forms of slavery, overlooking the differences between them."[118] Yet as Quirk comprehensively demonstrates, there are also serious political and analytical consequences to conflating "slavery" with "trafficking," much less with reducing slavery and servitude to examples of labor trafficking.[119] Likewise, while Efrat makes a strong case for the analytic utility of drawing a distinction between Israeli laws and policies that target "sex trafficking" and those that target "labor trafficking," this distinction also erases the perspective of sex workers' rights activists, who argue that sex work should be seen as a form of labor. Efrat contrasts the "relatively clear and specific practices" of organ removal and prostitution

---

[115] See, e.g., Aradau, *Rethinking Trafficking in Women: Politics Out of Security*; Berman; Asif Efrat, "Global Efforts against Human Trafficking: The Misguided Conflation of Sex, Labor, and Organ Trafficking," *International Studies Perspectives* 17, no. 1 (2016); Alex Kreidenweis and Natalie F. Hudson, "More Than a Crime: Re-imaging Anti-trafficking Policy," ibid. 16 (2015); Joel Quirk, *The Anti-slavery Project: From the Slave Trade to Human Trafficking* (Philadelphia: University of Pennsylvania Press, 2011).

[116] Efrat.

[117] Ibid., 34.

[118] Ibid., 37.

[119] Quirk, "Trafficked into Slavery"; *The Anti-Slavery Project: From the Slave Trade to Human Trafficking*.

with forced labor, slavery, and servitude, noting that "the border-line between labor-rights violations and labor trafficking is not easy to recognize."[120] Of course, one of the reasons that the Vienna negotiations surrounding the drafting of the Trafficking Protocol were so contentious in the first place is that questions of consent and the border line between rights violations and trafficking per se are only easy to recognize for those who believe that prostitution itself is fundamentally exploitative. Finally, it is far from obvious—due in part to reasons that Efrat identifies—that the sale of human organs is best understood or addressed as a form of human trafficking. If "organ trafficking has been nearly absent from social science research"[121] and has remained outside the purview of the US-led anti-trafficking campaign, the simplest answer may be that payment for human organs is not widely conceptualized in terms of human trafficking in the first place. In short, the claim that "[d]ifferentiating between sex, labor, and organ smuggling, rather than lumping them together, is essential not only for scholarly purposes, but also in order to formulate effective anti-trafficking policies"[122] must be recognized not only as an academic argument, but as a normative and political judgment as well.

A FEMINIST, CRITICAL CONSTRUCTIVIST APPROACH

Contrary to Kyle and Koslowski's finding that "both governments and activists socially construct 'the problem' in different ways depending on what or for whom they are advocating action,"[123] scholars have largely failed to appreciate the significance of the social construction of human trafficking.[124] Within IR, norms- and network-based analyses of human trafficking make the same error despite being situated within the constructivist tradition. In this section I lay out the details of my proposed remedy: a critical constructivist perspective. I show how genealogical methods such as discourse analysis reveal the productive power

---

[120] Efrat, 40, emphasis in the original.

[121] Ibid., 36.

[122] Ibid., 37.

[123] David Kyle and Rey Koslowski, "Introduction," in *Global Human Smuggling: Comparative Perspectives*, ed. David Kyle and Rey Koslowski (Baltimore: Johns Hopkins University, 2001), 6.

[124] Aradau and Berman are notable exceptions.

inextricably woven into the very fabric of anti-trafficking and the conceptual indeterminacy of "human trafficking" as an object of knowledge and governance.

Constructed, Contested, and Powerful

As an approach to world politics, Ann Towns describes critical constructivism as consisting of "post-structuralisms."[125] Jutta Weldes identifies three analytical commitments that undergird this perspective:

> (1) What we understand as "reality" is socially constructed and hence contestable, (2) constructions of reality both enact and reify relations of power, and (3) an expressly critical constructivism requires that dominant constructions be denaturalized.[126]

As one might expect, the position that reality is socially constructed is shared by constructivists of all stripes.[127] At the same time, although liberal constructivist trafficking scholars do refer to human trafficking as socially constructed, their analyses frequently neglect to address the multiple ways in which power operates in and through the production of sociopolitical "problems."[128]

Power, rather than resting in one particular location or acting as a tangible good that one can possess, inheres in all social relations.[129] Analyses of productive power—"the constitution of all social subjects with various social powers through systems of knowledge and discursive

---

[125] Ann E. Towns, *Women and States: Norms and Hierarchies in International Society* (Cambridge: Cambridge University Press, 2010), 17, 34–40.

[126] Jutta Weldes, "Bureaucratic Politics: A Critical Constructivist Assessment," *Mershon International Studies Review* 42, no. 2 (1998): 217. See also Jutta Weldes et al., "Introduction: Constructing Insecurity," in *Cultures of Insecurity: States, Communities and the Production of Danger* (Minneapolis, MN: University of Minnesota Press, 1999), 13.

[127] See, however, Patrick Thaddeus Jackson, "The Present as History," in *The Oxford Handbook of Contextual Political Analysis*, ed. Robert E. Goodin and Charles Tilly (Oxford: Oxford University Press, 2006), 493–96; Alexander Wendt, *Social Theory of International Politics* (Cambridge: Cambridge University Press, 1999); and Ian Hacking, *The Social Construction of What?* (Cambridge: Harvard University Press, 1999).

[128] See, e.g., Brysk.

[129] Wendy Brown, *States of Injury: Power and Freedom in Late Modernity* (Princeton: Princeton University Press, 1995), 32.

practices of broad and general social scope"[130]—depart from traditional conceptualizations of power in political science and international relations. While productive power is typically contrasted to compulsory power (e.g. "power over") or to material power (e.g., military and economic strength), one can also distinguish between analyses of TANs and social movements as enmeshed within relations of power and those that represent such movements as separable from power, or "speaking truth to power." Liberal constructivists, for example, too often portray the state as the sphere of power and transnational civil society as the sphere of values, presenting, as Michel Foucault put it, "opposition between a power-wielding state that exercises its supremacy over a civil society deprived of such processes of power."[131]

Critical constructivists and others working in a Foucauldian vein suggest an alternative way to understand how power functions in these circumstances. A critical constructivist approach

> conceives of power as much more pervasive. Specifically, it highlights the fact that policymaking is already imbued with power relations long before agendas are set or overt conflicts of interest erupt because all representational practices already entail—that is, enact and reify—power relations. Discourses bring with them the power to constitute worlds.[132]

In analyzing the constitution of worlds, this approach treats neither the state, nor transnational civil society, nor human trafficking as pre-given, natural or extrapolitical kinds, but focuses instead on how each is produced through discursive practices.[133]

[130] Michael N. Barnett and Raymond Duvall, "Power in International Politics," *International Organization* 59, no. 1 (2005): 55.

[131] Michel Foucault, "Questions of Method," in *Power*, ed. James D. Faubion (New York: The New Press, [1978] 1994), 290. See also Ole Jacob Sending and Iver B. Neumann, "Governance to Governmentality: Analyzing Ngos, States, and Power," *International Studies Quarterly* 50 (2006): 258.

[132] 221. See also Chantal Mouffe, *The Democratic Paradox* (Brooklyn: Verso, 2000), 21.

[133] As Towns writes, "In dramatic contrast with world polity and norms scholarship, which largely adopts realist understandings of power, discursive power is understood very broadly as *productive* social practices and structures of meaning that create the conditions of possibility of various international actors and modes of behavior." Towns, 35. Emphasis in the original. See also Judith Butler, *Undoing Gender* (New York: Routledge, 2004); Sandra Bartky, "Foucault, Femininity, and the Modernization of Patriarchal Power," in *Feminist Social Thought*, ed. Diana Tietjens Meyers (New York: Routledge, 1997).

Political problems, if they are seen as objective and measurable, can be managed through bureaucratic expertise without being mediated by politics—this is the "instrumental rationality" of Weber, the "technical reason" of Marcuse, and the "means-end rationality" of Habermas.[134] Yet as Joel Quirk puts it, "human trafficking is not so much a singular issue, as a powerful lodestone for a wide range of interests, orientations, and agendas."[135] *This is not a criticism of anti-trafficking efforts*—from a critical constructivist perspective, the situation could hardly be otherwise. Indeed, one could hardly dismiss the potential strategic benefits of claiming the "moral high ground," representing the anti-trafficking cause as a universal concern, and pursuing solutions in the technocratic realms of governmental bureaucracies and international law.[136] To accept the utility of such strategies, however, is not to say they must be taken at face value.[137] When self-described principled or moral actors depict themselves as beyond or untainted by power, they effectively place themselves beyond critique and contestation, i.e. beyond politics.[138]

Denaturalizing Dominant Constructions

In this book, I carry out a genealogical discourse analysis. Genealogy in the tradition of Michel Foucault and Friedrich Nietzsche calls into question "ready-made syntheses" of the supposedly real, concrete, or self-evident, revealing that which is taken as to be contingent and

---

[134] Brown, 24, 34. See also Chris Brown, "'Turtles All the Way Down': Anti-foundationalism, Critical Theory and International Relations," *Millennium*, no. 23 (1994): 216; James Ferguson, *The Anti-politics Machine: "Development," Depoliticization, and Bureaucratic Power in Lesotho* (Minneapolis: University of Minnesota Press, 1994).

[135] Quirk, "Trafficked into Slavery," 182.

[136] A point Brysk recognizes while still, I contend, minimizing its implications. Alison Brysk, "Sex as Slavery? Understanding Private Wrongs," *Human Rights Review* 12, no. 3 (2011).

[137] See, e.g., Bronwyn Leebaw, "The Politics of Impartial Activism: Humanitarianism and Human Rights," *Perspectives on Politics* 5, no. 2 (2007): 226; Arturo Escobar, *Encountering Development: The Making and Unmaking of the Third World* (Princeton: Princeton University Press, 1995).

[138] Brown, for example, describes hate speech codes as policies, born of social critique, that become reactionary and anti-political "insofar as [they seek] to preempt argument with a legislated and enforced truth." Wendy Brown, *Politics Out of History* (Princeton: Princeton University Press, 2001), 35.

contentious.[139] In short, genealogy "seeks to defamiliarize—to literally make strange—commonsense understandings and so to make their constructedness apparent."[140] A genealogical approach transforms how social scientific questions are asked. In contrast to scholars who start from the assumption that human trafficking is a rapidly growing problem, for example, I ask how anti-trafficking discourses in the United States "set the terms of intelligibility of thought, speech, and action,"[141] establishing the conditions of possibility for what can be meaningfully said or done in any given set of circumstances.

Genealogy lies in contrast to positivist approaches to policy analysis that, according to Dvora Yanow,

> share the presumption that the nature of the problem is real and concrete: that problems exist in the world as unambiguous facts, and that the purpose of policy and implementation analysis is to mirror that reality as closely as possible. In this view, we can take action to correct the problem when we are able to capture its definition appropriately and correctly [...] If we cannot narrow the 'gap' between policy intentions and outcomes, we simply have not grasped 'the nature' of the problem, seen it in the right light, or hit on the correct solution to it.

A genealogical approach to trafficking, for example, moves beyond critiques of policy implementation and rejects the position that a "trafficking victim" is a natural kind that investigators must simply "look harder" to find, or "do more" to help. Instead, a "trafficking victim" is seen as a person who occupies a particular subject position in domestic and international moral and political orders, and in trafficking discourses is distinguished from prostitutes and undocumented migrants among others. Along these lines, I hold that the challenges associated with establishing definitional parameters for "victims of trafficking" are interesting not because there should be greater precision and consistency, or because

---

[139] Michel Foucault, *The Archaeology of Knowledge and the Discourse on Language*, trans. A. M. Sheridan Smith (New York: Pantheon Books, 1972), 22.

[140] Weldes et al., 20.

[141] Neta C. Crawford, "Understanding Discourse: A Method of Ethical Argument Analysis," *Qualitative Methods: Newsletter of the American Political Science Association Organized Section on Qualitative Methods* 2, no. 1 (2004): 22.

this is possible, but because actors' difficulties in doing so provides a clearer glimpse into the discursive work and particular constellations of power necessary to produce the category in the first place.

REFERENCES

Abercrombie, Neil. "Remarks on Trafficking Victims Protection Act of 2000." Washington, DC: U.S. House of Representatives, 2000.

Adamson, Fiona B. "Crossing Borders: International Migration and National Security." *International Security* 31, no. 1 (2006): 165–99.

Agathangelou, Anna M. *The Global Political Economy of Sex: Desire, Violence, and Insecurity in Mediterranean Nation States.* New York: Palgrave Macmillan, 2004.

Alexander, Priscilla. "Feminism, Sex Workers, and Human Rights." In *Whores and Other Feminists,* edited by Jill Nagle, 83–97. New York: Routledge, 1997.

Apap, Joanna, Peter Cullen, and Felicita Medved. "Counteracting Human Trafficking: Protecting the Victims of Trafficking." Paper presented at the European Conference on Preventing and Combating Trafficking in Human Beings, Brussels, September 18–20, 2002.

Aradau, Claudia. "The Perverse Politics of Four-Letter Words: Risk and Pity in the Securitization of Human Trafficking." *Millennium Journal of International Studies* 33, no. 2 (2004): 251–77.

———. *Rethinking Trafficking in Women: Politics out of Security.* New York: Palgrave Macmillan, 2008.

Bales, Kevin. "The Social Psychology of Modern Slavery." *Scientific American* 286, no. 4 (2002): 80–8.

———. *Understanding Global Slavery.* Berkeley: University of California Press, 2005.

Barnett, Michael N., and Raymond Duvall. "Power in International Politics." *International Organization* 59, no. 1 (2005): 39–75.

Barry, Kathleen. *Female Sexual Slavery.* New York: New York University Press, 1979.

Bartky, Sandra. "Foucault, Femininity, and the Modernization of Patriarchal Power." In *Feminist Social Thought,* edited by Diana Tietjens Meyers. New York: Routledge, 1997.

Batstone, David B. *Not for Sale: The Return of the Global Slave Trade—And How We Can Fight It.* San Francisco: HarperCollins, 2007.

Bell, Shannon. *Reading, Writing, and Rewriting the Prostitute Body.* Bloomington and Indianapolis: Indiana University Press, 1994.

Berman, Jacqueline. "(Un)Popular Strangers and Crises (Un)Bounded: Discourses of Sex-Trafficking, the European Political Community and the Panicked State of the Modern State." *European Journal of International Relations* 9, no. 1 (2003): 37–86.

Bertone, Andrea M. "Human Trafficking on the International and Domestic Agendas: Examining the Role of Transnational Advocacy Networks between Thailand and United States." Washington, DC: University of Maryland, 2008.

———. "Sexual Trafficking in Women: International Political Economy and the Politics of Sex." *Gender Issues* 18, no. 1 (2000): 4–22.

———. "Transnational Activism to Combat Trafficking in Persons." *Brown Journal of World Affairs* 10, no. 2 (Winter/Spring 2004): 9–22.

Bindman, Jo. "An International Perspective on Slavery in the Sex Industry." In *Global Sex Workers: Rights, Resistance, and Redefinition,* edited by Kamala Kempadoo and Jo Doezema. New York: Routledge, 1998.

Bravo, Karen E. "Exploring the Analogy between Modern Trafficking in Humans and the Trans-Atlantic Slave Trade." *Boston University International Law Journal* 25 (2007): 207–95.

Britton, Hannah E., and Laura A. Dean. "Policy Responses to Human Trafficking in Southern Africa: Domesticating International Norms." *Human Rights Review* (2014): 1–24.

Brown, Chris. "'Turtles All the Way Down': Anti-foundationalism, Critical Theory and International Relations." *Millennium,* no. 23 (June 1994): 213–36.

Brown, Wendy. *Politics Out of History.* Princeton: Princeton University Press, 2001.

———. *States of Injury: Power and Freedom in Late Modernity.* Princeton: Princeton University Press, 1995.

Bruggeman, Willy. "Illegal Immigration and Trafficking in Human Beings Seen as a Security Problem for Europe." Paper presented at the European Conference on Preventing and Combating Trafficking in Human Beings, Brussels, 2002.

Brysk, Alison. "Beyond Framing and Shaming." *Journal of Human Security* 5, no. 3 (2009): 8–21.

———. "Sex as Slavery? Understanding Private Wrongs." *Human Rights Review* 12, no. 3 (2011): 259–70.

Brysk, Alison, and Austin Choi-Fitzpatrick, eds. *From Human Trafficking to Human Rights: Reframing Contemporary Slavery.* Philadelphia: University of Pennsylvania Press, 2012.

Butler, Judith. *Undoing Gender.* New York: Routledge, 2004.

CdeBaca, Luis. "Question and Answer on Human Trafficking." U.S. Department of State. Accessed December 1, 2010. http://www.state.gov/g/tip/rls/rm/2010/141642.htm.

Chapkis, Wendy. *Live Sex Acts: Women Performing Erotic Labor.* New York: Routledge, 1997.

Charnysh, Volha, Paulette Lloyd, and Beth Simmons. "Frames and Consensus Formation in International Relations: The Case of Trafficking in Persons." *European Journal of International Relations* 21, no. 2 (May 30, 2014): 323–51.

Chin, Christine B. N. *In Service and Servitude: Foreign Female Domestic Workers and the Malaysian 'Modernity' Project.* New York: Columbia University Press, 1988.

Chuang, Janie. "The United States as Global Sheriff: Using Unilateral Sanctions to Combat Human Trafficking." *Michigan Journal of International Law* 27 (2005/2006): 437–94.

Crawford, Neta C. "Understanding Discourse: A Method of Ethical Argument Analysis." *Qualitative Methods: Newsletter of the American Political Science Association Organized Section on Qualitative Methods* 2, no. 1 (Spring 2004): 22–25.

Derks, Annuska. *Combatting Trafficking in South-East Asia: A Review of Policy and Program Responses.* Geneva: International Organization for Migration, 2000.

DeStefano, Anthony M. *The War on Human Trafficking: U.S. Policy Assessed.* New Brunswick, NJ: Rutgers University Press, 2007.

Ditmore, Melissa, and Marjan Wijers. "The Negotiations on the UN Protocol on Trafficking in Persons." *Nemesis* 4 (2003): 79–88.

Doezema, Jo. "Forced to Choose: Beyond the Voluntary v. Forced Prostitution Dichotomy." In *Global Sex Workers: Rights, Resistance, and Redefinition*, edited by Kamala Kempadoo and Jo Doezema. New York: Routledge, 1998.

———. "Loose Women or Lost Women? The Re-emergence of the Myth of 'White Slavery' in Contemporary Discourses of 'Trafficking in Women'." *Gender Issues* 18, no. 1 (2000): 23–50.

———. "Now You See Her, Now You Don't: Sex Workers at the UN Trafficking Protocol Negotiation." *Social & Legal Studies* 14, no. 1 (2005): 61–89.

———. "Who Gets to Choose? Coercion, Consent, and the UN Trafficking Protocol." *Gender and Development* 10, no. 1 (2002): 20–27.

Donnelly, Jack. *Universal Human Rights in Theory and Practice.* 2nd ed. Ithaca: Cornell University Press, 2002.

Driscoll, Amy. "Federal Task Force Seeks to Root out Involuntary Servitude." *The Miami Herald*, July 11, 1999.

Dudas, Jeffrey. *The Cultivation of Resentment: Treaty Rights and the New Right.* Stanford: Stanford University Press, 2008.

Dudgeon V. United Kingdom, Council of Europe (1981).

Durkheim, Emile. *The Rules of Sociological Method*. New York: The Free Press, 1982.

Efrat, Asif. "Global Efforts against Human Trafficking: The Misguided Conflation of Sex, Labor, and Organ Trafficking." *International Studies Perspectives* 17, no. 1 (2016): 34–54.

Elliott, Michael A. "Human Rights and the Triumph of the Individual in World Culture." *Cultural Sociology* 1, no. 3 (2007): 343–63.

Enloe, Cynthia. *Bananas, Beaches & Bases: Making Feminist Sense of International Politics*. Berkeley: University of California Press, 1990.

Escobar, Arturo. *Encountering Development: The Making and Unmaking of the Third World*. Princeton: Princeton University Press, 1995.

European Union. "Fighting Trafficking in Human Beings: An Integrated Approach and Proposals for an Action Plan." Communication from the Commission to the European Parliament and the Council. Accessed September 29, 2009. http://europa.eu.int/eur-lex/lex/LexUriServ/LexUriServ.do?uri=COM:2005:0514:FIN:EN:PDF.

Evans, Christine, John Lantigua, Christine Stapleton, Jane Daugherty, and Connie Piloto. "Modern Day Slavery: A Palm Beach Post Special Report." *The Palm Beach Post*, 2003.

Ferguson, James. *The Anti-politics Machine: "Development," Depoliticization, and Bureaucratic Power in Lesotho*. Minneapolis: University of Minnesota Press, 1994.

Finckenauer, James O. "Russian Transnational Organized Crime and Human Trafficking." In *Global Human Smuggling: Comparative Perspectives*, edited by David Kyle and Rey Koslowski, 166–86. Baltimore: Johns Hopkins University Press, 2001.

Finnegan, William. "The Countertraffickers: Rescuing the Victims of the Global Sex Trade." *The New Yorker*, May 5, 2008.

Finnemore, Martha, and Kathryn Sikkink. "International Norm Dynamics and Political Change." *International Organization* 52, no. 4 (1998): 887–917.

Foucault, Michel. *The Archaeology of Knowledge and the Discourse on Language*. Translated by A.M. Sheridan Smith. New York: Pantheon Books, 1972.

———. "Questions of Method." In *Power*, edited by James D. Faubion, 223–38. New York: The New Press, [1978] 1994.

Friman, H. Richard, and Simon Reich. "Human Trafficking and the Balkans." In *Human Traficking, Human Security, and the Balkans*, edited by H. Richard Friman and Simon Reich, 1–19. Pittsburgh: University of Pittsburgh Press, 2007.

Gall, Gregor. *Sex Worker Union Organizing: An International Study*. Houndsmills, Basingstroke, Hampshire: Palgrave Macmillan, 2006.

Gallagher, Anne. "Trafficking, Smuggling and Human Rights: Tricks and Treaties." *Forced Migration Review* 12 (2002): 25–28.

Gómez-Mera, Laura. "Regime Complexity and Global Governance: The Case of Trafficking in Persons." *European Journal of International Relations* 22, no. 3 (September 1, 2016): 566–95.

Goodey, Jo. "Sex Trafficking in Women from Central and East European Countries: Promoting a 'Victimcentered' and 'Womancentered' Approach to Criminal Justice Intervention." *Feminist Review* 2006 (2004): 26–45.

Government Accountability Office. "Human Trafficking: Better Data, Strategy, and Reporting Needed to Enhance U.S. Antitrafficking Efforts Abroad." 2006.

———. "A Strategic Framework Could Help Enhance the Interagency Collaboration Needed to Effectively Combat Trafficking Crimes." 2007.

Gozdziak, Elzbieta M., and Elizabeth A. Collett. "Research on Human Trafficking in North America: A Review of Literature." *International Migration* 43, no. 1–2 (2005): 99–128.

Graycar, Adam. "Trafficking in Human Beings." Paper presented at the International Conference on Migration, Culture & Crime, Israel, 1999.

Grittner, Frederick. "Prostitutes in History: From Parables in Pornography to Metaphors of Modernity." *The American Historical Review* 140 (1990): 117–41.

Hacking, Ian. *The Social Construction of What?* Cambridge: Harvard University Press, 1999.

Haque, Md. Shahidul. "Ambiguities and Confusions in Migration-Trafficking Nexus: A Development Challenge." In *Trafficking and the Global Sex Industry*, edited by Delika Amir and Karen Beeks. Lanham, MD: Lexington Books, 2006.

Human Smuggling and Trafficking Center. "Report to Congress on the Establishment of the Human Smuggling and Trafficking Center." Washington, DC, 2005.

Huysmans, Jeff. "The European Union and the Securitization of Migration." *Journal of Common Market Studies* 38, no. 5 (2000): 751–77.

International Labor Organization. "Forced Labor, Child Labor, and Human Trafficking in Europe: An ILO Perspective." Paper presented at the European Conference on Preventing and Combating Trafficking in Human Beings, Geneva, September 18–22, 2002.

———. *ILO Action against Trafficking in Human Beings*. Geneva: International Labor Office, 2008.

Irwin, Mary Ann. "'White Slavery' as Metaphor: Anatomy of a Moral Panic." *Ex Post Facto: The History Journal* 5 (1996). Accessed September 29, 2009. http://userwww.sfsu.edu/~epf/1996/wslavery.html.

Jackson, Patrick Thaddeus. "The Present as History." In *The Oxford Handbook of Contextual Political Analysis*, edited by Robert E. Goodin and Charles Tilly, 490–505. Oxford: Oxford University Press, 2006.

Jeffreys, Sheila. "Trafficking in Women Versus Prostitution: A False Distinction." In *Townsville International Women's Conference*. Australia, 2002.

Jordan, Ann D. "The Annotated Guide to the Complete UN Trafficking Protocol." Washington, DC: International Human Rights Law Group, 2002.

———. "Human Rights or Wrongs? The Struggle for a Rights-Based Response to Trafficking in Human Beings." *Gender & Development* 10, no. 1 (2002): 28–37.

———. "Trafficking and Globalization." Center for American Progress. Accessed September 29, 2009. http://www.americanprogress.org/issues/2004/10/b222852.html.

Kapur, Ratna. "Cross-Border Movments and the Law: Renegotiating the Boundaries of Difference." In *Trafficking and Prostitution Reconsidered: New Perspectives on Migration, Sex Work and Human Rights*, edited by Kamala Kempadoo, Jyoti Sanghera, and Bandana Pattanaik, 25–41. Boulder: Paradigm Publishers, 2005.

Katrougalos, George. "The Rights of Foreigners and Immigrants in Europe: Recent Trends." Web Journal of Current Legal Issues. Accessed September 29, 2009. http://webjcli.ncl.ac.uk/articles5/katart5.html.

Keck, Margaret E., and Kathryn Sikkink. *Activists Beyond Borders: Advocacy Networks in International Politics*. Ithaca, NY: Cornell University Press, 1998.

Kelly, Liz. "'You Can Find Anything You Want': A Critical Reflection on Research on Trafficking in Persons within and into Europe." *International Migration* 43, no. 1/2 (January 2005): 235–65.

Kempadoo, Kamala. "From Moral Panic to Social Justice: Changing Perspectives on Trafficking." In *Trafficking and Prostitution Reconsidered: New Perspectives on Migration, Sex Work and Human Rights*, edited by Kamala Kempadoo, Jyoti Sanghera, and Bandana Pattanaik. Boulder: Paradigm Publishers, 2005.

———. "Introduction: Globalizing Sex Workers' Rights." In *Global Sex Workers: Rights, Resistance, and Redefinition*, edited by Kamala Kempadoo and Jo Doezema, 1–28. New York: Routledge, 1998.

Kentucky V. Wasson, 842 Kentucky 487 (1992).

Krause, Keith, and Michael C. Williams. "Broadening the Agenda of Security Studies: Politics and Methods." *Mershon International Studies Review* 40, no. 2 (October 1996): 229–54.

Kreidenweis, Alex, and Natalie F. Hudson. "More Than a Crime: Re-maging Anti-trafficking Policy." *International Studies Perspectives* 16, no. 1 (2015): 67–85.

Kristof, Nicholas D. "The Evil Behind the Smiles." *The New York Times*, January 1, 2009.

————. "Raiding a Brothel in India." *The New York Times*, May 25, 2011.

Kyle, David, and Rey Koslowski. "Introduction." In *Global Human Smuggling: Comparative Perspectives*, edited by David Kyle and Rey Koslowski, 1–25. Baltimore: Johns Hopkins University, 2001.

Laczko, Frank. "Data and Research on Human Trafficking." *International Migration* 43, no. 1–2 (2005): 5–16.

Laffey, Mark, and Jutta Weldes. "Beyond Belief: Ideas and Symbolic Technologies in the Study of International Relations." *European Journal of International Relations* 3, no. 2 (1997): 193–237.

Landesman, Peter. "The Girls Next Door." *The New York Times*, January, 25, 2004.

Leebaw, Bronwyn. "The Politics of Impartial Activism: Humanitarianism and Human Rights." *Perspectives on Politics* 5, no. 2 (2007): 223–39.

Leidholdt, Dorchen A. "Prostitution: A Modern Form of Slavery." In *Making the Harm Visible: Global Sexual Exploitation of Women and Girls*, edited by Donna M. Hughes and Claire M. Roche. Kingston, RI: Coalition Against Trafficking in Women, 1999.

Limoncelli, Stephanie A. *The Politics of Trafficking: The First International Movement to Combat the Sexual Exploitation of Women*. Palo Alto: Stanford University Press, 2010.

Lobasz, Jennifer K. "Beyond Border Security: Feminist Approaches to Human Trafficking." *Security Studies* 18, no. 2 (2009): 319–44.

Locher, Birgit. *Trafficking in Women in the European Union: Norms, Advocacy-Networks and Policy-Change*. 1. Aufl. ed. Wiesbaden: VS Verlag für Sozialwissenschaften, 2007. Thesis (doctoral) - Universität Bremen, 2002.

Lopez, Kathryn Jean. "Sexual Gulags: Facing and Fighting Sex Trafficking." National Review Online.

Mathews, Jessica Tuchman. "Redefining Security." *Foreign Affairs* 68, no. 2 (Spring 1989): 162–77.

Mertus, Julie, and Andrea Bertone. "Combating Trafficking: International Efforts and Their Ramifications." In *Human Trafficking, Human Security, and the Balkans*, edited by H. Richard Friman and Simon Reich, 40–60. Pittsburgh: University of Pittsburgh Press, 2007.

Miller, Ali, and Alison N. Stewart. "Report from the Roundtable on the Meaning of 'Trafficking in Persons': A Human Rights Perspective." *Women's Rights Law Reporter* 20, no. 1 (Fall/Winter 1998): 11–20.

Miller, John R. "Call It Slavery." *Wilson Quarterly* 32, no. 3 (Summer 2008): 52–56.

Moon, Katharine H. S. *Sex among Allies: Military Prostitution in U.S.-Korea Relations*. New York: Columbia University Press, 1997.

Mouffe, Chantal. *The Democratic Paradox*. Brooklyn: Verso, 2000.

Murray, Alison. "Debt Bondage and Trafficking: Don't Believe the Hype." In *Global Sex Workers: Rights, Resistance, and Redefinition*, edited by Kamala Kempadoo and Jo Doezema. New York: Routledge, 1998.

Nagle, Jill, ed. *Whores and Other Feminists*. New York: Routledge, 1997.

Naím, Moisés. *Illicit: How Smugglers, Traffickers, and Copycats Are Hijacking the Global Economy*. Doubleday, 2005.

Pearson, Elaine. *Human Rights and Trafficking in Persons: A Handbook*. Bangkok: Global Alliance Against Traffic in Women, 2000.

Price, Richard. "Transnational Civil Society and Advocacy in World Politics." *World Politics* 55 (2003): 579–606.

Quirk, Joel. *The Anti-slavery Project: From the Slave Trade to Human Trafficking*. Philadelphia: University of Pennsylvania Press, 2011.

———. "Trafficked into Slavery." *Journal of Human Rights* 6, no. 2 (2007): 181–207.

———. "Trafficked into Slavery." *Journal of Human Rights* 6 (2007): 181–207.

Raymond, Janice G. "Guide to the New Un Trafficking Protocol." North Amherst, MA: Coalition Against Trafficking in Women, 2001.

———. "Prostitution as Violence against Women: NG Stonewalling in Beijing and Elsewhere." *Women's Studies International Forum* 21, no. 1 (1998): 1–9.

Raymond, Janice G., and Donna M. Hughes. "Sex Trafficking of Women in the United States: International and Domestic Trends." New York: Coalition Against Trafficking in Women, 2001.

Rees, Wyn. "Organised Crime, Security and the European Union: Draft Paper for the ESRC Workshop, Grenoble." European Consortium for Political Research. Accessed September 29, 2009. http://www.essex.ac.uk/ecpr/events/jointsessions/paperarchive/grenoble/ws8/rees.pdf.

Sanghera, Jyoti. "Unpacking the Trafficking Discourse." In *Trafficking and Prostitution Reconsidered: New Perspectives on Migration, Sex Work and Human Rights*, edited by Kamala Kempadoo, Jyoti Sanghera and Bandana Pattanaik, 3–24. Boulder: Paradigm Publishers, 2005.

Scully, Eileen. "Pre-Cold War Traffic in Sexual Labor and Its Foes: Some Contemporary Lessons." In *Global Human Smuggling: Comparative Perspectices*, edited by David Kyle and Rey Koslowski. Baltimore: Johns Hopkins University, 2001.

Sending, Ole Jacob, and Iver B. Neumann. "Governance to Governmentality: Analyzing Ngos, States, and Power." *International Studies Quarterly* 50 (2006): 651–72.

Sharma, Nandita. "Anti-trafficking Rhetoric and the Making of a Global Apartheid." *NWSA Journal* 17, no. 3 (Fall 2005): 88–111.

Shelley, Louise I. "Trafficking in Women: The Business Model Approach." *Brown Journal of World Affairs* X, no. 1 (Summer/Fall 2003): 119–31.

———. "Transnational Organized Crime: An Imminent Threat to the Nation-State?" *Journal of International Affairs* 48, no. 2 (Winter 1995): 463.

Skinner, E. Benjamin. *A Crime So Monstrous: Face-to-Face with Modern-Day Slavery.* New York: Free Press, 2009.

Smith, Christopher H. "Remarks on Trafficking Victims Protection Act of 2000." Washington, DC: U.S. House of Representatives, 2000.

Soderlund, Gretchen. "Covering Urban Vice: The New York Times, 'White Slavery,' and the Construction of Journalistic Knowledge." *Critical Studies in Media Communication* 19, no. 4 (2002): 438–60.

———. "Running from the Rescuers: New U.S. Crusades against Sex Trafficking and the Rhetoric of Abolition." *NWSA Journal* 17, no. 3 (Fall 2005): 64–87.

Sontag, Deborah. "Deaf Mexicans Are Found in Forced Labor." *The New York Times,* June 20, 1997.

Specter, Michael. "Traffickers' New Cargo: Naïve Slavic Women." *The New York Times,* 11 January 1998.

Stange, Margit. *Personal Property: Wives, White Slaves, and the Market in Women.* Baltimore: Johns Hopkins University Press, 2002.

Subcommittee on International Operations and Human Rights of the Committee on International Relations. *Hearing on Trafficking of Women and Children in the International Sex Trade,* 106th Cong. 1st session, September 14, 1999.

Subcommittee on Near Eastern and South Asian Affairs of the Committee on Foreign Relations. *Hearings on International Trafficking in Women and Children: Prosecution, Testimonies, and Prevention,* 106th Cong. 2nd session, February 22 and April 4, 2000.

Tickner, J. Ann. *Gendering World Politics.* New York: Columbia University Press, 2001.

Towns, Ann E. *Women and States: Norms and Hierarchies in International Society.* Cambridge: Cambridge University Press, 2010.

"Traffic, N." In *OED Online.* Oxford University Press, 2011. http://www.oed.com/view/Entry/204333?rskey=QD1HFv&result=1&isAdvanced=false.

"Traffic, V." In *OED Online.* Oxford University Press, 2011. Accessed September 29, 2009. http://www.oed.com/view/Entry/204333?rskey=QD1HFv&result=1&isAdvanced=false.

Tyldum, Guri, and Anette Brunovskis. "Describing the Unobserved: Methodological Challenges in Empirical Studies on Human Trafficking." *International Migration* 43, no. 1/2 (2005): 17–34.

U.S. Immigration and Customs Enforcement. "Fact Sheet: Human Smuggling and Trafficking Center." Accessed September 29, 2009. http://www.ice.gov/news/library/factsheets/hstc.htm.

Uçarer, Emek M. "Trafficking in Women: Alternate Migration or Modern Slave Trade." In *Gender Politics in Global Governance,* edited by Mary K. Meyer and Elisabeth Prügl, 230–44. Lanham, MD: Rowman & Littlefield, 1999.

Ullman, Richard H. "Redefining Security." *International Security* 8, no. 1 (1983): 129–53.

United Nations. "Protocol against the Smuggling of Migrants by Land, Sea and Air, Supplementing the United Nations Convention against Transnational Crime." G.A. Res. 55/25, annex III, U.N. GAOR, 55th Sess., Supp. No. 49, at 65, U.N. Doc. A/45/49, 2001.

United Nations General Assembly. "Protocol to Prevent, Suppress and Punish Trafficking in Persons, Especially Women and Children, Supplementing the United Nations Convention against Transnational Organized Crime." Accessed September 29, 2009. http://www.unhcr.org/refworld/docid/4720706c0.html.

United Nations. "Special Rapporteur on Trafficking in Persons, Especially Women and Children." Accessed June 6, 2018. http://www.ohchr.org/EN/Issues/Trafficking/Pages/TraffickingIndex.aspx.

United States Department of State. "Victims of Trafficking and Violence Protection Act of 2000: Trafficking in Persons Report." Accessed September 29, 2009. http://www.state.gov/g/tip/rls/tiprpt/2004/.

Vance, Carol, ed. *Pleasure and Danger: Exploring Female Sexuality.* New York: Pandora Press, 1989.

Walkowitz, Judith R. *Prostitution and Victorian Society: Women, Class, and the State.* Cambridge University Press, 1982.

Wallace, Bill. "70 Immigrants Found in Raid on Sweatshop: Thai Workers Tell Horror Stories of Captivity." *The San Francisco Chronicle*, 4 August 1995.

Weldes, Jutta. "Bureaucratic Politics: A Critical Constructivist Assessment." *Mershon International Studies Review* 42, no. 2 (November 1998): 216–25.

Weldes, Jutta, Mark Laffey, Hugh Gusterson, and Raymond Duvall. "Introduction: Constructing Insecurity." In *Cultures of Insecurity: States, Communities and the Production of Danger*, 1–33. Minneapolis, MN: University of Minnesota Press, 1999.

Wendt, Alexander. *Social Theory of International Politics.* Cambridge: Cambridge University Press, 1999.

White House Office of the Press Secretary. "Fact Sheet on Migrant Smuggling and Trafficking." 2000.

Wolfers, Arnold. "'National Security' as an Ambiguous Symbol." *Political Science Quarterly* 67, no. 4 (1952): 481–502.

Wylie, Gillian. *The International Politics of Human Trafficking.* Palgrave Macmillan, 2016.

CHAPTER 3

The Trafficking Victims Protection Act of 2000

On September 14, 1999, Representative Chris Smith (R-NJ), Chairman of the US House of Representatives Subcommittee on International Operations and Human Rights, presided over a hearing "to investigate one of the world's most serious and most widespread human rights problems: The trafficking of women and children for the international sex trade."[1] Of the five witnesses called, one, in particular, stood out— Anita Sharma Bhattarai, a twenty-eight-year-old Nepalese woman identified as a trafficking survivor. Bhattarai, testifying with the aid of an interpreter, briefly recounted how a man and a woman she had met on a bus gave her a banana that had been drugged. The traffickers took her to a brothel in Mumbai, where she was forced to work as a prostitute. Bhattarai managed to escape, however, and a local International Justice Mission (IJM) worker helped her to free other girls enslaved in the same brothel.[2] A second witness, IJM President and CEO Gary Haugen, commended Bhattarai for her courage in sharing the story of her experience in "living hell."

> I believe the American people are compassionate people, and they will hear Anita's story, they will hear the story of those 950,000 others that you

---

[1] Subcommittee on International Operations and Human Rights of the Committee on International Relations, *Hearing on Trafficking of Women and Children in the International Sex Trade*, 106th Congress 1st session, September 14, 1999, 1.

[2] Ibid., 35–36.

© The Author(s) 2019
J. K. Lobasz, *Constructing Human Trafficking*, Human Rights Interventions, https://doi.org/10.1007/978-3-319-91737-5_3

mentioned, Congressman [Smith], and over time, it may not be today but tomorrow, sometime later, the American people will hear the story, and they will respond.[3]

In fact, Americans had already begun to hear and respond to stories such as these.[4] In addition to feminist abolitionist groups, some of whom had already spent decades working to end trafficking in women and children, the Clinton administration had already begun to address the issue.[5]

This chapter focuses on efforts of members of Congress, senior officials in the Clinton administration, and a wide range of highly active members of an abolitionist transnational advocacy network to place the United States at the forefront of global efforts to end human trafficking. I concentrate in particular on efforts within the US Congress from 1998 through 2000, a brief but highly significant period during which anti-trafficking legislation was introduced, vigorously debated, and ultimately signed into law. I ask how trafficking was constructed as a problem worthy of intervention, and what subjects and practices were produced, reproduced, challenged, and rendered invisible or undesirable through anti-trafficking discourses in the United States during this period. The answer, I find, begins with neo-abolitionist discourses featuring gendered and racialized invocations of the scourge of slavery, the ideal of human rights, and the responsibility of the United States to lead the anti-trafficking charge across the globe. And yet, despite the growing political significance of evangelical Christians—the driving force behind faith-based religious abolitionism—and their successful alliance on this issue with radical feminists, the final terms of the Trafficking Victims Protection Act of 2000 (TVPA) departed from abolitionists' proposals in important ways. Such differences, however, proved largely

---

[3]Statement of Gary A. Haugen, President and Chief Executive Office, International Justice Mission, ibid., 40.

[4]See, e.g., Anthony M. DeStefano, *The War on Human Trafficking: U.S. Policy Assessed* (New Brunswick, NJ: Rutgers University Press, 2007), 37.

[5]Francis T. Miko, "Trafficking in Women and Children: The U.S. and International Response," in *Trafficking in Women and Children: Current Issues and Developments*, ed. Anna M. Troubnikoff (New York: Nova Science, 2003). According to reporter Benjamin Skinner, then-First Lady Hillary Clinton encouraged her husband to address the issue after she was "deeply affected by meeting an HIV-positive sex slave during a 1994 trip to Thailand." E. Benjamin Skinner, *A Crime So Monstrous: Face-to-Face with Modern-Day Slavery* (New York: Free Press, 2009), 51.

insignificant during the first eight years following the law's passage inso-far as President George W. Bush's administration acceded to abolitionist demands concerning the TVPA's implementation.

The chapter begins with an overview of federal anti-trafficking efforts from 1998 through 2000, followed by a more thorough analysis of the competing ways in which human trafficking was conceptualized as a problem. I then turn to the two claims upon which all participants in the legislative process agreed: that human trafficking, whatever the final definition, represents an extraordinary violation of human rights and the manifestation of modern-day slavery. Finally, I address the gendered and racialized subjects produced through anti-trafficking discourses during this period as victims, villains, or virtuous.

A Capsule History

In 1998, President Clinton chose March 11—International Women's Day—to announce a government-wide anti-trafficking strategy.[6] Clinton's "Memorandum on Steps to Combat Violence against Women and Trafficking in Women and Girls" introduced a "3 P" approach centered on *prevention*, *protection*, and *prosecution*.[7] As the title of the presidential memorandum suggests, administration officials accepted abolitionists' gendered characterization of women and children as the populations most vulnerable to being trafficked. The administration rejected, however, abolitionist calls to focus primarily or exclusively on the sex trade, and Clinton noted that the federal government had already discovered "cases of trafficking for the purposes of forced prostitution, sweatshop labor, and exploitative domestic servitude."[8]

Likewise, while Smith's 1999 hearing was the first in a series that even-tually led to the passage of groundbreaking anti-trafficking legislation in

---

[6]William J. Clinton, "Memorandum on Steps to Combat Violence against Women and Trafficking in Women and Girls," *Weekly Compilation of Presidential Documents* 34, no. 11 (1998). Clinton also used the occasion to call on the Senate to ratify the UN Convention on the Elimination of All Forms of Discrimination Against Women (CEDAW), which has yet to occur.

[7]Francis T. Miko, "Trafficking in Persons: The U.S. and International Response" (Washington, DC: CRS Report for Congress, 2006), 8. The "3 Ps" framework would soon come to dominate the formation of anti-trafficking policy at the global level.

[8]Clinton.

2000, it was not the first time Congress had taken up the issue. In 1995, for example, Representative Louise Slaughter (D-NY) and Senator Patty Murray (D-WA) introduced resolutions condemning "the trafficking of Burmese women and girls into Thailand for the purposes of forced prostitution."[9] Three years later, Slaughter and Senator Paul Wellstone (D-MN) joined President Clinton in using International Women's Day to raise awareness of trafficking in persons (TIP) and its "disproportionate impact on women and girls."[10] The Slaughter and Wellstone resolutions urged bureaus within the Department of State and Department of Justice to expand their anti-trafficking efforts, and called for the President's Interagency Council on Women (PICW) to report to Congress on the success of these initiatives. Smith and Senator Sam Brownback (R-KS) carried the banner for religious abolitionists at the congressional level, while Wellstone and fellow Democrats pressed for a human rights-based approach more in line with that taken by the Clinton administration.

Congressional anti-trafficking activity intensified the following year. On March 11, 1999, Wellstone drew upon the symbolism of International Women's Day once again to introduce S. 600, the International Trafficking of Women and Children Victim Protection Act of 1999.[11] On March 25, Smith introduced a competing bill in the House: H.R. 1356, the Freedom from Sexual Trafficking Act of 1999, modeled on the successful International Religious Freedom Act of 1998.[12] Neither anti-trafficking bill would make it out of committee.

[9] *H. Con. Res. 21 Trafficking of Burmese Women and Girls into Thailand for the Purposes of Forced Prostitution*, 104th Congress, 1st Session, February 1, 1995; *S. Con. Res. 12 Trafficking of Burmese Women and Girls into Thailand for the Purposes of Forced Prostitution*, 104th Congress, 1st Session, May 4, 1995.

[10] *H. Con. Res. 239 Worldwide Trafficking of Persons*, 105th Congress, 2nd Session, March 10, 1998; *S. Con. Res. 82 Worldwide Trafficking of Persons*, 105th Congress, 2nd Session, March 10, 1998.

[11] *S. 600 International Trafficking of Women and Children Victim Protection Act of 1999*, 106th Congress, 1st Session, March 11, 1999. Slaughter introduced an identical bill in the House, H.R. 1238, on March 23. *H.R. 1238 International Trafficking of Women and Children Victim Protection Act of 1999*, 106th Congress, 1st Session, March 23, 1999.

[12] *H.R. 1356 Freedom from Sexual Trafficking Act of 1999*, 106th Congress, 1st Session, March 25, 1999. On the relationship between the Freedom from Sexual Trafficking Act and the International Religious Freedom Act, see *Hearing on Trafficking of Women and Children in the International Sex Trade*, 12; Allen D. Hertzke, *Freeing God's Children: The Unlikely Alliance for Global Human Rights* (Rowman & Littlefield, 2004). @322

Smith and Wellstone resumed their efforts in the fall. On October 27, 1999, Representative Sam Gejdenson (D-CT), introduced H.R. 3154, the Comprehensive Anti-Trafficking in Persons Act of 1999.[13] Wellstone introduced an identical bill, S. 1842, five days later.[14] Smith responded on November 8 with H.R. 3244, the Trafficking Victims Protection Act of 1999.[15] Noting "the different ideological perspectives of the lobbyist and legislator groups"[16] participating in the legislative process, Jayashri Srikantiah summarizes key differences among the bills:

> First, some applied only to sex trafficking while others covered labor trafficking as well. Second, the bills varied with respect to the level of coercion that a trafficked individual must have endured (ranging from "abuse of authority" to physical force) in order to be considered a "victim of trafficking" and thus entitled to immigration protections. Third, some bills additionally required fear of retribution if removed (deported), while others focused on whether the victim had suffered physical or mental abuse as a result of trafficking.[17]

In the months of heated negotiations that followed, Smith and his fellow abolitionists succeeded in establishing H.R. 3244 as the primary point of reference.[18] The two anti-trafficking bills subsequently introduced in the Senate—Wellstone's S. 2414, introduced on April 12, 2000, and Brownback's S. 2449, introduced the next day—took the Smith bill as their blueprint.[19] Conferees appointed by each chamber worked to resolve remaining points of dispute, and the Trafficking Victims

---

[13] *H.R. 3154 Comprehensive Anti-trafficking in Persons Act of 1999*, 106th Congress, 1st Session, October 27, 1999.

[14] *S. 1842 Comprehensive Anti-trafficking in Persons Act of 1999*, 106th Congress, 1st Session, November 2, 1999.

[15] *H.R. 3244 Trafficking Victims Protection Act of 1999*, 106th Congress, 1st Session, November 8, 1999.

[16] Jayashri Srikantiah, "Perfect Victims and Real Survivors: The Iconic Victim in Domestic Human Trafficking Law," *Boston University Law Review* 87 (2007): 169.

[17] Ibid.

[18] Committee on International Relations, "Report to Accompany H.R. 3244" (Washington, DC: U.S. House of Representatives, 1999).

[19] *S. 2414 Trafficking Victims Protection Act of 2000*, 106th Congress, 2nd Session, April 12, 2000; *S. 2449 International Trafficking Act of 2000*, 106th Congress, 2nd Session, April 13, 2000.

Protection Act of 2000 (TVPA) was subsequently passed as part of an omnibus bill and signed into law by President Bill Clinton on October 28, 2000.[20]

WHAT'S THE PROBLEM?

From 1998 to 2000, Congress held three hearings specifically concerned with TIP and introduced six distinct anti-trafficking bills. Comparison of hearing and bill titles provides an instructive first glimpse of how trafficking was initially conceptualized as a problem.

The titles listed in Tables 3.1 and 3.2 suggest at least four different conceptualizations of trafficking: (1) transporting women and children across international borders for forced prostitution; (2) transporting women and children across international borders for various types of forced labor, including prostitution; (3) transporting any person across international borders for various types of forced labor, including prostitution; and (4) subjecting any person to forced labor, including prostitution. Three elements of this list received the most attention: movement across international borders, the association between human trafficking and the sex trade, and the particular vulnerability of women and children. In this section I address the assumed relationships between trafficking, border crossing, and the sex trade. I return to the particular vulnerability of women and children later in the chapter.

Movement Across International Borders

The assumption that human trafficking entails movement across borders was commonly held and rarely questioned by participants in anti-trafficking debates of this period.[21] Smith's Freedom From Sexual

---

[20] "Remarks on Trafficking Victims Protection Act of 2000" (Washington, DC: U.S. House of Representatives, 2000). The TVPA faced only one dissenting vote in the House of Representatives, and was then unanimously approved in the Senate. For a more exhaustive account of legislative maneuvering surrounding the bill, see DeStefano; Hertzke; Skinner.

[21] This is consistent with a broader trend identified by Aradau, who finds that "almost all definitions of trafficking include the element of 'movement across borders.'" Claudia Aradau, *Rethinking Trafficking in Women: Politics Out of Security* (New York: Palgrave Macmillan, 2008), 22. See also the discussion regarding "Trafficking as Migration" in Chapter 2 of this book.

Table 3.1   Hearings regarding human trafficking

Date	Committee	Hearing title
September 14, 1999	Subcommittee on International Operations and Human Rights of the Committee on International Relations, House of Representatives	Trafficking of Women and Children in the International Sex Trade
February 22, 2000	Subcommittee on Near Eastern and South Asian Affairs, Committee on Foreign Relations, Senate	International Trafficking of Women and Children
April 4, 2000	Subcommittee on Near Eastern and South Asian Affairs, Committee on Foreign Relations, Senate	International Trafficking of Women and Children: Prosecution, Testimonies, and Prevention

Table 3.2   US Congress bills regarding human trafficking

Date	Sponsor(s)	Bill title
March 11, 1999	Rep. Louise Slaughter Sen. Paul Wellstone	International Trafficking of Women and Children Victim Protection Act of 1999
March 23, 1999	Rep. Chris Smith	Freedom From Sexual Trafficking Act of 1999
October 27, 1999	Rep. Sam Gejdenson Sen. Paul Wellstone	Comprehensive Anti-Trafficking in Persons Act of 1999
November 8, 2000	Rep. Chris Smith	Trafficking Victims Protection Act of 1999
April 12, 2000	Sen. Paul Wellstone	Trafficking Victims Protection Act of 2000
April 13, 2000	Sen. Sam Brownback	International Trafficking Act of 2000

Trafficking Act of 1999, for instance, applied only to "*international* sexual trafficking, in which women and children are brought across international boundaries by means of force or fraud for purposes of forced prostitution, sexual slavery, and similar practices."[22] Similarly, Assistant Secretary of State Harold Koh made the connection between trafficking and borders explicit in his testimony before the House Subcommittee on International Operations and Human Rights:

[22] *H.R. 1356 Freedom from Sexual Trafficking Act of 1999.* Emphasis added.

> Trafficking involves a vicious cycle in which victims are forced or lured from their home countries. They are shuttled across international borders and enslaved, with human rights violations occurring every step of the way.[23]

Koh made the same point in response to a question from Wellstone during hearings before the Senate Subcommittee on Near Eastern and South Asian Affairs, emphasizing that trafficking should be chiefly characterized by "the use of force, or fraud, and artifice, to get people across borders"[24] rather than any resultant sexual exploitation.

The belief that border crossing is a defining characteristic of human trafficking has two primary consequences. First, the association between trafficking and movement across international borders establishes human trafficking as an *external* problem facing the United States. The causes—and hence, the blame—for trafficking are portrayed as international rather than domestic. Wellstone, for example, routinely described trafficking as "one of the darkest aspects of globalization of the world economy, becoming more insidious and more widespread every day."[25] Blame was also attributed to the dissolution of the Soviet Union[26] and the purported growth of increasingly sophisticated transnational organized crime groups.[27] Externally-focused accounts allow other potential causal

---

[23] *Hearing on Trafficking of Women and Children in the International Sex Trade*, 9.

[24] Subcommittee on Near Eastern and South Asian Affairs of the Committee on Foreign Relations, *Hearings on International Trafficking in Women and Children: Prosecution, Testimonies, and Prevention*, 106th Congress, 2nd session, February 22 and April 4, 2000, 22. Koh's response notably reflects the Clinton Administration's changing stance on how broadly to define trafficking. Even as it was restricted to cross-border movement, its targets were "people" rather than only "women and children."

[25] Ibid., 3. Arguing along the same lines, Senator Kay Bailey Hutchison (R-TX) remarked, "It is a sad consequence of globalization that crime has become more international in its scope and reach. These seedy sex industries know no boundaries." Kay Bailey Hutchison, "Victims of Trafficking and Violence Protection Act of 2000 Conference Report" (Washington, DC: U.S. Senate, 2000), S101217. See also International Labor Organization, "Forced Labor, Child Labor, and Human Trafficking in Europe: An Ilo Perspective" (paper presented at the European Conference on Preventing and Combating Trafficking in Human Beings, Geneva, September 18–22, 2002).

[26] Paul Wellstone, "Victims of Trafficking and Violence Protection Act of 2000 Conference Report" (Washington, DC: U.S. Senate, 2000), S10167.

[27] Brownback, for example, castigated the "organized crime units and groups that are aggressively out making money off the trafficking of human flesh." Sam Brownback, "Victims of Trafficking and Violence Protection Act of 2000 Conference Report"

factors such as domestic demand for prostitution and cheap labor, lax oversight of the working conditions of migrant laborers, and the effects of strict immigration laws to evade scrutiny.[28]

The second effect of the association between trafficking and movement across international borders concerns the exclusion of domestic practices that could conceivably fit under alternative conceptualizations of trafficking. This is clearest with regard to prostitution. As I show in Chapter 4, feminist abolitionists recognize no meaningful difference between international trafficking and domestic prostitution.[29] In *Female Sexual Slavery*, for example, Kathleen Barry finds that "street pimps" and "international procurers" share similar strategies and goals, and that "practices used to force women into prostitution are the same whether they are trafficked across international boundaries or from one part of a city to another."[30] Drawing upon the groundbreaking analyses of rape published by her radical feminist contemporaries, Barry asserts that when "a woman or a girl is held in sexual slavery, sexual intercourse is, by definition, rape."[31] She continues, "Rape is the primordial core of female sexual slavery, extending from the most public international traffic in women for prostitution to the most private slavery in a suburban home, city tenement, or rural cottage."

Compare Barry's reasoning to Smith's call for Congress to take immediate action against international sex trafficking:

We must not delay even for a single day the effort to save these millions of women and children who are forced every day to submit to the most

---

(Washington, DC: U.S. Senate, 2000), S10166. See also Amy O'Neill Richard, "International Trafficking in Women to the United States: A Contemporary Manifestation of Slavery and Organized Crime," in *DCI Exceptional Intelligence Analyst Program* (Washington, DC: Center for the Study of Intelligence, 2000), 13.

[28]Wellstone made a rare reference to domestic causes such as demand for cheap labor on the same day that the TVPA was passed by the Senate. Wellstone, S10167. See also Julia O'Connell Davidson and Bridget Anderson, "The Trouble with 'Trafficking'," in *Trafficking and Women's Rights*, ed. Christien L. van der Anker and Jeroen Doomernik (Houndmills, Basingstoke, Hampshire: Palgrave Macmillan, 2006), 19.

[29]Kathleen Barry, *Female Sexual Slavery* (New York: New York University Press, 1979), 6–7.

[30]Ibid., 7.

[31]Ibid., 40.

atrocious offenses against their persons and against their dignity as human beings. Forcible and fraudulent trafficking of women and children for the commercial sex trade is a uniquely brutal practice. It is commercial rape, and it cries out for its own comprehensive and immediate solution.[32]

Much has been made of the "strange bedfellows" alliance between feminist and religious abolitionists,[33] yet in many respects Smith's forceful language echoes that of Barry. The discordant note sounds when Smith's statement is examined in its original context—i.e., in support of a bill that restricts relief for victims of "commercial rape" to those who have crossed international borders in the process. The construction of human trafficking as "international" enables the indefinite delay of consideration for women and children already in the United States "who are forced every day to submit to the most atrocious offenses against their persons."[34]

The assumed connection between trafficking and international migration likewise excludes domestic practices that the Department of Justice had at one time prosecuted as violations of the Thirteenth Amendment. Prosecution of many such cases had halted following the Supreme Court's 1988 ruling in *United States v. Kozminski*, which restricted the federal statute prohibiting slavery and involuntary servitude, 18 U.S.C. 241, to situations involving "the use or threatened use of physical or legal coercion."[35] William Yeomans, Chief of Staff for the Civil Rights

---

[32] *Hearing on Trafficking of Women and Children in the International Sex Trade*, 4.

[33] See, e.g., Jacqueline Berman, "The Left, the Right, and the Prostitute: The Making of U.S. Anti-trafficking in Persons Policy," *Tulane Journal of International and Comparative Law* 14 (2005–2006); Elizabeth Bernstein, "The Sexual Politics of the 'New Abolitionism'," *Differences* 18, no. 3 (2007); Elizabeth Bumiller, "Evangelicals Sway White House on Human Rights Issues Abroad: Liberals Join Effort on Aids and Sex Trafficking," *The New York Times, pp. A1* (2003); Wendy Chapkis, "Trafficking, Migration, and the Law: Protecting Innocents, Punishing Immigrants," *Gender & Society* 17, no. 6 (2003); Melissa Ditmore, "Trafficking in Lives: How Ideology Shapes Policy," in *Trafficking and Prostitution Reconsidered: New Perspectives on Migration, Sex Work and Human Rights*, ed. Kamala Kempadoo, Jyoti Sanghera, and Bandana Pattanaik (Boulder: Paradigm Publishers, 2005); Debbie Nathan, "Oversexed," *The Nation*, August 29, 2005; Nina Shapiro, "The New Abolitionists," *Seattle Weekly*, August 25, 2004; and Srikantiah.

[34] *Hearing on Trafficking of Women and Children in the International Sex Trade*, 4.

[35] *United States V. Kozminski*, 487 US 931 (1988). See also U.S. Department of Justice Civil Rights Division, "Statutes Enforced by the Criminal Section," accessed September 29, 2009, http://www.justice.gov/crt/about/crm/statutes.php; Srikantiah, 173. I thank Ambassador Luis Cdebaca for stressing the significance of this ruling to me.

Division of the Department of Justice, alludes to this issue in his testimony before the Senate on April 4, 2000. The limitations imposed on law enforcement by Kozminski, Yeomans explained, could only be addressed by an act of Congress "to expand the definition of 'coercion' to cover situations that fall short of force or threat of force, but in which the victim has no valid alternative but to submit to a condition of servitude."[36] While an expanded definition of coercion would presumably apply to victims irrespective of their immigration status,[37] Yeomans emphasized the particular need for federal law "to acknowledge that some immigrants and foreign nationals upon whom traffickers prey are particularly susceptible to coercion because of their unfamiliarity with our language, laws and customs."[38]

The Sex Trade

In the second chapter, I addressed the thoroughness with which human trafficking is identified with the sex trade. This association was reproduced at nearly every turn in the legislative process. As Srikantiah points out, "the bill that ultimately became law as the Trafficking Victims Protection Act, H.R. 3244, was incorrectly referred to as the Sexual Trafficking Victims Protection Act by some legislators as late as the date of the roll call vote for the bill."[39] Hearings on the anti-trafficking bills strongly emphasized the sex trade; the only trafficking survivors to testify, in fact, were those who had been trafficked into the United States from abroad and forced into prostitution. The choice of witnesses

---

[36] *Hearings on International Trafficking in Women and Children: Prosecution, Testimonies, and Prevention*, 78.

[37] In fact, "the TVPA does not specify movement across international boundaries as a condition of trafficking; it does not require the transportation of victims from one locale to another." Government Accountability Office, "Human Trafficking: Better Data, Strategy, and Reporting Needed to Enhance U.S. Anti-trafficking Efforts Abroad" (2006), 5.

[38] *Hearings on International Trafficking in Women and Children: Prosecution, Testimonies, and Prevention.*

[39] Srikantiah, 171, n. 72. See, e.g., Brownback's reference to "the sex trafficking bill." Brownback, "Victims of Trafficking and Violence Protection Act of 2000 Conference Report," S10211. Brownback's slip of tongue on the same day the Senate approved the TVPA is especially noteworthy given his leadership in reconciling competing versions of the bill. See also Jesse Helms, "Victims of Trafficking and Violence Protection Act of 2000 Conference Report" (Washington, DC: U.S. Senate, 2000), S101212.

provides one glimpse into the efforts of abolitionists lobbying behind the scenes. The 1999 Hearing on Trafficking of Women and Children in the International Sex Trade, for example, featured:

- Harold Koh and Theresa Loar, two prominent State Department officials.
- Anita Sharma Bhattarai, the Nepalese trafficking survivor referred to at the beginning of this chapter who had been working with the International Justice Mission.
- Laura Lederer, founder of the Protection Project, and largely responsible for the alliance between feminist and religious abolitionists.
- Gary Haugen, president and CEO of the International Justice Mission, and a prominent religious abolitionist.

The hearing was chaired, as previously noted, by Representative Chris Smith, himself a religious abolitionist. Likewise, the witness list for the two Senate hearings included Lauran D. Bethell, an American Baptist Churches missionary serving as director of the New Life Center in Chiang Mai, Thailand; sex trafficking survivors from Mexico, Russia, and Ukraine; and repeat appearances by Haugen, Koh, Lederer, and Loar.

The focus on international sex trafficking, though dominant, was not total.[40] Theresa Loar, director of the PICW,[41] testified that approximately half of the women and children trafficked into the United States were forced into domestic servitude and sweatshops rather than prostitution.[42] "Accordingly, US policy is not limited to addressing trafficking solely in the context of the sex trade."[43] Speaking in support of the TVPA, Gejdenson took the argument further, stating: "[The problem is] not just sexual slavery, but employment slavery. People are brought to this country as employees, often, legally and illegally, and are then

---

[40] See DeStefano, 37.

[41] President Clinton established PICW to coordinate implementation of U.S. obligations resulting from the 1995 United Nations Fourth World Conference on Women in Beijing. *Hearing on Trafficking of Women and Children in the International Sex Trade*, 73. Clinton's 1998 directive on trafficking placed PICW in charge of federal policy on trafficking in women and children. Clinton.

[42] *Hearing on Trafficking of Women and Children in the International Sex Trade*, 75.

[43] Ibid., 76.

worked beyond all reasonable length of time in completely abhorrent conditions."[44] Slaughter too applauded the final text of the bill for recognizing "the fact that trafficking is not exclusively a crime of sexual exploitation."[45]

In the end, the broader approach carried the day, and the TVPA defined "severe forms of trafficking" as

1. sex trafficking in which a commercial sex act is induced by force, fraud, or coercion, or in which the person induced to perform such act has not attained 18 years of age; or
2. the recruitment, harboring, transportation, provision, or obtaining of a person for labor or services, through the use of force, fraud, or coercion for the purpose of subjection to involuntary servitude, peonage, debt bondage, or slavery.[46]

Trafficking for sex and trafficking for non-sex labor were differentiated, but were nonetheless defined as different facets of the same overall phenomenon.

The inclusion of trafficking for purposes other than sexual exploitation in the TVPA may initially appear difficult to reconcile with Congress's predominant interest in sex trafficking. I suggest that one factor that enabled Wellstone and like-minded colleagues to expand the focus of the bill appears in one of Wellstone's earlier speeches in which he explains that women and children who are trafficked for purposes other than prostitution are still sexually abused. He states:

Women who are trafficked are subjected to other abuses—rape, beatings, physical confinement—squarely prohibited by human rights law. The human

---

[44]Sam Gejdenson, "Remarks on Trafficking Victims Protection Act of 2000" (Washington, DC: U.S. House of Representatives, 2000), H2684; See also Subcommittee on International Operations and Human Rights of the Committee on International Relations, *H.R. 1356, the Freedom from Sexual Trafficking Act of 1999, Markup*, 1st session, 106th Congress, August 4, 1999, 5.

[45]Louise McIntosh Slaughter, "Remarks on Trafficking Victims Protection Act of 2000" (Washington, DC: U.S. House of Representatives, 2000).

[46] *Victims of Trafficking and Violence Protection Act*, 106–386, 106th Congress, October 28.

abuses continue in the workplace, in the forms of physical and sexual abuse, debt bondage and illegal confinement, and all are prohibited.[47]

In other words, Wellstone was able to justify the difference between the Smith bill concerning the trafficking of women and children for sex and his own bill, S. 600, concerning the trafficking of women and children for all purposes on the grounds that the heinous violations described by Smith as rape were also prevalent in other forms of trafficking. This point is also made by feminist abolitionists in their efforts to classify all kinds of sexual exploitation as "female sexual slavery."[48] Subsequently, once the practices that counted as instances of trafficking were expanded to include debt bondage, domestic servitude, and other forms of forced labor, the exclusion of all victims of those practices became more difficult to legitimate.

Note, however, that the formal inclusion of multiple forms of trafficking within the TVPA did not guarantee equal enforcement of the statute. Just as the congressional debates were dominated by narratives of women and children trafficked for prostitution, so too was the early implementation of the law.[49] The George W. Bush administration echoed abolitionists' conflation of trafficking for sex and for all other purposes, and "soon made explicit its goal of eliminating all forms of sex work—not just sex trafficking—in its fight against trafficking in the

---

[47] *S. 600 International Trafficking of Women and Children Victim Protection Act of 1999*, S2598; See also McKinney, *Hearing on Trafficking of Women and Children in the International Sex Trade*, 5.

[48] See, e.g., Barry; Kathleen Barry, Charlotte Bunch, and Shirley Castley, eds., *International Feminism: Networking against Female Sexual Slavery; Report of the Global Feminist Workshop to Organize against Traffic in Women* (Rotterdam, the Netherlands: International Women's Tribune Center, 1983).

[49] In Feingold's assessment ten years after the TVPA was passed, "For the United States, it has been both politically more expedient and emotionally more rewarding to focus on trafficking for sexual exploitation, rather than for labor exploitation. Under the influence of a politically well-connected 'abolitionist' lobby, prostitution has been conflated with trafficking; a crusade against the former is seen as synonymous with a victory against the latter." David A. Feingold, "Trafficking in Numbers: The Social Construction of Human Trafficking Data," in *Sex, Drugs, and Body Counts: The Politics of Numbers in Global Crime and Conflict*, ed. Peter Andreas and Kelly M. Greenhill (Ithaca, NY: Cornell University Press, 2010), 62.

United States and worldwide."[50] Describing prostitution as "inherently harmful and dehumanizing," Bush directed the US government to restrict the granting of anti-trafficking funds to organizations willing to sign an anti-prostitution pledge.[51] Abolitionist discourse, in short, played a larger role in setting conditions of possibility for action than the text of the TVPA itself.[52]

Even with a more expansive definition of human trafficking, at least one set of individuals with a vested interested in the legislation was silenced altogether. At the same time that sex workers and sex workers' rights activists played a visible role in negotiating the UN Trafficking Protocol in Vienna, they were exiled from policy debates and mainstream news coverage of the issue in the United States.[53] In the last part of this section, I consider sex workers' absence from domestic anti-trafficking politics in order to suggest the consequences of their marginalization and to explain how it was accomplished.

Chapters 2 and 4 address the ways in which sex workers and rights activists allied with the International Human Rights Law Group, the GAATW, and the Asian Women's Human Rights Council in Vienna fought to construct "trafficking in persons" as a problem of exploitative

[50] Denise Brennan, "Competing Claims of Victimhood? Foreign and Domestic Victims of Trafficking in the United States," *Sexuality Research and Social Policy* 5, no. 4 (2008): 50.

[51] George W. Bush, "Trafficking in Persons National Security Presidential Directive," White House Office of the Press Secretary, accessed September 29, 2009, http://www.whitehouse.gov/news/releases/2003/02/20030225.html; See also Brennan, 50; Government Accountability Office, 23, fn. 22; Network of Sex Work Projects, "Taking the Pledge Curriculum," accessed September 29, 2009, http://www.sexworkersproject.org/downloads/TakingThePledgeCurriculum.pdf; Jayne Huckerby, "United States of America," in *Collateral Damage: The Impact of Anti-trafficking Measures on Human Rights Around the World*, ed. Mike Dottridge (Bangkok: Global Alliance Against Traffic in Women, 2007). On a similar "gag rule" limiting the funding of anti-HIV/AIDS campaigns, see Joanna Busza, "Having the Rug Pulled from under Your Feet: One Project's Experience of the U.S. Policy Reversal on Sex Work," *Health Policy and Planning* 21, no. 4 (2006).

[52] See, e.g., Huckerby.

[53] Regarding the presence of sex workers and sex workers' rights activists at the Vienna negotiations, see Melissa Ditmore and Marjan Wijers, "The Negotiations on the UN Protocol on Trafficking in Persons," *Nemesis* 4 (2003); Jo Doezema, "Now You See Her, Now You Don't: Sex Workers at the UN Trafficking Protocol Negotiation," *Social & Legal Studies* 14, no. 1 (2005).

labor rather than prostitution. For sex workers, problematizing trafficking in terms of labor serves two important functions, the first and foremost of which is legitimizing prostitution and other commercial sex industries as forms of work. The second function, in turn, concerns not the right to engage in sex work but the rights of those engaged in sex work. Recall that feminist abolitionists recognize—in fact, publicize—the dangers prostituted women face on the job insofar as the ever-present threat of harm is a key component in abolitionists' framing of prostitution as a form of violence against women and sexual slavery.[54] Sex workers' rights activists understand the threat differently, as the effects of society stigmatizing a class of workers and erecting barriers to reporting violence and exploitative labor practices to state authorities.[55] Recourse for the most vulnerable is the least available:

> While undocumented migrants *trafficked* for sex work can, in certain circumstances, avail themselves of the Act's protections, undocumented migrant workers who willingly perform sex work break the law both as undocumented migrants and as prostitutes.[56]

From this perspective, addressing human trafficking within a broader framework of workers' rights serves to protect men and women in the sex industry along the entire continuum of forced versus free labor from abuses ranging from theft to physical violence to slavery.

An additional cost of marginalizing the perspective of sex workers is the loss of potential alliances with anti-trafficking NGOs in identifying children and adults who have been forced into prostitution. The Durbar Mahila Samanwaya Committee (DMSC), an organization of 65,000 sex workers in West Bengal, India, for example, takes an active role in anti-trafficking work. The DSMC establishes self-regulatory boards "to prevent entry of minor girls and unwilling adult women into the sex sector, control the exploitative practices in the sector, regulate the rules and

[54] See, e.g., Donna M. Hughes and Claire M. Roche, eds., *Making the Harm Visible: Global Sexual Exploitation of Women and Girls* (Kingston, RI: Coalition Against Trafficking in Women, 1999).

[55] See, e.g., Jo Bindman, "An International Perspective on Slavery in the Sex Industry," in *Global Sex Workers: Rights, Resistance, and Redefinition*, ed. Kamala Kempadoo and Jo Doezema (New York: Routledge, 1998), 64–66.

[56] Huckerby, 242. See also Melissa Ditmore, "How Immigration Status Affects Sex Workers' Health and Vulnerability to Abuse," *Research for Sex Work* 5 (2002).

practices of the sector and institute social welfare measures for sex work-ers and their children."[57] Sex workers' advocacy groups in the United States, in contrast, are deterred from playing the same role.

Sex workers' exclusion from the floors of Congress might seem unre-markable given the nearly universal domestic prohibition of prostitution. The contemporaneous UN negotiations, however, remind us that alter-native political configurations were and are possible. Abolitionists' suc-cess in foreclosing opportunities for sex workers to participate in shaping federal anti-trafficking policy represents, in this light, a case in which the power of norm entrepreneurs is used to limit rather than enhance the status, safety, and freedoms of a marginalized population. Indeed, any gesture toward incorporating sex workers' perspectives is quickly denounced as morally reprehensible and beyond the pale. Abolitionist feminist and CATW member Donna Hughes, for example, condemned Clinton-era anti-trafficking grants that funded "groups that worked to 'empower' victims of trafficking rather than rescue them, and supported unionizing prostitutes as the solution to trafficking."[58] The loaded title of Bill Bennett and Chuck Colson's opinion piece in the *Wall Street Journal*, "The Clintons Shrug at Sex Trafficking," likewise illustrates a common abolitionist response to proposals challenging the dominant discourse.[59]

COMMON GROUND

Even as disagreements concerning what counted as an instance of human trafficking and who counted as a human trafficking victim threatened to derail the proposed legislation, unanimity reigned on two fronts. Administration officials, members of Congress, and represent-atives of civil society were united in expressing the notion that human

---

[57] Durbar Mahila Samanwaya Committee, "Anti-trafficking Website of Durbar: Our Mission," accessed September 29, 2009, http://antitrafficking-durbar.org/our_mission. html; See also William Finnegan, "The Countertraffickers: Rescuing the Victims of the Global Sex Trade," *The New Yorker*, May 5, 2008.

[58] Donna Hughes quoted in Kathryn Jean Lopez, "The New Abolitionist Movement: Donna Hughes on Progress Fighting Sex Trafficking," accessed September 29, 2009, http://old.nationalreview.com/interrogatory/hughes200601260824.asp.

[59] William J. Bennett and Charles W. Colson, "The Clintons Shrug at Sex Trafficking," *The Wall Street Journal*, January 10, 2000.

trafficking—however defined—represented a violation of human rights and a manifestation of modern-day slavery. In Loar's words, "subjecting women, men and children to slavery or slavery-like conditions in any context is an intolerable human rights violation and an evil that cannot be ignored."[60] Loar's testimony illustrates how the two themes were tied together, and how rhetoric associated with religious abolitionists, such as references to fighting evil, worked to create a sense of urgency and a moral imperative for action.

A Violation of Human Rights

In contrast to the EU and the UN, where the human rights approach was first introduced by TANs lobbying against anti-trafficking initiatives that prioritized security concerns above rights protections, politicians and policymakers in the United States began with the understanding that trafficking represented "a human rights problem that requires a human rights response."[61] Human trafficking was characterized as not only an assault on victims' human rights, but as "one of the most horrendous human rights violations of our time."[62] Brownback was among the many who forcefully made this point; the senator repeatedly stated that meeting girls and young women who had survived sex trafficking had convinced him that it was among "the cruelest human rights abuses existing."[63]

Clinton administration officials such as Koh located the justification for global anti-trafficking interventions within international human rights law. As the final text of the TVPA acknowledged:

> The United States and the international community agree that TIP involves grave violations of human rights and is a matter of pressing international concern. The international community has repeatedly condemned

---

[60] Hearing on Trafficking of Women and Children in the International Sex Trade, 76.

[61] S. 600 International Trafficking of Women and Children Victim Protection Act of 1999, S2598.

[62] Ibid., S2598. See also John Conyers, "Remarks on Trafficking Victims Protection Act of 2000" (Washington, DC: U.S. House of Representatives, 2000), H2687; Abercrombie, H2686.

[63] Hearings on International Trafficking in Women and Children: Prosecution, Testimonies, and Prevention, 72.

slavery and involuntary servitude, violence against women, and other elements of trafficking, through declarations, treaties, and United Nations resolutions and reports, including the Universal Declaration of Human Rights.[64]

International human rights law obligates states to protect individuals within their own territory against human rights abuses even if those individuals are not citizens of that state and even if the government itself is not the perpetrator.[65] This being the case, an appeal to international law could hardly have been expected to sway Republicans famously hostile to intergovernmental bodies such as the UN.[66] It did, however, resonate with State Department officials otherwise dissatisfied with TVPA provisions such as the establishment of a sanctions regime and the creation of a separate anti-trafficking bureaucracy.[67] Ideological qualms notwithstanding, Republicans within civil society and Congress continued to use the politically expedient language of human rights in constructing anti-trafficking as an unquestionably righteous endeavor.

Slavery

In the first years after the passage of the TVPA, abolitionists complained loudly that neither the Bush administration nor the State Department made sufficient use of the word "slavery" to describe human trafficking. In fact, no such reticence was displayed in public fora during the three years prior. Schakowsky (D-IL), quoted above, was far from the only politician or activist to observe that Americans were largely unaware of instances of trafficking-*qua*-slavery within their own communities, or to identify contemporary TIP with the trans-Atlantic slave trade. Under Secretary of State for Global Affairs Frank E. Loy, for example, declared that trafficking "is slavery, pure and simple. It is slavery in the

---

[64] *Trafficking Victims Protection Act*, 106–386, October 28, 2000.

[65] Elaine Pearson, *Human Rights and Trafficking in Persons: A Handbook* (Bangkok: Global Alliance Against Traffic in Women, 2000), 8. Feminist abolitionist Charlotte Bunch famously made this point in regards to women in "Women's Rights as Human Rights: Toward a Re-vision of Human Rights," *Human Rights Quarterly* 12 (1990).

[66] See, e.g. Ben Barber, "GOP's World View Frames Changes in Foreign Policy," *The Washington Times*, November 21, 1994; Arthur Schlesinger Jr., "Back to the Womb? Isolationism's Renewed Threat," *Foreign Affairs*, July/August 1995.

[67] *Hearing on Trafficking of Women and Children in the International Sex Trade*, 11–13.

21st century."[68] In the subsequent session of Senate hearings, Yeomans drew a direct parallel to the transatlantic slave trade:

> It is profoundly troubling that it is necessary to have this hearing as we move into the new millennium, but it is necessary. While we discuss this problem using such terms as "trafficking" and "forced labor," we should make no mistake about it: we are talking about slavery, slavery in its modern manifestations.[69]

Yeomans' repeated references to the time period—e.g. "the new millennium," "slavery in its modern manifestations"—reflect the frequently expressed sense of surprise and historical anachronism gestured to by Schakowsky. He continued:

> While some of the schemes and practices employed reflect the sophistication of the modern world, others are as basic and barbaric as the trade that brought African-Americans to this continent.[70]

The continued presence of a scourge Americans had long thought defeated is figured as a moment of crisis, a threat to the progress of Western civilization and a sign that history had not, as Fukuyama proposed,[71] come to an end.

As with the similarly unifying claim that human trafficking should be considered an abuse of human rights, the notion that trafficking should also be considered a manifestation of slavery was supported with a range of assertions and arguments. Brownback justified his description of international sex trafficking as "the new slavery" by identifying elements historically associated with chattel slavery as also present in modern-day sex trafficking. These elements included

> being abducted from your family and home, taken to a strange country where you do not speak the language, losing your identity and freedom,

---

[68] Christopher H. Smith, "Remarks on Trafficking Victims Protection Act of 2000" (Washington, DC: U.S. House of Representatives, 2000).

[69] *Hearings on International Trafficking in Women and Children: Prosecution, Testimonies, and Prevention*, 76.

[70] Ibid.

[71] Francis Fukuyama, *The End of History and the Last Man* (New York: Simon and Schuster, 1992).

being forced to work against your will with no pay, being beaten and raped, having no defense against the one who rules you, and eventually dying early because of this criminal misuse.[72]

Yeomans, in comparison, focused less on naming similar details pertaining to contemporary and historical forms of slavery in favor of emphasizing the common bottom line: like slave traders, human traffickers "all deny the essential humanity of the victims and turn them into objects for profit."[73]

The equation of human trafficking and historic enslavement of Africans constructs trafficking as a form of a recognizably abhorrent practice that can and should be eradicated once again.[74] Chapkis points to another facet of the claim:

From [the slavery] perspective, abuse of migrants becomes fully the fault of traffickers who must be stopped, not the by-product of exploitive employment practices, restrictive immigration policies, and vast economic disparities between rich and poor nations. Attempts to restrict immigration can then be packaged as antislavery measures; would-be migrants are would-be victims whose safety and well-being are ostensibly served by more rigorously policing of the borders.[75]

In other words, the articulation of trafficking to slavery works in much the same way as the coupling of "trafficking" and "international," pointing away from a context in which states such as the United States share responsibility for creating the underlying conditions for trafficking problems, and toward a context in which the state's responsibility to address such problems stems only from its status as a benevolent global power. This articulation also serves to reinforce constructions of trafficked persons as victims lacking agency—and therefore culpability—akin to

---

[72] *Hearings on International Trafficking in Women and Children: Prosecution, Testimonies, and Prevention*, 72. As I discuss in the latter part of this chapter, Brownback's depiction of the iconic sex trafficking victim matches the experiences of only some of the persons identified as claiming to be survivors of sex trafficking.

[73] Ibid., 76.

[74] Joel Quirk, "Trafficked into Slavery," *Journal of Human Rights* 6 (2007); See also John T. Picarelli, "Historical Approaches to the Trade in Human Beings," in *Human Trafficking*, ed. Maggy Lee (Portland, OR: Willan Publishing, 2007).

[75] Chapkis, 927.

the historical kidnap and capture of persons for the purpose of chattel slavery.

While the slavery analogy can serve to obscure state culpability and to legitimate restrictions on border-crossing, it also provides opportunities to reconfigure the meaning of human trafficking. In Chapter 5, I show how the Salvation Army, among others, draws on its long history of opposition to multiple practices identified as slavery in order to justify its comparatively expansive conceptualization of human trafficking today. Conversely, the popular association in the United States between the concept of slavery and the historical practice of enslaving black Africans and their descendants might instead make it more difficult for someone whose situation does not resemble chattel slavery to gain recognition—and therefore services, benefits, and protections—as a "genuine" trafficking victim.[76]

Building on Common Ground

Today's abolitionists have, according to Bales, already won the "moral argument"—human trafficking, like traditional forms of slavery, is seen as an abominable violation of human rights that no moral person or government can support.[77] In contrast to the fractious process of negotiating anti-trafficking legislation, nearly everyone involved emphasized the diversity of supporters united in support of the TVPA. Brownback, for instance, thanked the "people of heart, courage, and intelligence whose advocacy made a way for this bill—whose dedication pried open the doors and let the light shine in the darkness."[78] Underscoring that support for the bill came from the entirety of the political spectrum, the politically and socially conservative Brownback added meaningfully that "Gloria Steinem, whom I am not noted to thank, is part of this coalition."[79] Wellstone echoed his colleague's remarks, stating that

[76] Nora Demleitner, "The Law at a Crossroads: The Construction of Migrant Women Trafficked into Prostitution," in *Global Human Smuggling: Comparative Perspectives*, ed. David Kyle and Rey Koslowski (Baltimore: The Johns Hopkins University Press, 2001).

[77] Committee on Foreign Relations, *Hearing on Slavery Throughout the World*, 106th Congress, 2nd Session, September 28, 2000, 22.

[78] Brownback, "Victims of Trafficking and Violence Protection Act of 2000 Conference Report," S10166.

[79] Ibid.

"something important is in the air when such a broad coalition of people, including Bill Bennett, Gloria Steinem, Rabbi David Saperstein, Ann Jordan, and Chuck Colson work together for the passage of this legislation."[80] In one sense, the rounds of mutual congratulations and generous displays of gratitude to those across the aisle can be understood as par for the course after the passage of a major piece of legislation, particularly one garnering only a single "nay" vote. Yet paired with Bales' contention quoted above that "the" moral issue of trafficking has already been settled, repeated references to the broad spectrum of support function more like claims of universally recognized normative validity. In this way, the human trafficking problem was moved from the agonistic realm of the political to the seemingly neutral realm of technocracy.

The Subjects of Trafficking

I hope we do not lose sight, in our discussions here on legislative points and whether this is the way to go or that one is, of that 13-year-old girl that is locked in a brothel in Bombay and beaten regularly, submitting to this trade and returning to Nepal with tuberculosis and AIDS. I hope we keep focused on that is what this is about.

—Senator Sam Brownback[81]

From the perspective of the first half of this chapter, which focused on the construction of human trafficking as a problem, the above quotation is significant insofar as it conceptualizes trafficking as a transnational problem of forcing young women into brutal commercial sex enterprises. In the latter half of this chapter, I shift my focus from the construction of problems to the production of subjects. Brownback's reference to the Nepalese trafficking survivors to whom he had been introduced illustrates how problematizations of human trafficking expressed in Congress emphasized elements such as youth, femininity, sexual brutality, and death in order to produce a particular kind of subject—a sympathetic victim that it would be politically unpalatable to criminalize as a prostitute or undocumented migrant. Brownback furthermore demonstrates how

---

[80] Wellstone, S10169. Virtually identical statements were made by members of both parties in the House. See Smith, "Remarks on Trafficking Victims Protection Act of 2000," H2683.

[81] *Hearing on Trafficking of Women and Children in the International Sex Trade*, 22.

the anti-trafficking cause is set apart from politics, which he casts as a distraction from the moral obligation to save trafficked girls.

Innocents Abroad

The received picture of the trafficking victim depicts a young, naïve woman seeking a better life away from her rural home, who answers an advertisement to become a waitress or nanny only to be forced into sexual slavery.[82] Jahic and Finckenauer depict the challenge of mustering support for all but the most pitiable victims:

> While trafficking involves deception, many victims reportedly do have some idea of what kind of work they will be expected to do. Many are aware that they will be entering countries illegally. And, victims are rarely kidnapped or abducted. Despite this, such women are nevertheless trafficking victims. They are just not those with whom the public will be particularly empathetic and would want to help.[83]

In order to garner financial and institutional support for the rescue, care, and protection of trafficked persons, those persons needed to be rendered unthreatening and worthy of assistance.[84] In the iconic narrative repeated by expert witnesses and members of Congress, the young woman is wholly unable to consent, undergoes a brutal period of acculturation or "breaking in," lives in a prison-like environment where she is frequently raped, becomes addicted to drugs, catches sexually transmitted infections, is forced to abort any pregnancies, and is fearful and demoralized upon being released from her traffickers.[85]

---

[82] Galma Jahic and James O. Finckenauer, "Representations and Misrepresentations of Human Trafficking," *Trends in Organized Crime* 8, no. 3 (2005); Jacqueline Berman, "(Un)Popular Strangers and Crises (Un)Bounded: Discourses of Sex-Trafficking, the European Political Community and the Panicked State of the Modern State," *European Journal of International Relations* 9, no. 1 (2003); and Srikantiah, 187.

[83] Jahic and Finckenauer, 26–27.

[84] See Claudia Aradau, "The Perverse Politics of Four-Letter Words: Risk and Pity in the Securitization of Human Trafficking," *Millennium Journal of International Studies* 33, no. 2 (2004).

[85] My summary of the iconic narrative relies in particular on the story of "Lydia," a composite character created by Laura Lederer to represent a typical victim of trafficking. "Lydia" is meant to be a sixteen-year-old girl from a Slavic country, drugged and kidnapped by strangers posing as modeling scouts. The story was retold several times, not

As I noted earlier, each of the trafficking survivors who testified before Congress had been trafficked for sex, and their testimony closely followed the same lines. Inez, for example, told her story of leaving Mexico at eighteen because she had been guaranteed a job as a waitress, but then being brutally forced into prostitution in a Florida trailer park. Senators also heard from Marsha, a Russian woman trafficking into prostitution in Germany, and from Olga, a Russian woman trafficked into prostitution in Israel. Both women had been immediately deported to Russia after being discovered by police in their destination countries.[86] Members of Congress also shared stories they had seen and heard.[87] These personal stories put names and faces to the statistics, eliciting an emotional response. Loar, for example, attributed the Clinton administration's commitment to address trafficking to meeting trafficking victims from the former Soviet Union in the mid-1990s, "and hearing from people whose villages were wiped out because girls were being sold away."[88]

Although female survivors of sex trafficking were the only victims to testify in person before Congress, the traffic of men and women for forced labor eventually received mention during subsequent TVPA negotiations and floor debates. Yet positive—or even nuanced—depictions of prostitution were omitted altogether. Domestic sex worker organizations received no hearing; the notion that prostitution might represent a legitimate career path remained unspoken.[89] Admittedly, the exclusion of current sex workers and of sex workers' rights proponents is not unexpected given that prostitution is currently illegal in all but a few US counties. Their absence is rendered more conspicuous, however, by the influential role that domestic and transnational sex workers' rights advocacy networks played during the UN Trafficking Protocol negotiations

only by Lederer, but also by members of Congress such as Smith. *Hearing on Trafficking of Women and Children in the International Sex Trade*, 37; Smith, "Remarks on Trafficking Victims Protection Act of 2000," H2683.

[86] *Hearings on International Trafficking in Women and Children: Prosecution, Testimonies, and Prevention.*

[87] Hutchison, S10217.

[88] *Hearing on Trafficking of Women and Children in the International Sex Trade*, 27.

[89] I discuss sex workers' rights advocacy in greater detail in the second and fourth chapters of this book.

occurring at the same time.[90] Sex workers' perspectives were marginalized even further in 2003 as abolitionists successfully lobbied the George W. Bush administration for a federal "gag rule" that required recipients of federal anti-trafficking funding to explicitly oppose the legalization or decriminalization of prostitution.[91]

At times, the depiction of trafficked women became paternalistic in the most literal sense. Anti-trafficking advocates made explicit appeals to their colleagues' humanity, frequently comparing trafficked women and children to their own daughters and granddaughters.[92] In Koh's words, "some of the young girls in that institute were no older than my daughter, who is only 13 years old. That experience reminded me that trafficking hits us so hard because it so often involves children like our own."[93] Brownback was even more explicit in his quest to see the trafficking bill made law: "If I can encourage you anymore, I say pull out a picture from your billfold, pull out a picture of a child or grandchild. Those are the ages, somewhere between 9 and 15, who are the most frequently trafficked victims."[94] This rhetorical strategy encouraged lawmakers to emotionally identify with women and girls who might otherwise be dismissed as undocumented migrant prostitutes.

The strategy likewise casts victims as young and potentially lacking in judgment and, therefore, culpability. Consider the following exchange between Koh and Brownback from the Senate's first hearing on trafficking:

> Mr. KOH. And Senator, if I could just add, I think the key to the approach that we are supporting is that the victims and survivors be the target of the protection and prevention efforts, but it is the traffickers who are the target of the prosecutorial efforts. In other words, in the prosecutorial extraditions phase of this operation, we are not looking at the state of mind of the victim, because as you said, the state of mind of the victim may be clouded, misled, change over time.

---

[90] See Ditmore and Wijers; Doezema.

[91] See Busza.

[92] *Hearing on Trafficking of Women and Children in the International Sex Trade*, 19.

[93] Ibid., 9.

[94] Brownback, "Victims of Trafficking and Violence Protection Act of 2000 Conference Report," S10212.

Senator BROWNBACK. She may be an 11-year-old girl. She probably is, which I have a 13-year-old daughter, and she can move—her mind can frequently be clouded.

Mr. KOH. Well, I have a 13-year-old daughter as well, and she actually has a quite unclouded mind, but nevertheless, the main point I think is in the prosecutorial side of this, targeting the traffickers.

In this excerpt, Koh's expressed desire to shift legal standards of evidence away from the difficult task of needing to prove that the victim had a certain state of mind is reinterpreted in Brownback's words as a claim about the flighty nature of preteen girls.

Constituting the victim as young and foolish serves to privilege certain policy responses over others. If the problem of trafficking occurs when "unsuspecting families allow their daughters to leave,"[95] then the logical solution must include "getting the messages back to the villages so families will not be fooled."[96] The agency of the potential victim is assumed away, and potential reasons for young women to migrate are dismissed out of hand as not worth the risk.[97] In a widely commented upon *New York Times* feature, Peter Landesman describes an "epidemic" of sex slavery in the United States, run in part by Mexican crime families that prey on young girls:

The father controls the organization and the money, while the sons and their male cousins hunt, kidnap and entrap victims. The boys leave school at 12 and are given one or two girls their age to rape and pimp out to begin their training, which emphasizes the arts of kidnapping and seduction. [These men] troll the bus stations and factories and school dances where under-age girls gather, work and socialize. They first ply the girls like prospective lovers, buying them meals and desserts, promising affection and then marriage. Then the men describe rumors they've heard about America, about the promise of jobs and schools. Sometimes the girls are easy prey. Most of them already dream of El Norte. But the theater

---

[95] Barbara Mikulski, "Victims of Trafficking and Violence Protection Act of 2000 Conference Report" (Washington, DC: U.S. Senate, 2000), S10175.

[96] Gejdenson, "Remarks on Trafficking Victims Protection Act of 2000," H2684.

[97] Laura María Agustín, *Sex at the Margins: Migration, Labor Markets, and the Rescue Industry* (London: Zed Books, 2007), 39.

often ends as soon as the agent has the girl alone, when he beats her, drugs her or simply forces her into a waiting car.[98]

Yet according to Nora Demleitner, kidnapped women represent the least likely scenario of human trafficking, as many women willingly leave their homes to join traffickers, and that it is the subsequent enslavement or coercion that constitutes trafficking.[99] She argues that kidnapped women are used as paradigmatic cases because "these women represent the innocent, the 'true' victim, a victim who did not choose to migrate illegally, let alone prostitute herself."[100]

In addition to prevention strategies focused on discouraging female migration, another result of portraying trafficking victims as brutalized young women trafficked for sex and entirely lacking in agency is that a hierarchy of victims is created. Women who have chosen to work as sex workers, but not as sex slaves, do not garner the same kind of sympathy, and men and women trafficked for non-sex labor are easily relabeled "illegal immigrants."[101] This approach puts even sex-trafficked women themselves at a disadvantage if they cannot portray their status as entirely involuntary, or if the conditions of their exploitation were merely undesirable instead of horrifically brutal. Such women fail both the test of innocence and the test of pain, lacking the "raw physical suffering" required to distinguish insufficiently "innocent" trafficking victims from illegal immigrants and prostitutes. In other words, the "legal process may tend to declare any woman not fitting this childlike image—and most

[98] Peter Landesman, "The Girls Next Door," *The New York Times*, January 25, 2004. For a critical view of Landesman, and his response, see Jack Shafer et al., "Assessing Landesman," Slate, accessed September 29, 2009, http://www.slate.com/articles/news_and_politics/press_box/2004/01/assessing_landesman.html.

[99] The most common recruitment strategies focus not on kidnapping or abduction, but on deceptive job advertisements, and promises of employment. See Louise I. Shelley, "Human Trafficking as a Form of Transnational Crime," in *Human Trafficking*, ed. Maggy Lee (Portland, OR: Willan Publishing, 2007); Kevin Bales, *Understanding Global Slavery* (Berkeley: University of California Press, 2005), 142–43.

[100] Demleitner, 264.

[101] Chapkis, 925; Quirk, 188. In the European Union, for example, Europol Deputy Director Willy Bruggeman distinguishes between exploited, deceived, and kidnapped sex trafficking victims, arguing that only kidnapped victims "are sex slaves in the truest sense." Willy Bruggeman, "Illegal Immigration and Trafficking in Human Beings Seen as a Security Problem for Europe" (paper presented at the European Conference on Preventing and Combating Trafficking in Human Beings, Brussels, 2002), 5.

victims of unscrupulous traffickers will not conform to this model—as unworthy of support and protection."[102] Regarding the gendering of sympathetic victims, the GAO reports:

> In most countries where trafficking data are gathered, women and children are seen as victims of trafficking, and men are predominantly seen as migrant workers, reflecting a gender bias in existing information. Men are also perceived as victims of labor exploitation that may not be seen as a crime but rather as an issue for trade unions and labor regulators.[103]

The bias is not simply in the collection of information, but in the constitution of the trafficking victim as a subject lacking agency. The failure to represent male migrants forced into labor as victims of trafficking rests upon stereotypes of men actively going out into the world to make their way, and women passively staying at home unless duped, seduced, or kidnapped by a trafficker.[104]

Representations of trafficking based upon women's assumed lack of agency often conflict with how many women who were trafficked perceive themselves. Mertus and Bertone explain, "The narrative of individuals labeled as victims in this process, however, often reflects a far more complicated self-understanding of their own status, one that is not static and devoid of agency."[105] Likewise, Bindman argues that analyses of trafficking must recognize that women, like men, make choices and take risks within the international labor market for a wide range of reasons, from the need to financially support themselves and their families to the desire to seek adventure and new experiences.[106] This should not be read

---

[102] Demleitner, 273.

[103] Government Accountability Office, "Human Trafficking: Better Data, Strategy, and Reporting Needed to Enhance U.S. Antitrafficking Efforts Abroad," 15.

[104] Julia O'Connell Davidson and Bridget Anderson, "The Trouble with 'Trafficking'," in *Trafficking and Women's Rights*, ed. Christien L. van der Anker and Jeroen Doomernik (Houndmills, Basingstoke, Hampshire: Palgrave Macmillan, 2006).

[105] Julie Mertus and Andrea Bertone, "Combating Trafficking: International Efforts and Their Ramifications," in *Human Trafficking and the Balkans*, ed. H. Richard Friman and Simon Reich (Pittsburgh: University of Pittsburgh Press, 2007), 51.

[106] Bindman, "An International Perspective on Slavery in the Sex Industry," 70; See also Ann D. Jordan, "Human Rights or Wrongs? The Struggle for a Rights-Based Response to Trafficking in Human Beings," *Gender & Development* 10, no. 1 (2002): 20; Chapkis, 924; and Ratna Kapur, "Cross-Border Movements and the Law: Renegotiating the Boundaries of Difference," in *Trafficking and Prostitution Reconsidered: New Perspectives on Migration,*

as a call to ignore or downplay the sense in which individuals *are* coerced or misled, but rather to begin analysis of human trafficking with the recognition that it occurs within a larger context in which labor migration is a reasonable pursuit.

For all of the concern expressed on behalf of daughters and granddaughters, sons and grandsons were nowhere to be found. The gendering of the iconic victim rendered invisible not only male migrant laborers, but also male prostitutes/sex workers. Granted, one could argue that prostituted boys under the age of eighteen were technically included within references to "women and children," but such a claim is misleading. In practice, the subject category of trafficked "women and children" was strictly female. Consider, for example, the following excerpt from Rep. Chris Smith's opening statement to a 1999 hearing of the House Subcommittee on International Operations and Human Rights:

> Each year up to a million innocent victims, of whom the overwhelming majority are women and children, are brought by force and/or fraud into the international commercial sex industry. [...] Every day we read of news accounts of women and girls who are abducted in places as diverse as Burma, Kosovo, and Vietnam, and sold into sexual slavery in countries from Thailand to Israel, from China to the United States.[107]

Within the course of a single paragraph the population Smith describes as "innocent victims" shifts from women and *children* to women and *girls*. Smith was followed by Rep. Cynthia McKinney, who thanked the congressman for his efforts to publicize "this issue of sexual trafficking, a practice that involves tens of thousands of *women* all around the world."[108] McKinney went on to criticize both the Clinton administration and the international community as a whole for failing to devote an appropriate amount of attention to "this grave abuse of *women and children*."[109] As with the other congressional hearings on human trafficking

---

Sex Work and Human Rights, ed. Kamala Kempadoo, Jyoti Sanghera, and Bandana Pattanaik (Boulder: Paradigm Publishers, 2005), 29.

[107] *Hearing on Trafficking of Women and Children in the International Sex Trade.*

[108] Ibid. Emphasis added.

[109] Ibid. Emphasis added.

during this time period, adult men were represented as agents engaged in purposeful, if illicit, action: as traffickers, johns, corrupt public officials, or rescuers, but not as victims. Boys, meanwhile, were absent from the discussion.

While the victim subject was consistently gendered as a woman, styles of racialization were more likely to shift according to context. Recall that a number of scholars connect contemporary trafficking discourses to the racially-charged "white slave panic."[110] Some argue that human trafficking only rose to international prominence as an issue once again in the context of increasing numbers of *white* sex workers. Jahic and Finckenauer note that the influx of trafficked women from Eastern Europe and the former Soviet Union during the early 1990s contributed to the resurgence of interest in human trafficking, particularly the so-called "Natasha trade" in white women of Slavic origin.[111] They write:

> Until it became possible to present the victims as like 'one of our own,' trafficking was a low priority. Unlike the women from Asia and Africa, who were women of color, the new trafficking victims were more likely to be recognized as just like 'girls next door.' The old image of white slaves was invoked, and this resonated with the developed countries of the West.[112]

Loar's testimony lends support to this idea, as she states that the federal government had originally seen trafficking as an Asian problem that did not affect the United States:

> What we have seen is a big increase after the fall of the former Soviet Union. It is something I think we were all aware of and has been documented in South Asia and Southeast Asia. I think it hit home when the numbers coming into the United States really increased in the last few

[110]See Berman, "The Left, the Right, and the Prostitute: The Making of U.S. Anti-trafficking in Persons Policy," 278.

[111]Jahic and Finckenauer. See, e.g., Hughes, who writes, "as a result of trafficking, Russian women are in prostitution in over 50 countries. In some parts of the world, such as Israel and Turkey, women from Russia and other republics of the former Soviet Union are so prevalent, that prostitutes are called 'Natashas'." Donna M. Hughes, "The 'Natasha' Trade: The Transnational Shadow Market of Trafficking in Women," *Journal of International Affairs* 53, no. 2 (2000); See also Victor Malarek, *The Natashas: Inside the New Global Sex Trade* (New York: Arcade Publishing, 2004).

[112]Jahic and Finckenauer, 26.

years and when we saw more visible areas of criminal activity in the former Soviet Union.[113]

Yet even if Jahic and Finckenauer are correct in stating that it was the whiteness of the victims that provoked the scandal, this does not mean that the trafficked subject is always, or even usually, represented as white. Sex worker's rights advocates and other feminists have also criticized abolitionist portrayals of the victim subject as "backward," "Third World," and women of color.[114]

The Foreign Menace

In contrast to the feminized victims, other subjects produced through anti-trafficking discourses are typically portrayed as masculine. The masculine subjects represented as threatening—i.e., migrants, traffickers, and corrupt bureaucrats and police—are also typically portrayed as foreign, thereby drawing a sharp contrast between virtuous Americans and villainous "foreigners." Most notably, sympathetic female victims of trafficking are established in opposition to male migrants, a group portrayed by conservative media figures and some politicians as a growing menace to the American economy and the safety of the American people.[115]

Opposing representations sympathetic and unsympathetic migrants can be seen most clearly in the debate concerning T visas

> specifically designed for certain human trafficking victims who cooperate with law enforcement against those responsible for their enslavement. The statute allows victims to remain in the United States if it is determined that such victims could suffer, "extreme hardship involving unusual and severe harm" if returned to their home countries. After three years in T status, victims of human trafficking may apply for permanent residency.[116]

---

[113] *Hearing on Trafficking of Women and Children in the International Sex Trade*, 27.

[114] See Agustín; Jo Doezema and Kamala Kempadoo, eds., *Global Sex Workers: Rights, Resistance, and Redefinition* (New York: Routledge, 1998); and Kamala Kempadoo, Jyoti Sanghera, and Bandana Pattanaik, eds., *Trafficking and Prostitution Reconsidered: New Perspectives on Migration, Sex Work and Human Rights* (Boulder: Paradigm Publishers, 2005).

[115] DeStefano, The War on Human Trafficking, 5.

[116] United States Department of Justice, "Department of Justice Issues T Visa to Protect Women, Children and All Victims of Human Trafficking" (Washington, DC, 2002).

There was bitter disagreement regarding a proposed cap on the number of trafficking victims eligible to receive the visa each year. Representative Lamar Smith (R-TX) argued against an unlimited number of visas because of the likelihood that undocumented immigrants might "take advantage of the system and abuse the privilege." He further asserted, "Whenever a new form of immigration relief is created, many aliens apply for that relief. Too often, these applications do not contain bona fide claims of relief."[117] The position of the losing side was summarized by Representative Mel Wyatt (D-NC), who argued that a cap on humanitarian visas was "beneath our dignity as a nation," and listed the Catholic Conference, the National Organization for Women, the Legal Defense and Educational Fund, and the National Immigration Law Center as fellow opponents of the cap.[118] Conyers disapprovingly blamed Republican shenanigans for the outcome, noting that

> a compromise bill was substituted by the Republicans immediately prior to the Judiciary Committee mark-up to satisfy their unrealistic concerns that the bill would enable persons to fraudulently obtain a lawful status by claiming that they were a victim of sex trafficking or involuntary servitude.[119]

"Maria," a trafficking survivor from Mexico, addressed the issue directly in her testimony before the Senate. After sharing her story of enslavement, she concluded:

> If anyone thinks that providing protection to trafficking survivors by affording them permanent residence is a magnet for other immigrants like myself, they are wrong. No woman or child would want to be a sex slave and endure the evil that I have gone through. I am in fear for my life more than ever. I helped put these evil men in jail. Please help me. Please help us. Please do not let this happen to anyone else.[120]

---

[117] Lamar Smith, "Appointment of Conferees on H.R. 3244, Trafficking Victims Protection Act of 2000" (Washington, DC: U.S. House of Representatives, 2000), H7629.

[118] Melvin Watt, "Appointment of Conferees on H.R. 3244, Trafficking Victims Protection Act of 2000" (Washington, DC: U.S. House of Representatives, 2000), H7628.

[119] Conyers, H2687.

[120] *Hearings on International Trafficking in Women and Children: Prosecution, Testimonies, and Prevention*, 92.

Maria's plea reinforced the representation of innocent female and child victims and reinscribed the threatening image of male migrants.

Feminist abolitionist discourse also contributed to the constitution of male migrants as threatening, arguing that among sex trafficking operations in the United States, "many of the brothels housing international women catered to buyers in specific immigrant or migrant worker communities. Some brothels had a selective entrance for men from their own ethnicity, nationality or race."[121] The CATW report quoted above, and written with the support of a federal grant, went on to emphasize that the notorious Cadena case[122] was another instance of women trafficked for sexual exploitation by migrant co-nationals.

> One well-publicized 1996 Florida trafficking case depicted only a small snapshot of the prostitution industry in rural Florida. Known as the Cadena case, seventeen members and associates of the Cadena family engaged in trafficking and prostitution until they were indicted and prosecuted. In this case, women and girls from Mexico were trafficked for prostitution to isolated rural Florida locations around farmworker camps in Avon Park, Fort Myers, Fort Peters, Lake Worth, Oceobe, Ocoee, Zolfo Springs and also in neighboring South Carolina.[123]

This portrayal also serves to locate the blame for trafficking—the demand side emphasized by feminist abolitionists—with subjects represented as culturally exterior to the United States. Traffickers were described as foreign, often co-nationals of their victims[124]—in Senator Jesse Helms' vivid words, "human beasts who thrive on prostitution."[125] Kempadoo takes the influential O'Neill Richard report to task for eliding the harms caused by forced labor within the formal economy in favor of emphasizing "groups of middle-persons who are held up as the 'real'

---

[121] Janice G. Raymond and Donna M. Hughes, "Sex Trafficking of Women in the United States: International and Domestic Trends" (New York: Coalition Against Trafficking in Women, 2001), 11; See Barry, 80. For the same argument.

[122] The young Mexican women who testified in the House and Senate hearings had been trafficked by the Cadena family.

[123] Raymond and Hughes, 37.

[124] Wellstone, S10167; O'Neill Richard.

[125] Helms, S10212.

menaces—recruiting agents and those who assist others to move without legal documents or money—who are commonly identified as greedy, immoral men from the global South and postsocialist states."[126]

The representation of foreign government officials and law enforcement officers was scarcely more positive.[127] Smith described Russian and Ukrainian officials he had met with as either complicit or in denial, prompting him to reply that "These are your daughters, these are people you should be putting sandbags around to protect them."[128] Speaking from his experience with IJM, Haugen described cities where "you can set your watch" by the arrival of police officers collecting bribes from brothel owners.[129] The overarching theme, however, was less of criminality than of cultural backwardness. Comparing the abolitionists of today to those of past centuries, Brownback reminded his audience of Christian missionary Amy Carmichael's efforts to rescue young girls from forced temple prostitution in India at the turn of the twentieth century. "It bears noting," Brownback added, "that this terrible practice continues today, in lesser degree, in rural villages throughout South Asia, including India."[130] Wellstone, too, described trafficking as induced, in part, by the "horribly low status of women in many cultures."[131] Echoing Barry's description of trafficking as barbarous and Yeomans' references to the basic and barbaric slave trade, Loy summarized the state of affairs with the observation that "it seems almost incomprehensible that at the dawn of the twenty-first century the primitive and barbaric practice of buying and selling human beings occurs at all."[132]

[126] Kamala Kempadoo, "From Moral Panic to Social Justice: Changing Perspectives on Trafficking," in *Trafficking and Prostitution Reconsidered: New Perspectives on Migration, Sex Work and Human Rights*, ed. Kamala Kempadoo, Jyoti Sanghera, and Bandana Pattanaik (Boulder: Paradigm Publishers, 2005), xvii.

[127] Wellstone, S10168.

[128] *Hearing on Trafficking of Women and Children in the International Sex Trade*, 19.

[129] *Hearings on International Trafficking in Women and Children: Prosecution, Testimonies, and Prevention*, 38.

[130] Brownback, "Victims of Trafficking and Violence Protection Act of 2000 Conference Report," S10167.

[131] *Hearings on International Trafficking in Women and Children: Prosecution, Testimonies, and Prevention*, 4.

[132] Ibid., 6–7.

American Exceptionalism

Smith's incredulity that Russians and Ukrainians would, in his estimation, hesitate to protect their daughters complements the concern for daughters and granddaughters expressed multiple times by Koh and Brownback quoted earlier in the chapter. In stark contrast to the backwardness and unreliability attributed to other governments, the United States was lauded as "the human rights leader. We are the ones, we have to stand up and make these things an issue, because we're finding other places just do not make them that much of an issue."[133] Helms, rarely a proponent of international engagement, spoke of restoring the "moral underpinning in U.S. foreign policy,"[134] while others connected anti-trafficking to the promotion of "American values" such as freedom.[135]

Senator John Ashcroft (R-MO) was emphatic in calling for action by "the leading industrialized nation, founded on principles of freedom and justice."[136] The future US Attorney General continued:

> We must strive to see that every man, woman, and child be afforded the opportunity to live in a world of freedom. President Ronald Reagan, and other cold war warriors, fought diligently to see peace, democracy, and freedom throughout the world. We have achieved a small part of their vision, and the protection of women and children throughout the world who are tortured and de-humanized through international human trafficking is another step closer to that vision.[137]

Ashcroft's appeal, couched in explicitly normative terms, was hardly unusual in casting the United States as not only virtuous, but as at the apex of the moral hierarchy of states.[138] Divided on questions concerning the conceptual boundaries of the problem and how it should be handled,

---

[133] Ibid., 56.

[134] Helms, S10212.

[135] Hutchison, S10217.

[136] *Hearings on International Trafficking in Women and Children: Prosecution, Testimonies, and Prevention.*

[137] Ibid.

[138] Towns makes a similar argument at greater length regarding the function of international norms regarding women's rights. *Women and States: Norms and Hierarchies in International Society* (Cambridge: Cambridge University Press, 2010).

anti-traffickers were unified in their portrayal of the American subject as exemplary, indispensable, and empowered to intervene abroad to defend civilization itself against the threat posed by human trafficking. Is such ethnocentrism surprising or remarkable? Surely not. American exceptionalism is notable in this context not because it is unexpected but in terms of the specific possibilities thereby enabled or disallowed, from the annual TIP reports mandated by the TVPA for the purpose of ranking and assessing the efforts of other states to address human trafficking to abolitionists' inclusion of a mandatory sanctions regime in the legislation, which succeeded despite the strenuous opposition of many congressional Democrats, the Clinton White House, and the Department of State.[139]

Conclusion

The TVPA stands alongside the UN Trafficking Protocol as evidence of a purported increasingly successful international norm against human trafficking. Assertions that an anti-trafficking norm exists, however, assume more than they reveal. On what grounds could an account concerning the content of the norm be justified in the first place? Looking specifically to the United States, even when legislators, diplomats, and activists agree on the terms of debate, as with characterizations of human trafficking as an egregious violation of human rights and a modern-day form of slavery, consensus regarding the actual practices and populations involved remains elusive. Yet disputes concerning the meaning of trafficking reflect more than the simple empirical fact of disagreement among interested parties; competing representations draw attention to the processes through which human trafficking is constructed as a problem. In the unlikely event that a consensus definition was to gain supremacy the result would be no less constructed, and an agreement would render the consensus no less political. To present a specific conceptualization of trafficking as neutral, apolitical, or otherwise unproblematic is to ignore both the gendered and racialized politics of its construction and the productive effects of subsequent anti-trafficking interventions. To imagine that the question of definition is closed,

---

[139] See Janie Chuang, "The United States as Global Sheriff: Using Unilateral Sanctions to Combat Human Trafficking," *Michigan Journal of International Law* 27 (2005/2006); DeStefano, 34.

moreover, is to miss the contradictions and instabilities central to the making of meaning.

In order to understand how and with what effects public officials, scholars, and activists in the United States conceptualized human trafficking as a problem at the end of the twentieth century, one must look further than the definition of crime codified in the TVPA. The discourse analysis of congressional hearings and floor debates in this chapter demonstrates that participants typically understood trafficking as referring exclusively to the international transportation and subsequent exploitation of women and children forced into prostitution. I argued that the association between human trafficking and movement across state borders served to locate the causes—and therefore, the blame—in forces external to the United States The role of plausible domestic causal factors, including demand for prostitution and inexpensive consumer goods, minimal and under-enforced labor protections, state and federal immigration policies, and the proliferation of free-trade agreements was ignored accordingly. I further argued that articulations of human trafficking to international border-crossing also exclude the forced prostitution and involuntary servitude of non-migrants even though both practices have been characterized in other venues as instances of trafficking.

The construction of subjects was no less consequential for those figured as victims, villains, or the virtuous—or erased from the political imaginary altogether. The rhetorical trappings of innocence served anti-traffickers well in transforming women and girls potentially cast as transgressors of moral and geographic boundaries into pitiable, non-threatening victims worthy of assistance. This success of abolitionist norm entrepreneurs represents, from a liberal constructivist standpoint, a skillful deployment of persuasive frames and symbolic politics.[140] A critical constructivist perspective, however, reveals that there is more at stake. Representations of iconic victims do indeed draw attention to the needs of the marginalized, but they do so by further marginalizing the perspectives and positions of others: sex workers who desire workplace safety

---

[140] Margaret E. Keck and Kathryn Sikkink, *Activists Beyond Borders: Advocacy Networks in International Politics* (Ithaca, NY: Cornell University Press, 1998), 16–17; Alison Brysk, "Beyond Framing and Shaming," *Journal of Human Security* 5, no. 3 (2009); and Joshua William Busby, "Bono Made Jesse Helms Cry: Jubilee 2000, Debt Relief, and Moral Action in International Politics," *International Studies Quarterly* 51, no. 2 (2007): 251.

rather than rescue, laborers in dangerous and frequently exploitative occupations, and migrants deemed "insufficiently innocent." Likewise, exhortations to action that appeal to American values and past victories motivate laudable and even desirable initiatives. So too do these appeals enable the US government and its partners in civil society to impose standards and sanctions on others, to resist self-reflection or criticism, and to bolster xenophobic and anti-immigrant sentiment in the service of defending besieged borders.

REFERENCES

Abercrombie, Neil. "Remarks on Trafficking Victims Protection Act of 2000." Washington, DC: U.S. House of Representatives, 2000.

Agustín, Laura María. *Sex at the Margins: Migration, Labor Markets, and the Rescue Industry*. London: Zed Books, 2007.

Aradau, Claudia. "The Perverse Politics of Four-Letter Words: Risk and Pity in the Securitization of Human Trafficking." *Millennium Journal of International Studies* 33, no. 2 (2004): 251–77.

———. *Rethinking Trafficking in Women: Politics Out of Security*. New York: Palgrave Macmillan, 2008.

Bales, Kevin. *Understanding Global Slavery*. Berkeley: University of California Press, 2005.

Barber, Ben. "GOP's World View Frames Changes in Foreign Policy." *The Washington Times*, November 21, 1994, A12.

Barry, Kathleen. *Female Sexual Slavery*. New York: New York University Press, 1979.

Barry, Kathleen, Charlotte Bunch, and Shirley Castley, eds. *International Feminism: Networking against Female Sexual Slavery; Report of the Global Feminist Workshop to Organize against Traffic in Women*. Rotterdam, the Netherlands: International Women's Tribune Center, 1983.

Bennett, William J., and Charles W. Colson. "The Clintons Shrug at Sex Trafficking." *The Wall Street Journal*, January 10, 2000.

Berman, Jacqueline. "The Left, the Right, and the Prostitute: The Making of U.S. Anti-trafficking in Persons Policy." *Tulane Journal of International and Comparative Law* 14 (2005–2006): 269–93.

———. "(Un)Popular Strangers and Crises (Un)Bounded: Discourses of Sex-Trafficking, the European Political Community and the Panicked State of the Modern State." *European Journal of International Relations* 9, no. 1 (2003): 37–86.

Bernstein, Elizabeth. "The Sexual Politics of the "New Abolitionism"." *Differences* 18, no. 3 (2007): 128.

Bindman, Jo. "An International Perspective on Slavery in the Sex Industry." In *Global Sex Workers: Rights, Resistance, and Redefinition*, edited by Kamala Kempadoo and Jo Doezema. New York: Routledge, 1998.

Brennan, Denise. "Competing Claims of Victimhood? Foreign and Domestic Victims of Trafficking in the United States." *Sexuality Research and Social Policy* 5, no. 4 (2008): 45–61.

Brownback, Sam. "Victims of Trafficking and Violence Protection Act of 2000 Conference Report." Washington, DC: U.S. Senate, 2000.

Bruggeman, Willy. "Illegal Immigration and Trafficking in Human Beings Seen as a Security Problem for Europe." Paper presented at the European Conference on Preventing and Combating Trafficking in Human Beings, Brussels, 2002.

Brysk, Alison. "Beyond Framing and Shaming." *Journal of Human Security* 5, no. 3 (2009): 8–21.

Bumiller, Elizabeth. "Evangelicals Sway White House on Human Rights Issues Abroad: Liberals Join Effort on Aids and Sex Trafficking." *The New York Times*, A1 (2003).

Bunch, Charlotte. "Women's Rights as Human Rights: Toward a Re-vision of Human Rights." *Human Rights Quarterly* 12 (1990): 486–98.

Busby, Joshua William. "Bono Made Jesse Helms Cry: Jubilee 2000, Debt Relief, and Moral Action in International Politics." *International Studies Quarterly* 51, no. 2 (2007): 247–75.

Bush, George W. "Trafficking in Persons National Security Presidential Directive" White House Office of the Press Secretary. Accessed September 29, 2009. http://www.whitehouse.gov/news/releases/2003/02/20030225.html.

Busza, Joanna. "Having the Rug Pulled from Under Your Feet: One Project's Experience of the U.S. Policy Reversal on Sex Work." *Health Policy and Planning* 21, no. 4 (2006): 329–32.

Chapkis, Wendy. "Trafficking, Migration, and the Law: Protecting Innocents, Punishing Immigrants." *Gender & Society* 17, no. 6 (2003): 923–37.

Chuang, Janie. "The United States as Global Sheriff: Using Unilateral Sanctions to Combat Human Trafficking." *Michigan Journal of International Law* 27 (2005/2006): 437–94.

Civil Rights Division, U.S. Department of Justice. "Statutes Enforced by the Criminal Section." Accessed September 29, 2009. http://www.justice.gov/crt/about/crm/statutes.php.

Clinton, William J. "Memorandum on Steps to Combat Violence against Women and Trafficking in Women and Girls." *Weekly Compilation of Presidential Documents* 34, no. 11 (1998): 412.

Committee on Foreign Relations. *Hearing on Slavery Throughout the World*, 106th Congress, 2nd Session, September 28, 2000.

Committee on International Relations. "Report to Accompany H.R. 3244." Washington, DC: U.S. House of Representatives, 1999.

Conyers, John. "Remarks on Trafficking Victims Protection Act of 2000." Washington, DC: U.S. House of Representatives, 2000.

Demleitner, Nora. "The Law at a Crossroads: The Construction of Migrant Women Trafficked into Prostitution." In *Global Human Smuggling: Comparative Perspectives*, edited by David Kyle and Rey Koslowski. Baltimore: The Johns Hopkins University Press, 2001.

DeStefano, Anthony M. *The War on Human Trafficking: U.S. Policy Assessed*. New Brunswick, NJ: Rutgers University Press, 2007.

Ditmore, Melissa. "How Immigration Status Affects Sex Workers' Health and Vulnerability to Abuse." *Research for Sex Work* 5 (June 2002): 3–5.

———. "Trafficking in Lives: How Ideology Shapes Policy." In *Trafficking and Prostitution Reconsidered: New Perspectives on Migration, Sex Work and Human Rights*, edited by Kamala Kempadoo, Jyoti Sanghera, and Bandana Pattanaik, 107–26. Boulder: Paradigm Publishers, 2005.

Ditmore, Melissa, and Marjan Wijers. "The Negotiations on the UN Protocol on Trafficking in Persons." *Nemesis* 4 (2003): 79–88.

Doezema, Jo. "Now You See Her, Now You Don't: Sex Workers at the UN Trafficking Protocol Negotiation." *Social & Legal Studies* 14, no. 1 (2005): 61–89.

Doezema, Jo, and Kamala Kempadoo, eds. *Global Sex Workers: Rights, Resistance, and Redefinition*. New York: Routledge, 1998.

Durbar Mahila Samanwaya Committee. "Anti-trafficking Website of Durbar: Our Mission." Accessed September 29, 2009. http://antitrafficking-durbar.org/our_mission.html.

Feingold, David A. "Trafficking in Numbers: The Social Construction of Human Trafficking Data." In *Sex, Drugs, and Body Counts: The Politics of Numbers in Global Crime and Conflict*, edited by Peter Andreas and Kelly M. Greenhill, 46–74. Ithaca, NY: Cornell University Press, 2010.

Finnegan, William. "The Countertraffickers: Rescuing the Victims of the Global Sex Trade." *The New Yorker*, May 5, 2008.

Fukuyama, Francis. *The End of History and the Last Man*. New York: Simon and Schuster, 1992.

Gejdenson, Sam. "Remarks on Trafficking Victims Protection Act of 2000." Washington, DC: U.S. House of Representatives, 2000.

Government Accountability Office. "Human Trafficking: Better Data, Strategy, and Reporting Needed to Enhance U.S. Antitrafficking Efforts Abroad." 2006.

H. Con. Res. 21 Trafficking of Burmese Women and Girls into Thailand for the Purposes of Forced Prostitution, 104th Congress, 1st Session, February 1, 1995.

H. Con. Res. 239 Worldwide Trafficking of Persons, 105th Congress, 2nd Session, March 10, 1998.

Helms, Jesse. "Victims of Trafficking and Violence Protection Act of 2000 Conference Report." Washington, DC: U.S. Senate, 2000.

Hertzke, Allen D. *Freeing God's Children: The Unlikely Alliance for Global Human Rights*. Lanham, MD: Rowman & Littlefield, 2004.

H.R. 1238 International Trafficking of Women and Children Victim Protection Act of 1999, 106th Congress, 1st Session, March 23, 1999.

H.R. 1356 Freedom from Sexual Trafficking Act of 1999, 106th Congress, 1st Session, March 25, 1999.

H.R. 3154 Comprehensive Anti-trafficking in Persons Act of 1999, 106th Congress, 1st Session, October 27, 1999.

H.R. 3244 Trafficking Victims Protection Act of 1999, 106th Congress, 1st Session, November 8, 1999.

Huckerby, Jayne. "United States of America." In *Collateral Damage: The Impact of Anti-trafficking Measures on Human Rights Around the World*, edited by Mike Dottridge, 230–56. Bangkok: Global Alliance Against Traffic in Women, 2007.

Hughes, Donna M. "The 'Natasha' Trade: The Transnational Shadow Market of Trafficking in Women." *Journal of International Affairs* 53, no. 2 (2000): 625–51.

Hughes, Donna M., and Claire M. Roche, eds. *Making the Harm Visible: Global Sexual Exploitation of Women and Girls*. Kingston, RI: Coalition Against Trafficking in Women, 1999.

Hutchison, Kay Bailey. "Victims of Trafficking and Violence Protection Act of 2000 Conference Report." Washington, DC: U.S. Senate, 2000.

International Labor Organization. "Forced Labor, Child Labor, and Human Trafficking in Europe: An Ilo Perspective." Paper presented at the European Conference on Preventing and Combating Trafficking in Human Beings, Geneva, September 18–22, 2002.

Jahic, Galma, and James O. Finckenauer. "Representations and Misrepresentations of Human Trafficking." *Trends in Organized Crime* 8, no. 3 (Spring 2005): 24–40.

Jordan, Ann D. "Human Rights or Wrongs? The Struggle for a Rights-Based Response to Trafficking in Human Beings." *Gender & Development* 10, no. 1 (2002): 28–37.

Kapur, Ratna. "Cross-Border Movments and the Law: Renegotiating the Boundaries of Difference." In *Trafficking and Prostitution Reconsidered: New Perspectives on Migration, Sex Work and Human Rights*, edited by Kamala Kempadoo, Jyoti Sanghera, and Bandana Pattanaik, 25–41. Boulder: Paradigm Publishers, 2005.

Keck, Margaret E., and Kathryn Sikkink. *Activists Beyond Borders: Advocacy Networks in International Politics.* Ithaca, NY: Cornell University Press, 1998.

Kempadoo, Kamala. "From Moral Panic to Social Justice: Changing Perspectives on Trafficking." In *Trafficking and Prostitution Reconsidered: New Perspectives on Migration, Sex Work and Human Rights*, edited by Kamala Kempadoo, Jyoti Sanghera, and Bandana Pattanaik. Boulder: Paradigm Publishers, 2005.

Kempadoo, Kamala, Jyoti Sanghera, and Bandana Pattanaik, eds. *Trafficking and Prostitution Reconsidered: New Perspectives on Migration, Sex Work and Human Rights.* Edited by Kamala Kempadoo. Boulder: Paradigm Publishers, 2005.

Landesman, Peter. "The Girls Next Door." *The New York Times*, January 25, 2004.

Lopez, Kathryn Jean. "The New Abolitionist Movement: Donna Hughes on Progress Fighting Sex Trafficking." Accessed September 29, 2009. http://old.nationalreview.com/interrogatory/hughes200601260824.asp.

Malarek, Victor. *The Natashas: Inside the New Global Sex Trade.* New York: Arcade Publishing, 2004.

Miko, Francis T. "Trafficking in Persons: The U.S. and International Response." Washington, DC: CRS Report for Congress, 2006.

———. "Trafficking in Women and Children: The U.S. and International Response." In *Trafficking in Women and Children: Current Issues and Developments*, edited by Anna M. Troubnikoff. New York: Nova Science, 2003.

Mikulski, Barbara. "Victims of Trafficking and Violence Protection Act of 2000 Conference Report." Washington, DC: U.S. Senate, 2000.

Nathan, Debbie. "Oversexed." *The Nation*, August 29, 2005.

Network of Sex Work Projects. "Taking the Pledge Curriculum." Accessed September 29, 2009. http://www.sexworkersproject.org/downloads/TakingThePledgeCurriculum.pdf.

O'Connell Davidson, Julia, and Bridget Anderson. "The Trouble with 'Trafficking'." In *Trafficking and Women's Rights*, edited by Christien L. van der Anker and Jeroen Doomernik. Houndmills, Basingstoke, Hampshire: Palgrave Macmillan, 2006.

O'Neill Richard, Amy. "International Trafficking in Women to the United States: A Contemporary Manifestation of Slavery and Organized Crime." In *DCI Exceptional Intelligence Analyst Program*. Washington, DC: Center for the Study of Intelligence, 2000.

Pearson, Elaine. *Human Rights and Trafficking in Persons: A Handbook.* Bangkok: Global Alliance Against Traffic in Women, 2000.

Picarelli, John T. "Historical Approaches to the Trade in Human Beings." In *Human Trafficking*, edited by Maggy Lee, 26–48. Portland, OR: Willan Publishing, 2007.

Quirk, Joel. "Trafficked into Slavery." *Journal of Human Rights* 6 (2007): 181–207.

Raymond, Janice G., and Donna M. Hughes. "Sex Trafficking of Women in the United States: International and Domestic Trends." New York: Coalition Against Trafficking in Women, 2001.

S. Con. Res. 12 Trafficking of Burmese Women and Girls into Thailand for the Purposes of Forced Prostitution, 104th Congress, 1st Session, May 4, 1995.

S. Con. Res. 82 Worldwide Trafficking of Persons, 105th Congress, 2nd Session, March 10, 1998.

S. 600 International Trafficking of Women and Children Victim Protection Act of 1999, 106th Congress, 1st Session, March 11, 1999.

S. 1842 Comprehensive Anti-trafficking in Persons Act of 1999, 106th Congress, 1st Session, November 2, 1999.

S. 2414 Trafficking Victims Protection Act of 2000, 106th Congress, 2nd Session, April 12, 2000.

S. 2449 International Trafficking Act of 2000, 106th Congress, 2nd Session, April 13, 2000.

Schlesinger, Arthur, Jr. "Back to the Womb? Isolationism's Renewed Threat." *Foreign Affairs*, July/August 1995.

Shafer, Jack, Peter Landesman, Gerald Marzorati, and Daniel Radosh. "Assessing Landesman." Slate. Accessed September 29, 2009. http://www.slate.com/articles/news_and_politics/press_box/2004/01/assessing_landesman.html.

Shapiro, Nina. "The New Abolitionists." *Seattle Weekly*, August 25, 2004.

Shelley, Louise I. "Human Trafficking as a Form of Transnational Crime." In *Human Trafficking*, edited by Maggy Lee, 116–37. Portland, OR: Willan Publishing, 2007.

Skinner, E. Benjamin. *A Crime So Monstrous: Face-to-Face with Modern-Day Slavery*. New York: Free Press, 2009.

Slaughter, Louise McIntosh. "Remarks on Trafficking Victims Protection Act of 2000." Washington, DC: U.S. House of Representatives, 2000.

Smith, Christopher H. "Remarks on Trafficking Victims Protection Act of 2000." Washington, DC: U.S. House of Representatives, 2000.

Smith, Lamar. "Appointment of Conferees on H.R. 3244, Trafficking Victims Protection Act of 2000." Washington, DC: U.S. House of Representatives, 2000.

Srikantiah, Jayashri. "Perfect Victims and Real Survivors: The Iconic Victim in Domestic Human Trafficking Law." *Boston University Law Review* 87 (2007): 157–211.

Subcommittee on International Operations and Human Rights of the Committee on International Relations. *H.R. 1356, the Freedom from Sexual Trafficking Act of 1999, Markup*, 106th Congress, 1st session, August 4, 1999.

Subcommittee on International Operations and Human Rights of the Committee on International Relations. *Hearing on Trafficking of Women and Children in the International Sex Trade*, 106th Congress, 1st session, September 14, 1999.

Subcommittee on Near Eastern and South Asian Affairs of the Committee on Foreign Relations. *Hearings on International Trafficking in Women and Children: Prosecution, Testimonies, and Prevention*, 106th Congress, 2nd session, February 22 and April 4, 2000.

Towns, Ann E. *Women and States: Norms and Hierarchies in International Society*. Cambridge: Cambridge University Press, 2010.

Trafficking Victims Protection Act, 106–386, October 28, 2000.

United States Department of Justice. "Department of Justice Issues T Visa to Protect Women, Children and All Victims of Human Trafficking." Washington, DC, 2002.

United States V. Kozminski, 487 US 931 (1988).

U.S. Department of State. "Trafficking in Persons Report." Accessed September 29, 2009. http://www.state.gov/j/tip/rls/tiprpt/index.htm.

Victims of Trafficking and Violence Protection Act, 106–386, 106th Congress, October 28.

Watt, Melvin. "Appointment of Conferees on H.R. 3244, Trafficking Victims Protection Act of 2000." Washington, DC: U.S. House of Representatives, 2000.

Wellstone, Paul. "Victims of Trafficking and Violence Protection Act of 2000 Conference Report." Washington, DC: U.S. Senate, 2000.

CHAPTER 4

"Especially Women and Children"

A 2009 *New York Times* article investigating the low number of state-level human trafficking arrests opens with the story of "a typical recent case" in which a 22-year-old woman moved from Mexico to New York to join a boyfriend who had promised to find her work as a waitress:

> Instead, she said she worked for his uncle in Queens as a prostitute, servicing 10 men a night across the five boroughs for $35 to $45 a trick. Friendless, stranded on alien streets, frightened that the police would discover she was here illegally, she felt she had no choice, said the woman, who is pregnant. "I felt so bad, so bad," she said, drying tears as she spoke softly with the help of a translator. "I didn't know what I could do. I was alone." In July, the boyfriend was arrested after, she said, he beat her so brutally that she finally fled and sought out a stranger, who led her to the police. But he was charged only with a misdemeanor assault for domestic violence.[1]

According to the article, the police did not consider that the young woman may have been a human trafficking victim, or that her abusive boyfriend was also her pimp and trafficker. On this last point, reporter Joseph Berger quotes Dorchen Leidholdt, the legal director of an agency for battered women that is helping the woman. Regarding the police

---

[1] Joseph Berger, "Sex Trafficking Arrests Are Few, Despite Laws," *The New York Times*, December 4, 2009.

© The Author(s) 2019   115
J. K. Lobasz, *Constructing Human Trafficking*, Human Rights
Interventions, https://doi.org/10.1007/978-3-319-91737-5_4

response, Leidholdt scoffs, "If you're looking at a frightened immigrant woman in a brothel, it doesn't take a Ph.D. in political science to know what you're dealing with."[2]

Leidholdt's response is noteworthy for a number of reasons, including her prominence as a feminist abolitionist within domestic and international anti-trafficking circles.[3] What I find most significant, however, is Leidholdt's implied claim that certain people—specifically, certain women—are *obviously* victims of human trafficking.[4] Even to the layperson,[5] in other words, it should be manifestly clear that a "frightened immigrant woman in a brothel" has been trafficked for sexual exploitation. Underlying this claim is the feminist abolitionist position that all female prostitutes are, in fact, sex trafficking victims. The possibility that Leidholdt's client might have consented to work as a prostitute is deemed irrelevant—consent to prostitution is akin to consent to slavery, a contradiction in terms.[6]

Given the authority of feminist abolitionism within global anti-trafficking politics, such assumptions about who victims are and where they can be found are far from trivial, and merit careful examination. Hence, in this chapter, I construct a genealogy of feminist abolitionism, tracing the influential anti-trafficking discourse from its roots in US-based radical feminist theory and activism to its present-day incarnation as a transnational advocacy network (TAN). My purpose is to investigate radical feminists' construction of human trafficking as a problem by asking how subjects are made intelligible and practices made possible through feminist abolitionist discourse. In this chapter and the next I treat each

---

[2] Quoted in ibid.

[3] In addition to directing the Center for Battered Women's Legal Services at Sanctuary for Families in New York, Leidholdt is a founding member of the Coalition Against Trafficking in Women (CATW). "Biography of Dorchen A. Leidholdt," Coalition Against Trafficking in Women, accessed September 29, 2009, http://www.catwinternational.org/bio_DorchenLeidholdt.php.

[4] I also question Leidholdt's assumptions that (1) women in brothels are necessarily prostitutes (as opposed to managers, owners, waitresses, bartenders, cleaners, clients, or researchers); (2) "frightened immigrant women" are readily identifiable as such; and (3) women in brothels are frightened because they have been trafficked, and not because they fear deportation, jail, or public shaming.

[5] The notion that having obtained a doctorate in Political Science might confer a special ability to identify trafficked persons is questionable, to say the least.

[6] Kathleen Barry, *The Prostitution of Sexuality* (New York: New York University Press, 1995), 79.

abolitionist network as if they are separable from the sociopolitical relations in which they are embedded. Please note, however, that this treatment reflects a specific analytical choice to highlight certain features of abolitionism rather than a belief that advocacy networks can or should be theorized as independent variables.[7]

I find that feminist abolitionism constructs the human trafficking problem, along with its victims, villains, and liberators, through a series of gendered and racialized demarcations. Surprisingly, I also find that feminist abolitionist discourse is less settled than conventionally depicted by either its champions or its critics. Significant points of tension emanate from deeply buried questions of theory and practice that abolitionists have yet to satisfactorily address, although this has not prevented the feminist abolitionist advocacy network from gaining considerable influence in global anti-trafficking policy circles.

The chapter begins with a brief account of historical precursors to modern-day feminist abolitionism. I note in particular contemporary abolitionist assertions of continuity between their efforts to end human trafficking and earlier feminist campaigns against the Contagious Disease Acts in Great Britain and the *fin de siècle* menace of "white slavery." In the next section, I situate feminist abolitionism within the context of US radical feminist theory and practice, paying particular attention to the work of Catherine MacKinnon and Andrea Dworkin. I emphasize that while radical feminist epistemology is used to validate women's experiences as authoritative grounds for knowledge, in doing so radicals necessarily exclude or marginalize women with divergent testimony, introducing a major fault line in feminist abolitionism. I then turn to the work of Kathleen Barry, whose 1979 *Female Sexual Slavery* has been credited with placing human trafficking back on feminist agendas. I show how Barry's writings established the parameters for feminist abolitionism as an outgrowth of radical feminism. In the final section of this chapter, I explore the growth of feminist abolitionism as a TAN, focusing in particular on the discursive production of subjects. I suggest that although feminist abolitionists' adoption of the rhetoric of "human trafficking" in the place of "female sexual slavery" may have contributed to their initial political success, it has become an impediment to efforts to fix the meaning of trafficking to include all forms of prostitution.

---

[7] Patrick Thaddeus Jackson and Daniel H. Nexon, "Relations before States," *European Journal of International Relations* 5, no. 3 (1999): 296–97.

HISTORICAL PRECURSORS

Josephine Butler and the Contagious Disease Acts

Although contemporary accounts of human trafficking are prone to describe the condition of trafficked persons as one of slavery,[8] I noted in Chapter 2 that anti-trafficking discourses today share more in common with the Victorian and Progressive Era uproar regarding migratory prostitution than with movements to end the slave trade of black Africans. Barry, for example, devotes the second chapter of *Female Sexual Slavery* to the subject, situating her own advocacy against sex trafficking in the tradition of British feminist Josephine Butler, who "single-handedly raised a national and then international movement against forced prostitution in the nineteenth century."[9]

Forced prostitution became a subject for concern within the context of Victorian debates about regulation versus abolition of prostitution.[10] These debates were motivated in turn by the British Contagious Disease (CD) Acts of 1864, 1866, and 1869 intended to curtail sexually transmitted diseases within the British military by targeting the class that Parliament held responsible for the problem: prostitutes. Under the CD Acts, women suspected to be prostitutes were detained by police, forcibly examined internally by doctors, and could be imprisoned in hospital wards and institutions until the state deemed their moral and physical health sufficiently improved.[11] Butler's campaign to repeal

---

[8] See, e.g., Kevin Bales, *Understanding Global Slavery* (Berkeley: University of California Press, 2005).

[9] Kathleen Barry, *Female Sexual Slavery* (New York: New York University Press, 1979), 5. See also Sheila Jeffreys, "Sexology and Antifeminism," in *The Sexual Liberals and the Attack on Feminism*, ed. Dorchen A. Leidholdt and Janice G. Raymond (New York: Pergamon Press, 1990), 5.

[10] Jo Doezema, "Loose Women or Lost Women? The Re-emergence of the Myth of 'White Slavery' in Contemporary Discourses of 'Trafficking in Women'," *Gender Issues* 18, no. 1 (2000): 26.

[11] Shannon Bell, *Reading, Writing, and Rewriting the Prostitute Body* (Bloomington and Indianapolis: Indiana University Press, 1994), 56. I thank David Blaney for pointing out the parallels between the Contagious Diseases Acts and 1970s campaigns to "clean up" *kijich'on* (camptown) prostitution connected to US military installations in the Republic of Korea. Regarding the latter, see Katharine H. S. Moon, *Sex Among Allies: Military Prostitution in US-Korea Relations* (New York: Columbia University Press, 1997).

the Acts[12] rested on the belief that organized prostitution was an evil to be abolished rather than regulated. Abolitionists considered the Acts objectionable both in principle, for establishing a legal framework for sinful activities, and in practice, for denying suspected prostitutes the rights of habeas corpus and due process.[13] Butler and her fellow abolitionists held, furthermore, that the blame for prostitution lay not with the prostitutes themselves but with the men who frequented them and with the states that permitted or encouraged prostitution through regulatory measures such as the Acts.

White Slavery

Abolitionists' efforts came to fruition in 1886 when the CD Acts were repealed at last, twenty-two years after their first passage. Still, the uproar regarding migratory prostitution, soon referred to as "white slavery," continued to gather momentum. By the early twentieth century, feminists, religious organizations, and other social reformers had succeeded in eliciting broad public outrage stoked by dire reports of formerly "innocent" young white women seduced or abducted, violated, and forced into a brutal life of prostitution.[14] The wave of public interest

[12] Butler's Ladies National Association for the Repeal of the Contagious Disease Acts metamorphosed into the British, Continental and General Federation for the Abolition of the Government Regulation of Vice in 1875, and eventually settled upon the more concise and euphonious International Abolitionist Federation in 1898. Stephanie A. Limoncelli, *The Politics of Trafficking: The First International Movement to Combat the Sexual Exploitation of Women* (Palo Alto: Stanford University Press, 2010), 45–46.

[13] Ibid., 50.

[14] Questions as to the actual existence of coerced prostitution and enslavement of white women on a large scale remain, becoming, in fact, another front in the disputes regarding contemporary measurements of human trafficking. Wendy Chapkis, for example, argues, "The belief in a pervasive sexual slave trade in the absence of widespread evidence suggests that the notion of white slavery was not dependent on large numbers of documented cases. Instead, it was fueled by more general anxieties about changing gender, sex, class, and race relations at the turn of the century. The idea of a 'white slave' unconsciously spoke not only to the experience of the white working class laboring under harsh conditions of early industrial capitalism, but also to the racial fears of an increasingly ethnically diverse population." *Live Sex Acts: Women Performing Erotic Labor* (New York: Routledge, 1997), 42. See also Doezema. In contrast, Mary Ann Irwin writes, "Many Victorians were convinced that white slavery existed, while many others were just as certain that it did not; what is of concern is the dialogue itself. The issue is essentially one of definition: acceptance of the white slavery idea depends a great deal upon how one defines it." "'White Slavery' as Metaphor: Anatomy of a Moral Panic," *Ex Post Facto: The History Journal* 5 (1996),

surrounding white slavery and prostitution crested in 1949 with the UN's passage of the International Convention for the Suppression of the Traffic in Persons and of the Exploitation of the Prostitution of Others, only to lay dormant for the next several decades.[15]

RADICAL FEMINISM

At the same time, public and state interest in the issue of human trafficking was receding in the 1950s, a "second wave" of feminism was beginning to gather strength, mobilizing the activists who would successfully place trafficking back onto the American public's agenda by the end of the century. Susan Brownmiller, author of the landmark feminist analysis of rape *Against Our Will,* identifies two wings of the this new feminist movement: reformers, who gravitated toward the National Organization for Women (NOW), and radicals, who dubbed themselves the vanguard of "Women's Liberation."[16] Both wings of the movement echoed Carol Hanisch's rallying cry that "the personal is political," mobilizing around rape, wife battering, sexual harassment, reproductive rights, and other

accessed September 29, 2009, http://userwww.sfsu.edu/~epf/1996/wslavery.html. For feminist abolitionists such as Barry, those who deny the existence of "white slavery" ignore not only the documented cases of international sex trafficking during that time period, but also the high levels of domestic prostitution. *Female Sexual Slavery,* 33. Barry emphasizes, however, that Butler herself used the term rarely, and to refer to all exploitation of women in prostitution. For Barry, the term "embodied all the sexist, classist, and racist bigotry that was ultimately incorporated within the movement dominated by religious morality." Ibid., 32.

[15] See Kathleen Barry, "The Network Defines Its Issues: Theory, Evidence and Analysis of Female Sexual Slavery," in *International Feminism: Networking against Female Sexual Slavery; Report of the Global Feminist Workshop to Organize against Traffic in Women,* ed. Kathleen Barry, Charlotte Bunch, and Shirley Castley (Rotterdam, the Netherlands: International Women's Tribune Center, 1983), 23; Penelope Saunders, "Traffic Violations: Determining the Meaning of Violence in Sexual Trafficking Versus Sex Work," *Journal of Interpersonal Violence* 20, no. 3 (2005): 346.

[16] Susan Brownmiller, *In Our Time: Memoir of a Revolution* (New York: Dial Press, 1999), 7. Brownmiller's typology excludes a significant third wing of socialist feminists such as Barbara Ehrenreich, Gloria Martin, and Juliet Mitchell, among many others. See Barbara Ehrenreich, "What Is Socialist Feminism?" *WIN,* June 3, 1976; Alison M. Jaggar, *Feminist Politics and Human Nature* (Totowa, NJ: Rowman & Allanheld, 1983), 123–71, 303–50.

"personal" issues that had previously been excluded from discussion in the public sphere. Radical feminists such as Hanisch, however, departed from the reformers in their identification of sexuality as the root cause of all of these issues, and it was from within this theoretical framework that the feminist movements against pornography, prostitution, and trafficking in women would emerge.[17]

Theory of Gender

Since the early days of the women's liberation movement, radical feminists have sought, along with their liberal and socialist counterparts, to establish "women" as a meaningful political category. Early radical feminists argued that "women are oppressed not by virtue of their class or race, but simply by the fact of their womanhood. That is, women are oppressed *as women*."[18] Women, in short, are akin to a social class.[19] In order for feminists to assert women's common oppression, however, they had to address a more fundamental question: What do women have in common at all? What unites women as a collective subject such that "there exists ONE universal patriarchal oppression of women which takes different forms in different cultures and different regions"?[20]

[17] See Dorchen A. Leidholdt, "Demand and the Debate," Coalition Against Trafficking in Women, accessed September 29, 2009, http://www.childtrafficking.com/Docs/leidholdt_2003_demand_and_the_debate.pdf. I use "feminist abolitionist" when referring to activists and ideas associated solely or primarily with the traffic of women for sex, and "radical feminist" when referring to activists and ideas associated with all forms of female sexual exploitation. The latter group subsumes the former.

[18] Judith Grant, *Fundamental Feminism: Contesting the Core Concepts of Feminist Theory* (New York: Routledge, 1993), 20. Emphasis in original. See also Robin Rowland and Renate Klein, "Radical Feminism: History, Politics, Action," in *Radically Speaking: Feminism Reclaimed*, ed. Diane Bell and Renate Klein (North Melbourne: Spinifex Press, 1996), 19.

[19] Rowland and Klein, 12.

[20] Charlotte Bunch, "Network Strategies and Organizing against Female Sexual Slavery," in *International Feminism: Networking against Female Sexual Slavery; Report of the Global Feminist Workshop to Organize against Traffic in Women*, ed. Kathleen Barry, Charlotte Bunch, and Shirley Castley (Rotterdam, the Netherlands: International Women's Tribune Center, 1983), 53. Emphasis in original. Diane Bell and Renate Klein go on to claim that identity is the basis of political action: "Radical feminists have always understood that race, class, sexuality, age are intertwined, but they hold fast to the identity of woman." Diane Bell and Renate Klein, "Beware: Radical Feminists Speak, Read, Write, Organize, Enjoy Life, and Never Forget," in *Radically Speaking: Feminism Reclaimed*, ed. Diane Bell

For radical feminists in the tradition of Catharine MacKinnon the answer lies within a single mechanism: male supremacist sexuality, the "primary social sphere of male power."[21] In MacKinnon's words, "Women and men are divided by gender, made into the sexes as we know them, by the social requirements of its dominant form, heterosexuality, which institutionalizes male sexual dominance and female sexual submission."[22] Identification of sexuality as the root cause[23] rather than a symptom of women's subjugation represented a marked departure from earlier feminist analyses that had variously posited nature, the family, religion, and the state as initial impetuses for the oppression of women.[24]

While specific instantiations of male supremacist sexuality vary according to context,[25] radical feminists argue that its scope is universal: "Prostitution [...] wife battery, rape, incest, bride burning, excision and

and Renate Klein (North Melbourne: Spinifex Press, 1996), xviii. Feminist philosopher Judith Butler, who is critical of the notion of universalist subjects herself, notes, "For the most part, feminist theory has assumed that there is some existing identity, understood through the category of women, who not only initiates feminist interests and goals within discourse, but constitutes the subject for whom political representation is pursued." Judith Butler, *Gender Trouble: Feminism and the Subversion of Identity* (New York: Routledge, 1999), 3. See also Chandra Talpade Mohanty, *Feminism without Borders: Decolonizing Theory, Practicing Solidarity* (Durham: Duke University Press, 2003), 22.

[21] Catharine MacKinnon, *Toward a Feminist Theory of the State* (Cambridge: Harvard University Press, 1989), 109. See also Barry, *Female Sexual Slavery*, 194. Rowland and Klein define patriarchy as "a system of structures and institutions created by men in order to sustain and recreate male power and female subordination" 15. MacKinnon and Dworkin both use the term "male supremacy" in place of "patriarchy" to avoid the impression that male-led family structures rather than sexuality ground the oppression of women. See MacKinnon. Following conventional feminist practice, I use the terms interchangeably.

[22] Ibid., 113. See also Dorchen A. Leidholdt, "When Women Defend Pornography," in *The Sexual Liberals and the Attack on Feminism*, ed. Dorchen A. Leidholdt and Janice G. Raymond (New York: Pergamon Press, 1990).

[23] Writing about the meaning of "radical feminism," Robin Morgan muses that "etymology is usually revealing: the word 'radical,' for example, refers to 'going to the root' (as in radish) of an issue or subject. (That is to say, why waste time on political superficialities when you can wrestle with the most primary, basic oppression of all?)" Robin Morgan, "Light Bulbs, Radishes, and the Politics of the 21st Century," in *Radically Speaking: Feminism Reclaimed*, ed. Diane Bell and Renate Klein (North Melbourne: Spinifex Press, 1996), 5.

[24] MacKinnon, 109.

[25] See Bunch.

pornography [...] are carefully woven into the structure and content of patriarchal power and male domination around the globe."[26] Indeed, Barry declares that *all* women, regardless of class, ethnicity, or nationality, have their sexual victimhood in common.[27] Sonia Johnson further elaborates on this theme in *The Sexual Liberals and the Attack on Feminism*, a collection of radical feminist writings inspired by a 1987 conference of the same name. Drawing upon the sexual slavery narrative, Johnson writes:

> All of us—all women in patriarchy—are seasoned to be slaves, are seasoned to be prostitutes. All of us, in some sense, are, or have been, prostitutes and slaves, and most of us will continue to be for the rest of our lives.[28]

In this way, radical feminists argue that female oppression under patriarchy is a universal phenomenon, and that "women" constitute a coherent, unified subject with common interests despite differences such as race and class.[29]

Although male sexual supremacy is institutionalized as heterosexuality, lesbians are not freed from the sexual victimization common to all women.[30] Even as the binary distinction between dominance and submission and its mapping onto men and women are central to patriarchal oppression, this excludes neither homosexual acts nor solitary sexual activity.[31] Radical feminists identify the vast majority of contemporary

[26] Kathleen Barry, "The Network Defines Its Issues: Theory, Evidence and Analysis of Female Sexual Slavery," ibid., 21.

[27] *Female Sexual Slavery*, 41. In Jaggar's words, "Radical feminists believe that women, whether they recognize it or not, are the sexual slaves of men. Consequently, women's sexual relation with men is typically that of rape," 261.

[28] Sonia Johnson, "Taking Our Eyes Off the Guys," in *The Sexual Liberals and the Attack on Feminism*, ed. Dorchen A. Leidholdt and Janice G. Raymond (New York: Pergamon Press, 1990), 56.

[29] According to MacKinnon, radical feminists believed "that we didn't all have to be the same in order to be part of this common condition [...] [Radical feminism was premised] as much on diversity as on commonality. It did not assume that commonality meant sameness." Catharine A. MacKinnon, "Liberalism and the Death of Feminism," ibid., 5.

[30] See Andrea Dworkin, "Dworkin on Dworkin," in *Radically Speaking: Feminism Reclaimed*, ed. Diane Bell and Renate Klein (North Melbourne: Spinifex Press, 1996), 210.

[31] Radical feminists criticized gay male sexuality in particular, and rejected the idea that gay political activism had much affinity with lesbian political activism. See Adrienne Rich, "Compulsory Heterosexuality and Lesbian Existence," *Signs: Journal of Women in Culture &*

sexual practices, including those occurring solely with oneself or between or among same-sex partners, as sexually exploitative insofar as they reproduce "the eroticization of dominance and submission"[32] constitutive of male supremacy. Especially problematic practices include "sado-masochism, pornography, prostitution, cruising (promiscuous sex with strangers), adult/child sexual relations, and sexual role playing (e.g., butch/femme relationships)."[33] Moreover, the domain of sexuality is not limited to sex acts, but rather encompasses a much larger sphere of human experience. MacKinnon writes:

> Sexuality is not confined to that which is done as pleasure in bed or as an ostensible reproductive act; it does not refer exclusively to genital contact or arousal or sensation, or narrowly to sex-desire or libido or eros. Sexuality is conceived as a far broader social phenomenon, as nothing less than the dynamic of sex as social hierarchy, its pleasure the experience of power in its gendered form.[34]

Importantly, MacKinnon's articulation of sexuality to hierarchy is meant to be read as a commentary on *male supremacist* sexuality. Although, as we have seen, all forms of sexuality are suspect within a patriarchal or male supremacist system, radical feminists have also sought to theorize and create space for the realization of feminist sexuality.[35]

Building on their argument that male supremacist sexuality is faced by women universally—though not identically—radical feminists further contend that these harms are not discrete: all female sexual exploitation contributes to the oppression of all women. In other words, women are linked not only by their common experiences of sexual exploitation, but by the patriarchal mindset that is both cause and effect of the sexual

---

Society (1980): 631–60, which includes an extensive discussion of Barry's Female Sexual Slavery.

[32] MacKinnon, 113.

[33] Ann Ferguson, "Sex War: The Debate between Radical and Libertarian Feminists," *Signs: Journal of Women in Culture and Society* 10, no. 1 (1984): 106–12. See also Barry, *The Prostitution of Sexuality*, Jeffreys, "Eroticizing Women's Subordination."

[34] MacKinnon, xiii.

[35] See Robin Rowland, "Politics of Intimacy: Heterosexuality, Love and Power," in *Radically Speaking: Feminism Reclaimed*, ed. Diane Bell and Renate Klein (North Melbourne: Spinifex Press, 1996).

exploitation of any woman. Leidholdt, for example, argues that "sexually exploited women and children are the sex industry's primary casualties but not its only victims. Commercial sexual exploitation diminishes the lives of all women and girls by inculcating in men and boys profoundly misogynistic beliefs and attitudes."[36] In a paper presented at the Holy See 20th anniversary conference on trafficking in persons hosted by the Pontifical Gregorian University, Leidholdt reiterates the radical feminist argument that forms of sexual exploitation such as sex trafficking and pornography are responsible for women's universal inequality, "coloring the way husbands treat their wives and daughters, bosses treat female employees, and men and boys treat the women and girls they encounter on the street."[37] Barry likewise classifies sexual violence as a form of terrorism that "goes beyond one women's experience of sexual violence [to] create a state of existence that captures the hearts and minds of all those who may be potentially touched by it."[38]

Positing women as universally subject to sexual violence such that harm to one is harm to all enables feminist abolitionists to begin erasing distinctions between the helpers and the helped within any single feminist campaign. In MacKinnon's contribution to *The Sexual Liberals and the Attack on Feminism*, she makes this point explicitly:

> When women were hurt, this movement defended them. Individually and in groups, it organized and started shelters and groups of and for all women: battered women, incest survivors, prostitutes. We did this not because these women were thought 'bad' by society or considered outlaws or shunned. We did it because what was done to them was a systematic act of power against each one of us, although they were taking the brunt of it. This was not a sentimental identification. We knew that whatever could be done to them could be, was being, would be done to us. We *were* them, also.[39]

[36] Dorchen A. Leidholdt, "Presentation to UN Special Seminar on Trafficking, Prostitution and the Global Sex Industry—Postion Paper for CATW," Coalition Against the Trafficking of Women, accessed September 29, 2009, http://action.web.ca/home/catw/readingroom.shtml.

[37] "A Call to Action: Joining the Fight against Trafficking in Persons" (paper presented at the US Embassy to the Holy See 20th Anniversary Conference—A Call to Action: Joining the Fight against Trafficking in Persons, The Pontifical Gregorian University, June 17 2004).

[38] Barry, *Female Sexual Slavery*, 42.

[39] MacKinnon, 5.

MacKinnon's comments here are instructive. For radical feminists, the claim that "we" (the movement) were or are identical to "them" (the hurt women to be defended) is a powerful one used to rebut charges of racism and western imperialism. Compare MacKinnon's comment, for instance, to Doezema's charge that "CATW's construction of 'third world prostitutes' is part of a wider western feminist impulse to construct a damaged 'other' as the main justification for its own interventionist impulses."[40]

Radical feminists' assertion of a universal female subject has the additional effect of granting all women standing to challenge instances of systemic oppression of any woman. Anti-pornography protests and legal action in the late 1970s and 1980s provide an early example of how this worked in practice. Drawing connections "between media violence to women and real-life violence to them,"[41] radical feminists claim that pornography is a "blueprint for female enslavement and gynocide,"[42] a tool of patriarchal oppression that cannot be countenanced under any circumstances due to the dangerous cultural environment it reinforces for women.[43] In Robin Morgan's words, "Pornography is the theory, and

---

[40] Jo Doezema, "Ouch! Western Feminists' 'Wounded Attachment' to the 'Third World Prostitute'," *Feminist Review* 67, no. 1 (2001): 17. Doezema does not limit her criticism to CATW. She goes on to argue, "CATW feminists are not alone in their attachment to 'third world prostitutes' suffering bodies'. Feminist anti-trafficking organizations that nominally support the recognition of prostitution as a legitimate profession can slip into orientalist representations of third world sex workers." Ibid., 18.

[41] Laura Lederer, *Take Back the Night: Women on Pornography* (New York: Harper Perennial, 1980), 16.

[42] Barry, *Female Sexual Slavery*, 252. Leidholdt notes, "To radical feminist at the beginning of the Second Wave, pornography was nothing more or less than a codification of a male supremacist value system and the reification of male sexual power over women [...]." Vance and Snitow, in contrast, challenge the anti-pornography movement's conflation of categories. They argue that "the failure to make distinctions—between violent pornography and pornography, between pornography and sex, and between sex and violence—makes it hard to describe complex relations that involve both similarity *and* difference." Carol S. Vance and Ann Barr Snitow, "Toward a Conversation About Sex in Feminism: A Modest Proposal," *Signs: Journal of Women in Culture and Society* 10, no. 1 (1984): 182.

[43] Barry, *Female Sexual Slavery*, 252. MacKinnon, for example, baldly states that "[pornography] is sexual reality," 98. The precise distinction between the pornographic and the erotic, and the question of whether such a distinction is meaningful under patriarchy, remains an area of disagreement among radical feminists.

rape is the practice."[44] In the introduction to *Take Back the Night*, Laura Lederer's foundational anthology on pornography and violence against women, Lederer describes pornography as "the ideology of a culture which promotes and condones rape, woman-battering, and other crimes of violence against women."[45] Insofar as the existence of pornography is understood to be *inherently abusive to all women*, radical feminists oppose harm reduction strategies such as working to improve conditions within sex industries and protecting performers against sexually transmitted infections. Such measures are themselves harmful, propping up a male supremacist system that must be destroyed entirely.[46]

Radical Feminist Epistemology

Mackinnon contends that radical feminists first ascertained the fundamental role of sexuality in explaining women's oppression as a result of feminist practices such as consciousness-raising,[47] a "face-to-face social experience that strikes at the fabric of meaning of social relations between and among women and men by calling their givenness into question and reconstituting their meaning in a transformed and critical way."[48] Consciousness-raising sessions frequently began with "going around the room in a meeting to hear each woman's testimony."[49]

[44] Robin Morgan, "Theory and Practice: Pornography and Rape," in *Take Back the Night: Women on Pornography*, ed. Laura Lederer (New York: William Morrow, 1980), 139–40, quoted in Jaggar, 265.

[45] Lederer, 19–20. Following the publication of the anthology, "Take Back the Night" became the rallying cry for feminist protest marches against pornography, and Lederer went on to play a prominent role in activist, academic, and government circles in the feminist abolitionist campaigns against trafficking. Ibid., 19. Take Back the Night is now a charitable foundation that organizes events about violence against women and sexual violence. See http://www.takebackthenight.org.

[46] Ibid., 29. The question of harm reduction strategies reappears in similar guise within anti-trafficking debates.

[47] MacKinnon, 109.

[48] Ibid. For criticism of the ethnocentrism of early feminist consciousness-raising sessions, see María C. Lugones and Elizabeth V. Spelman, "Have We Got a Theory for You! Feminist Theory, Cultural Imperialism, and the Demand for 'the Woman's Voice'," *Women's Studies International Forum* 6, no. 6 (1983).

[49] Kathie Sarachild, "Consciousness-Raising: A Radical Weapon," *Feminist Revolution* (1978), accessed September 29, 2009, http://scriptorium.lib.duke.edu/wlm/fem/sarachild.html.

Kathie Sarachild, one of the initial radicals who developed and popularized the practice, cautions that the purpose of consciousness-raising was not, as opponents on both ends of the political spectrum characterized it, simply therapeutic:

> The purpose of hearing from everyone was never to be nice or tolerant or to develop speaking skill or the "ability to listen." It was to get closer to the truth. Knowledge and information would make it possible for people to be "able" to speak. The purpose of hearing people's feelings and experience was not therapy, was not to give someone a change to get something off her chest [...] that is something for a friendship. It was to hear what she had to say. The importance of listening to a woman's feelings was collectively to analyze the situation of women, not to analyze *her*. The idea was not to change women, was not to make "internal changes" except in the sense of knowing more. It was and is the conditions women face, it's male supremacy, we want to change.[50]

Brownmiller provides an example of how such a session unfolded, beginning with the question posed by Sarachild of whether participants preferred having male or female children and moving on to testimonies of secret abortions. She writes, "Saying 'I've had three illegal abortions' aloud was my feminist baptism, my swift immersion in the power of sisterhood [...] The simple technique of consciousness-raising had brought my submerged truths to the surface, where I learned that I wasn't alone."[51]

Consciousness-raising and related practices are significant for feminists not only in terms of the truths they uncover, but also for the manner in which they disrupt male-established theories of truth itself. Radical feminists maintain that the realities of sexual exploitation and its foundational support of patriarchy are rendered invisible by male supremacist notions of objectivity and verifiability. In practice, these putatively neutral standards for knowledge are used to sustain patriarchal oppression and delegitimate opposition from the oppressed. As Dworkin declared in a speech delivered at the University of Michigan School Of Law's symposium on prostitution:

---

[50] Ibid.

[51] Brownmiller, 7.

There is a middle-class presumption that one knows everything worth knowing. It is the presumption of most prostituted women that one knows nothing worth knowing. In fact, neither thing is true. What matters here is to try to learn what the prostituted woman knows, because it is of immense value. It is true and it has been hidden. It has been hidden for a political reason: to know it is to come closer to knowing how to undo the system of male dominance that is sitting on top of all of us.[52]

In order to recover hidden knowledge, feminist epistemologists reject pretentions of objectivity, "the male epistemological stance,"[53] and profess instead the necessity of building theory from the starting point of women's lived experiences. Dworkin provides a clear example of this position in her 1986 testimony before the Attorney General's Commission on Pornography in New York City. Here she introduces justification for radical feminist activism against "snuff films," the empirical existence of which had not been verified by the US Department of Justice:

My information comes from a journalist, whose sources I trust, that such films exist, from women who have seen them, whom I believe, whom no law-enforcement official would, that the films exist, that they have seen them. And so far, all that I could tell you is that it doesn't mean we won't

---

[52]Andrea Dworkin, "Prostitution and Male Supremacy," *Michigan Journal of Gender & Law* 1 (1993): 5.

[53]Catharine MacKinnon, "Feminism, Marxism, Method, and the State: An Agenda for Theory," in *Feminist Social Thought: A Reader*, ed. Diana Tietjens Meyers (New York: Routledge, 1997), 75. See also *Toward a Feminist Theory of the State*. Cherríe Moraga and Gloria Anzaldúa, eds., *This Bridge Called My Back: Writings by Radical Women of Color* (New York: Kitchen Table: Women of Color Press, 1983 [1981]); Carol Gilligan, *In a Different Voice: Psychological Theory and Women's Development* (Cambridge, MA: Harvard University Press, 1982); Sara Ruddick, *Maternal Thinking: Towards a Politics of Peace* (New York: Ballantine Books, 1989); Sandra Harding, ed., *The Feminist Standpoint Theory Reader: Intellectual and Political Controversies* (New York: Routledge, 2004); and Patricia Hill Collins, *Black Feminist Thought: Knowledge, Consciousness, and the Politics of Empowerment* (New York: Routledge, 2000). Other feminists such as Joan W. Scott and Chandra Talpade Mohanty have argued that "experience" is a problematic notion in itself. Uncritical reliance upon experience as the foundation for knowledge runs the risk of reifying difference rather than critically understanding its construction and possibilities. See Joan Wallach Scott, "The Evidence of Experience," *Critical Inquiry* 17, no. 4 (1991); Chandra Talpade Mohanty, "Feminist Encounters: Locating the Politics of Experience," *Copyright* 1, Fall (1987). Mohanty, 78–84.

be wrong, but so far we have said battery exists and the FBI has said it doesn't, and we have been right. And we've said rape exists and law-enforcement people have said, no; and we have been right. And we said incest is rife in this country and law-enforcement people first said no, and we were right. Our big secret is that we listen to the people to whom it happens. And that's what we are doing here.[54]

Claims such as these directly challenge what radical feminists take to be patriarchal distortions of reality by shifting "the reference point for truth and thereby the definition of reality as such."[55]

Women's testimony to their experiences is established as trustworthy through collective practices such as consciousness-raising that alter "the terms of validation by creating community through a process that redefines what counts as verification."[56] The notion that standards of verification are necessary, even if radically different from those said to support male supremacist knowledge, suggests that radical feminists are cognizant of the dangers of simplistic appeals to experience, and recognize that accounts of experience require at least some sort of mediation in order to be accepted as true or valid. Moreover, truth claims based on the experience are particularly vulnerable to competing truth claims based on different experiences, or on different interpretations of similar experiences. For radical feminists, a persistent puzzle appears. What happens when women's experiences and interpretations of those experiences produce conflicting accounts of the truth?

For MacKinnon, however, the mere fact of disagreement among women's interpretations of their experiences is unproblematic for radical feminism, which "recognizes that cognitive judgments need not be universally agreed upon to be true."[57] Women's "nonfeminist perception of their situation" simply reflects an absence of feminist consciousness.[58] Barry, the preeminent theorist of feminist abolitionism, is unequivocal on this point:

---

[54] Andrea Dworkin, *Letters from a War Zone: Writings, 1976–1989* (New York: E.P. Dutton, 1989).

[55] MacKinnon, *Toward a Feminist Theory of the State*, 87.

[56] Ibid.

[57] Ibid., 102.

[58] Ibid.

Things simply do not exist only as perceptions. There is an objective reality which precedes perception and is presumed by perceived reality. Objective reality is, where or not it is perceived. It is not merely a matter of perception or opinion that women are sexually enslaved. It is a fact. But social perception is presently inconsistent with objective reality. The decision to suppress the evidence of sex slavery is but one means of maintaining the disparity between social perception and objective reality.[59]

Barry argues that claims to the contrary represent "false consciousness."[60] Though MacKinnon eschews the terminology of "false consciousness,"[61] she makes clear that "in contemporary philosophical terms, nothing is 'indeterminate' in the post-structuralist sense here; it is all too determinate."[62] The most significant aspect of this position is that which unites radical feminists: the notion that female sexual slavery is a universal fact of female existence today.

Note that Mackinnon and Barry both emphasize that women's perceptions of reality may be unreliable—this holds true for physiological perceptions as well. Several contributors to *The Sexual Liberals and the Attack on Feminism,* for example, contend that women's sexual fantasies, desires, and orgasms represent more the insidious reach of male supremacist sexuality than women's authentic or true bodily responses.[63] Sheila Jeffreys writes:

We have got to understand that sexual response for women and orgasm for women is not necessarily pleasurable and positive. It can be a very real problem. It can be an accommodation of our oppression. It can be the eroticizing of our domination.[64]

---

[59] Barry, *Female Sexual Slavery,* 118.

[60] On "false consciousness" as a theory, see ibid., 217–18.

[61] MacKinnon, *Toward a Feminist Theory of the State,* 116.

[62] Ibid., 137. She continues, "The reality of pervasive sexual abuse and its eroticization does not shift relative to perspective, although whether or not one will see it or accord it significance may."

[63] See, e.g. Leidholdt, "When Women Defend Pornography"; Catharine A. MacKinnon, "Liberalism and the Death of Feminism," ibid.; Sheila Jeffreys, "Eroticizing Women's Subordination," ibid.

[64] "Sexology and Antifeminism," 22.

Leidholdt makes a similar point about pornography in the same edited volume:

> Acting out the roles of dominance and submission that the system forces on us is not the same as choosing them. Experiencing arousal and orgasm in the course of acting out these roles is not defining our own sexuality. I've come to believe that a human being can eroticize anything—including banging one's head against a brick wall.[65]

Given the suspicion cast upon critics' personal testimony—even to the extent of questioning the authenticity of one's own perception of sexual arousal and climax—it is unsurprising that radical feminists' commitment to "women" as a universal subject, and their subsequent attempts to police the boundaries of what authentically belongs to that domain will continue to be sites of tension, and will carry over to radical anti-trafficking campaigns.

FROM MALE SEXUAL SUPREMACY TO FEMALE SEXUAL SLAVERY

As stated in the introduction to this chapter, Kathleen Barry's 1979 opus *Female Sexual Slavery* is largely responsible for renewing feminist interest in stopping sex trafficking and setting the discursive parameters of contemporary feminist abolitionism.[66] In this section I examine Barry's two most prominent works—*Female Sexual Slavery* and *The Prostitution of Sexuality*—as well as her contributions to the 1983 *Report of the Global Feminist Workshop to Organize Against Traffic in Women*.[67]

Building upon Mackinnon's radical feminist theory of women's oppression, Barry starts from the position that male supremacist sexuality results in female sexual slavery. The linkages that constitute female sexual slavery connect all women living in patriarchal orders such that

---

[65] Dorchen A. Leidholdt, "When Women Defend Pornography," ibid., 129.

[66] In addition to her career as an activist, Barry received her Ph.D. in sociology from the University of Berkeley in 1977. She is currently Professor Emerita of Human Development at Pennsylvania State University.

[67] Barry, *Female Sexual Slavery*, *The Prostitution of Sexuality*, and Kathleen Barry, Charlotte Bunch, and Shirley Castley, eds., *International Feminism: Networking against Female Sexual Slavery; Report of the Global Feminist Workshop to Organize against Traffic in Women* (Rotterdam, the Netherlands: International Women's Tribune Center, 1983).

women, regardless of class, ethnicity, or nationality, have their sexual victimhood in common.[68] The commonality of women's experiences as victims therefore suggests the possibility for a transnational movement informed by these experiences to fight female sexual slavery. Barry reasserts the universality of women's condition under patriarchy in order to argue for the necessity for broadly targeted transnational activism:

> To confront the whole, the female class condition, strategically and politically, I launched action in an international arena of human rights because sex is power over all women. As the female condition is a class condition, sex power must be addressed as a global issue, inclusive of all of its occurrences in the subordination of women.[69]

While prostitution is but a single facet of women's oppression, it is "the model, the most extreme and most crystallized form of all sexual exploitation."[70] Thus, while Barry understands "prostitute women not as a group set apart, which is a misogynist construction, but as women whose sexual exploitation is consonant with that of all women's experience of sexual exploitation,"[71] she nonetheless makes prostitution the center of what will become the feminist abolitionism movement.

Lines of Demarcation

Female Sexual Slavery begins with the contention that there is no meaningful distinction between prostitution and what Barry refers to as "the traffic in women." She explains, "From interviews and other research I learned that virtually the only distinction that can be made between traffic in women and street prostitution is that the former involves crossing international borders."[72] For Barry this means that opposition to the traffic in women necessitates opposition to domestic prostitution and vice versa, as both represent essentially the same form of female sexual slavery. There are two facets of this position worth noting, both of which will be explored at greater length below. First, Barry's position entails a

---

[68] Barry, *Female Sexual Slavery*, 41.
[69] *The Prostitution of Sexuality*, 10.
[70] Ibid., 11.
[71] Ibid., 9.
[72] *Female Sexual Slavery*, 7.

rejection of any distinction between "forced" prostitution and "voluntary" prostitution. *All* forms of prostitution, regardless of recruitment mechanism or participants' purported consent are to be opposed on the grounds that "experientially rape and prostitution sex are undifferentiated for the women who are its vehicles."[73] Second, Barry's terminology will result in definitional difficulties for feminist abolitionists further down the line. In *Female Sexual Slavery*, Barry takes "trafficking in women" to mean migration across international borders for commercial sex. This poses no issue for Barry insofar as she subsumes both trafficking and prostitution under the more general category of "female sexual slavery." When the terminology of "female sexual slavery" is replaced by "trafficking in women" and "human trafficking," however, feminist abolitionists will have fewer rhetorical resources with which to connect trafficking and domestic prostitution.

Just as Barry rejects the distinction between trafficking and domestic prostitution, so too does she refuse to differentiate between the prostitution of children and of adult women:

> Child prostitution has always been part of the sex slave trade. Separating the enslavement of children from that of women distorts the reality of the practices and conveys the impression that on some level it is tolerable to enslave women while child slavery is still reprehensible. Within that distinction lies the implication that one form of slavery is intolerable and worth attention while the other is not.[74]

Barry makes the same argument with regards to pornography, which she identifies as a form of prostitution.[75] Her case against pornography *qua* prostitution takes the form of a lengthy discussion of the harms of *child* pornography rather than adult pornography, passing over any differences in rationality, maturity, and legal ability to provide consent between adult women and children.[76]

Barry's sexually enslaved female subject is established in opposition to a sexually supremacist male subject, rendering the latter group ineligible to be considered true victims of prostitution and sex trafficking. While

---

[73] *The Prostitution of Sexuality*, 37.

[74] *Female Sexual Slavery*, 11.

[75] Ibid., 252.

[76] Ibid., 99–100.

Barry resists the "false" lines drawn between domestic and international prostitution, and between prostitution and pornography, she firmly upholds a distinction between the sexual traffic in women and the sexual traffic in men:

> The sex-power relationship between men and women makes male prostitution quite a different practice than female prostitution. The victimization and enslavement to which women are subject in male-dominated society find no equivalent in male experience.[77]

The statement above is unique in abolitionist writing insofar as it refers to male prostitution at all. For subsequent feminist abolitionists, the category of male prostitutes/trafficking victims is either empty or unworthy of mention.

If men cannot be sexually victimized, so too are they limited as allies. While later feminist abolitionists formed a strong political alliance in the United States with the largely male-led network of religious abolitionists, Barry herself specifically takes to task the nineteenth-century anti-trafficking activists she describes as "religious moralists." Returning again to Josephine Butler's movement opposing the1864 and 1869 Contagious Disease Acts in Great Britain, Barry sees Butler's feminist campaign as undermined by two forces who sought to join her—men, who would engage in sensationalist rescue work while disregarding any harm they might cause to actual victims of sexual slavery, and religious moralists, whose purity crusades reinforced the Madonna/whore binary, and focused exclusively on saving redeemable "innocents."[78]

One of the main offenders, in Barry's opinion, was Alfred Dyer, a Quaker author who investigated and wrote about the case of a nineteen-year-old British girl tricked into sexual slavery in Brussels. Dyer discovered the girl in captivity in Brussels, but took her case to the authorities, whom Butler believed to be corrupt, rather than rescuing the girl himself. The girl later disappeared.[79] Describing the incident, Barry writes,

---

[77] *The Prostitution of Sexuality*, 11. Barry defines male prostitution as the prostitution of "teenage boys and adult men," but does not specify the point at which male children lose the vulnerability that had previously deemed them worthy of protection from sexual exploitation. Ibid. On the rape of adult men, see Jaggar, 262–63.

[78] Barry, *Female Sexual Slavery*, 23–30.

[79] Ibid., 22.

"When men entered the campaign against regulated prostitution, particularly in rescue work and investigations, one notes that consistently their behavior was dominated by righteous heroics in which the fate of the victim is secondary to the escapade they are performing."[80]

The paternalism demonstrated by men such as Dyer was matched, in Barry's opinion, by religious moralists such as the Salvation Army. Their standards for victimhood excluded many of the prostitutes that Butler herself was attempting to help, so that "the victim became redefined; the less sweet, innocent, and young she was the less likely she could be a victim."[81] In the end, Butler's campaign was co-opted, done in by "the tactical mistake of resorting to coalition politics."[82] Barry concludes, "The inherently feminist politics of liberation with which Josephine had so carefully built and guided this movement were to be swept aside by the religious moralists who began *en masse* to take over the movement."[83]

A second line of demarcation—between those whose stories can be taken seriously and those whose stories can be dismissed—is more implicit than explicit, but is nonetheless essential to Barry's position. As the previous section documents, feminists have long recognized "Who can speak?"[84] as a central question for the movement, and it is revealing who Barry allows to speak through her writings. *Female Sexual Slavery* and *The Prostitution of Sexuality* incorporate numerous narratives in the third person as well as a smaller number of direct quotations, all of which are said to represent the experiences of women victimized by prostitution. On the one hand, Barry claims that stories of immense bodily and psychological harm and the representation of those who have experienced sexual violence as "victims" have been necessary in order to force courts and the public to take rape seriously.[85] On the other hand, Barry also recognizes that repetition of these narratives runs the risk of placing women in the permanent role of victim, with a corresponding

---

[80] Ibid., 23.

[81] Ibid., 32.

[82] Ibid., 28.

[83] Ibid.

[84] See also Judith Roof and Robyn Wiegman, eds., *Who Can Speak? Authority and Critical Identity* (Urbana and Champaign: University of Illinois Press, 1995).

[85] Barry, *Female Sexual Slavery*, 43–44.

loss of agency and the necessity to "play the part" or risk losing sympathy.[86] Thus, although Barry describes the victims of female sexual slavery at great lengths as victims, she specifies that these women are also "survivors," that is, women who have made necessary and often difficult choices in their attempts to survive.[87] This tension is evident throughout *Female Sexual Slavery*, with narratives occasionally focusing on women's escape and survival strategies, but more generally emphasizing women's abject abuse and victimhood under conditions of slavery. Readers are introduced to a slew of victims/survivors, such as Marie, an eighteen-year-old Frenchwoman who was raped, beaten, and sold to a brothel by a couple she met at a dance club,[88] and Jennifer, a fourteen-year-old runaway from Long Island who was beaten, raped, and tortured by a pimp attempting to break her spirit before putting her on the streets.[89] In *The Prostitution of Sexuality*, Barry's 1995 follow-up to *Female Sexual Slavery*, representations of survivors are almost wholly eclipsed by representations of victims.[90]

Significantly, Barry does not quote women engaged in prostitution who claim not to have been victimized by prostitution; rather, as I discussed previously, Barry ascribes women's pro-sex work testimony to false consciousness.[91] In Doezema's critical reading of this move:

> Barry constructs the 'injury' of sex in prostitution in a circular manner. Prostitution is considered always injurious because the sex in it is dehumanizing. However, the sex takes on this dehumanizing character because it takes place within prostitution. In this neat, sealed construction, there is no place for the experiences of sex workers who claim their work is not harmful or alienating. For Barry and CATW, the notion of a prostitute who is unharmed by her experience is an ontological impossibility: that which cannot be.[92]

[86] Ibid., 11, 44–46. For a dissenting radical feminist view, see Andrea Dworkin, "Woman-Hating Right and Left," in *The Sexual Liberals and the Attack on Feminism*, ed. Dorchen A. Leidholdt and Janice G. Raymond (New York: Pergamon Press, 1990), 38.

[87] Barry, *Female Sexual Slavery*, 47–49.

[88] Ibid., 80–81.

[89] Ibid., 92–93.

[90] See, e.g., *The Prostitution of Sexuality*, 11, 35, 171, 82.

[91] *Female Sexual Slavery*, 120; *The Prostitution of Sexuality*, 23, 37, 69–73, 79, 296.

[92] Doezema, "Ouch! Western Feminists' 'Wounded Attachment' to the 'Third World Prostitute'," 27.

In sum, for radical feminists the notion that women can consent to prostitution is rejected out of hand: "Consent to oppression or an apparent 'will' to be objectified is a condition of oppression. It is never a state of freedom."[93] In fact, Barry suggests, prostituted women who claim to have chosen their work may actually be reacting to histories of sexual abuse that they have repressed. She laments that "we may never know how many among these women do not remember and cannot yet know that they were sexualized as children by uncles, fathers, stepfathers, grandfathers."[94]

FEMINIST ABOLITIONISM

In addition to Barry, key figures in the burgeoning radical feminist anti-trafficking movement included scholars such as Donna Hughes and Janice Raymond, community activists and self-described survivors of prostitution such as Vednita Carter and Norma Hotaling, and other veterans of the anti-pornography movement such as feminist attorneys Laura Lederer and Dorchen Leidholdt and clinical psychologist Melissa Farley. Despite the ubiquity of Americans in formal and informal leadership roles, the feminist abolitionist community strongly emphasizes both the transnational existence of women's oppression and the transnational membership of abolitionist organizations.[95] Abolitionists' litanies of female oppression include widespread practices, such as rape, prostitution, incest, and battering as well as culturally specific practices such as dowry deaths and female genital mutilation.[96]

---

[93] Barry, *The Prostitution of Sexuality*, 79.

[94] Ibid. See also Evelina Giobbe, "Confronting the Liberal Lies About Prostitution," in *The Sexual Liberals and the Attack on Feminism*, ed. Dorchen A. Leidholdt and Janice G. Raymond (New York: Pergamon Press, 1990). Barry, "The Opening Paper: International Politics of Female Sexual Slavery," 79; For a critical discussion of studies that claim to document a high percentage of childhood rape and sexual abuse reported by prostituted women, see Ine Vanwesenbeeck, "Another Decade of Social Scientific Work on Sex Work: A Review of Research 1990–2000," *Annual Review of Sex Research* 12 (2001).

[95] See Barry, *The Prostitution of Sexuality*, 10; Leidholdt, "Demand and the Debate."

[96] Aurora Javarte de Dios, "Confronting Trafficking, Prostitution and Sexual Exploitation in Asia–the Struggle for Survival and Dignity," in *Making the Harm Visible: Global Sexual Exploitation of Women and Girls*, ed. Donna M. Hughes and Claire M. Roche (Kingston, RI: Coalition Against Trafficking in Women, 1999). "Female genital mutilation" is itself a highly contested concept, and is alternatively described as "female circumcision" and "female genital cutting." See, e.g., Rogaia Mustafa Abusharaf, "Virtuous

Barry credited the passion attached to human rights advocacy with her decision to situate feminist abolitionism within the context of the international human rights movement.[97] "Human-rights philosophy matches radical feminist moral outrage," she wrote, "recognizing any acts that are destructive to human beings—anything that dehumanizes the human condition—as barbarous."[98] Even more important than outrage,[99] however, was the universalism of the human rights approach, making it an appropriate "foundation for global feminist struggle based on the common dimensions of women's oppression."[100] Indeed, both of the major feminist advocacy networks that participated in the Trafficking Protocol negotiations prioritized a human rights approach, pitting the abolitionist "International Human Rights Network" led by the CATW against the pro-sex workers' rights "Human Rights Caucus" led by the International Human Rights Law Group, the GAATW, and the Asian Women's Human Rights Council.[101]

Cuts: Female Genital Circumcision in an African Ontology," in *Going Public: Feminism and the Shifting Boundaries of the Private Sphere*, ed. Joan W. Scott and Debra Keates (Urbana and Champaign: University of Illinois Press, 2004).

[97] Barry does not claim to have accomplished this single-handedly. In fact, Charlotte Bunch is most closely associated with the slogan, "Women's Rights Are Human Rights." See, e.g., Charlotte Bunch, "Women's Rights as Human Rights: Toward a Re-vision of Human Rights," *Human Rights Quarterly* 12 (1990). See also Margaret E. Keck and Kathryn Sikkink, *Activists Beyond Borders: Advocacy Networks in International Politics* (Ithaca, NY: Cornell University Press, 1998), 184–88. The distinction that Barry is drawing is between the field of international human rights—the chosen battleground for her coterie of radical feminists—and the field of individual civil rights, the ground upon which MacKinnon and Dworkin had staked their radical feminist campaign against pornography in the 1980s. Barry, *The Prostitution of Sexuality*, 10.

[98] *The Prostitution of Sexuality*, 302.

[99] The importance of which should not be underestimated. As Bunch and Shirley Castley wrote in their introduction to the published proceedings of the 1983 Rotterdam workshop, "We wish, ultimately, to outrage." "Introduction," in *International Feminism: Networking against Female Sexual Slavery; Report of the Global Feminist Workshop to Organize against Traffic in Women*, ed. Kathleen Barry, Charlotte Bunch, and Shirley Castley (Rotterdam, the Netherlands: International Women's Tribune Center, 1983), 8.

[100] *The Prostitution of Sexuality*, 303.

[101] Jo Doezema, "Now You See Her, Now You Don't: Sex Workers at the UN Trafficking Protocol Negotiation," *Social & Legal Studies* 14, no. 1 (2005): 68.

As the other chapters of this book attest, rights rhetoric is a powerful tool with which to legitimate one's own claims and silence those of others. Consider, for example, Hughes' contention that "most everyone agrees that the sex-trafficking networks that enslave millions of women and children each year are among the most egregious systems of human-rights violations in the world."[102] At the same time, Hughes reiterates the importance of her issue, so too does she reinforce the abolitionist position that (1) "millions of women and children" are enslaved by sex traffickers each year; (2) that trafficking women and children for sex represent a more egregious rights violation than other forms of exploitation or enslavement; and (3) that these beliefs are validated by public consensus.

Feminist abolitionists point to the 1980 World Conference on the United Nations Decade for Women in Copenhagen as a foundational moment in the history of their movement.[103] Barry had just published *Female Sexual Slavery*, and she was invited to lead six workshops at the conference and its associated NGO forum along with Uri Kondo, who had been doing similar work on male sex tourism with the Asian Women's Association.[104] According to Barry, "It was in these workshops, discussing female sexual slavery and sex tourism that a feminist momentum built which resulted in the governmental conference adopting into the World Plan of Action for Women a resolution against the traffic in women."[105] The resolution focused specifically on adult women and children of both sexes, urging governments "to recognize that women and children are not a commodity and that every woman and every child has the right to legal protection against abduction,

---

[102]Donna M. Hughes, "Accommodation or Abolition? Solutions to the Problem of Sexual Trafficking and Slavery," National Review Online, accessed September 29, 2009, http://www.nationalreview.com/articles/206761/accommodation-or-abolition/donna-m-hughes.

[103]Barry, "The Opening Paper: International Politics of Female Sexual Slavery." The objective of the conference, attended by delegations from more than 140 states, was to assess the improvement in women's status since 1975, the UN-designated International Women's Year. See Fran P. Hosken, "Toward a Definition of Women's Human Rights," *Human Rights Quarterly* 3, no. 2 (1981): 3.

[104]Bunch and Castley, 9.

[105]Kathleen Barry, "The Opening Paper: International Politics of Female Sexual Slavery," ibid., 22.

rape, and prostitution."[106] 64 UN member states concluded the conference by signing the Convention on the Elimination of All Forms of Discrimination Against Women (CEDAW),[107] which included the mandate that "States Parties shall take all appropriate measures, including legislation, to suppress all forms of traffic in women and exploitation of prostitution of women."[108]

Buoyed by their successes in Copenhagen, a core group of feminists immediately began making plans for another workshop.[109] The 1983 Global Feminist Workshop to Organize Against Traffic in Women succeeding in drawing participants from Africa, Australia, Western Europe, the Middle East, Asia, Latin America, and the United States to the meeting in Rotterdam.[110] 26 women, including activists, social service providers, Catholic nuns and other religious figures, academics, and lawyers, participated in the 10-day workshop, which concluded with an affirmation of the need for a global network to counter the sexual exploitation of women.[111]

The Rotterdam workshop was followed by the 1988 Conference on Trafficking in Women organized in New York by Leidholdt, Women against Pornography, and the Minneapolis-based organization WHISPER (Women Hurt in Systems of Prostitution Engaged in Revolt).[112] Notably, conference attendees settled upon a definition of trafficking in women as "a broad, umbrella concept that encompassed

[106] United Nations, "Report of the World Conference of the United Nations Decade for Women, Equality, Development, and Peace" (Copenhagen 1980), Resolution 43.

[107] CEDAW, which has been ratified by 185 states (not including the U.S.), is a UN convention that requires state parties to seek to eliminate gender discrimination by codifying women's equality in domestic law and establishing domestic institutions to further women's equality. UNHCHR, "Committee on the Elimination of Discrimination against Women," Office of the United Nations High Commisioner for Human Rights, accessed September 29, 2009, http://www2.ohchr.org/english/bodies/cedaw/index.htm.

[108] CEDAW article 6.

[109] Keck and Sikkink, 178.

[110] Bunch and Castley, 9.

[111] Ibid., 10.

[112] The Trafficking in Women conference was funded in part through the efforts of *Take Back the Night*'s Laura Lederer, who along with Leidholdt would go on to take a leading role in anti-trafficking politics. Leidholdt, "Demand and the Debate," 1.

all practices of buying and selling women's and children's bodies."[113] Participants concluded the meeting with the founding of the network envisioned in Rotterdam, the Coalition Against Trafficking in Women (CATW), and Aurora Javate de Dios, a scholar-activist from the Philippines, was named president.[114]

The rapid growth of feminist abolitionism paralleled what activists describe as the dramatic worldwide expansion of trafficking in women. Hughes, for example, concluded in 1999:

> At the end of the twentieth century, local and international forces have merged to escalate the sexual exploitation of women and girls. Policies, practices and crises are combining to increase both the supply of women and girls vulnerable to exploitation and the demand by men for women and girls to be used for their profit and sexual gratification.[115]

Determined to resist this trend, abolitionists coordinated largely by the CATW pursued a multitiered lobbying campaign targeting the UN, states with liberal prostitution policies, such as the Netherlands, Germany, and Sweden, and all levels of US government. The two most significant focuses of abolitionist efforts both reached fruition in 2000: the UN Trafficking Protocol and the US Trafficking Victims Protection Act.[116] These more explicitly political activities have been further supported by research of sex trafficking and prostitution undertaken by scholar-activists informed by analyses of sexuality with a distinct radical feminist influence.[117]

---

[113] Ibid.

[114] Ibid.

[115] Donna M. Hughes, "Introduction," in *Making the Harm Visible: Global Sexual Exploitation of Women and Girls*, ed. Donna M. Hughes and Claire M. Roche (Kingston, RI: Coalition Against Trafficking in Women, 1999).

[116] I discuss the TVPA at length in Chapter 3. Regarding the Trafficking Protocol, see Ann D. Jordan, "The Annotated Guide to the Complete UN Trafficking Protocol" (Washington, DC: International Human Rights Law Group, 2002).

[117] See, e.g., Janice G. Raymond and Donna M. Hughes, "Sex Trafficking of Women in the United States: International and Domestic Trends" (New York: Coalition Against Trafficking in Women, 2001). This study was supported by a grant from the National Institute of Justice (NIJ), an agency within the US Department of Justice.

From Trafficking in Women to Trafficking in Persons

In many respects, the Trafficking Protocol and the TVPA represented victories for feminist abolitionists. In one specific regard, however, both agreements signaled a failure. Despite their clear emphasis on the trafficking of women and children for sexual exploitation,[118] both the Protocol and the TVPA disappointed abolitionists in yoking a wide range of practices and affected persons together under the umbrella term of "trafficking in persons."[119] In fact, feminist abolitionists explicitly oppose grouping trafficking for sex and trafficking for forced nonsexual labor. Abolitionists do not deny that forced labor exists or that it is a violation of human rights, but rather they weigh it against the severity of sexual exploitation and what they claim to be the growing incidence of sexual exploitation, arguing that including forced labor in the definition of trafficking would redirect essential resources away from the more important problem of sex trafficking. While Leidholdt acknowledges, for example, that "being trafficked into exploitative farm or factory work is incompatible with fundamental human rights and is harmful to those who [are] subjected to this form of trafficking," she goes on to ask rhetorically, "but is that harm really as severe as the harm to women and girls trafficked into prostitution in brothels and over and over again subjected to intimate violation—to rape?"[120] For feminist abolitionists, the traffic of women and children for sex represents a uniquely horrifying violation of human rights hardly comparable to labor trafficking or sex trafficking in adult men. As we saw in the previous chapter, men (and often boys) are thereby excluded from the category of worthy victims, rendered ineligible for assistance or protection, and positioned for further abuse or exploitation.

The Victims Are the Same

Following Barry, feminist abolitionists hold that the fight against trafficking is a fight against prostitution—i.e., all prostitution of women and children. Both international sex trafficking and domestic prostitution are

---

[118] In the case of the Protocol, for example, the full title describes it as a Protocol to Prevent, Suppress and Punish Trafficking in Persons, *Especially Women and Children.* Emphasis added.

[119] See Janice G. Raymond, "Guide to the New UN Trafficking Protocol" (North Amherst, MA: Coalition Against Trafficking in Women, 2001).

[120] Leidholdt, "Demand and the Debate," 10.

said to involve the same sets of oppressive practices—procuring women, selling women's sexual services (pimping), and engaging in or facilitating rape.[121] Leidholdt's discussion of the similarities between international and domestic prostitution is worth quoting at length for her candor in depicting the gendered and racialized subjects at the heart of feminist abolitionism:

> The fact is that sex trafficking and organized prostitution are inextricably connected and share fundamental characteristics. The victims who are targeted are the same—poor, minority, or so-called Third World women and children, frequently with histories of physical and sexual abuse.[122]

Again echoing Barry, Leidholdt elides the distinction between adult women and children, emphasizing their vulnerability and attributing it to social and geographic location.[123]

Sex workers' rights activists criticize abolitionists for reproducing and strengthening stereotypical representations of helpless girls and predatory men. Barry's discussion of Filipina "bar women" in *The Prostitution of Sexuality* is similarly emblematic of critics' targets:

> Most of [the Filipina bar women] still had the naiveté of many of the women who migrate from the distant rural countryside, some previously victimized sexually by incest abuse and rape, others without any knowledge or sexual experience, many not even fully comprehending what is happening to them, many still believing that their American "boyfriends" who left when the United States withdrew its bases from the Philippines are still coming back for them, some gagging into towels after each blow job, and others, those in the cheapest bars [...] who are known as 'three holers' because no orifice of the human body is protected from sale and customer intrusion.[124]

---

[121] Barry, *Female Sexual Slavery*, 86; See also Leidholdt, "Demand and the Debate," 11–12; Raymond and Hughes, 13.

[122] Dorchen A. Leidholdt, "Prostitution: A Modern Form of Slavery," in *Making the Harm Visible: Global Sexual Exploitation of Women and Girls*, ed. Donna M. Hughes and Claire M. Roche (Kingston, RI: Coalition Against Trafficking in Women, 1999).

[123] See also "Presentation to UN Special Seminar on Trafficking, Prostitution and the Global Sex Industry-Postion Paper for CATW."

[124] Barry, *The Prostitution of Sexuality*, 11.

For Doezema, passages such as the above "ironically echo traditional, religious/patriarchal moralizing against prostitutes."[125] She writes that "third world sex workers' organizations reject this racist portrayal of themselves as deluded and despairing,"[126] citing as an example the 1997 "Sex Workers' Manifesto" produced at the First National Conference of Sex Workers in India.[127]

Abolitionists' representations of women's experiences as victims/survivors are deeply informed by radical feminist epistemology; consequently, such representations entail the same tensions discussed previously. As early as 1983, Charlotte Bunch emphasized that abolitionists' primary task is "to make the different forms of violence against women and their relationship to female sexual slavery more visible in all our countries, since they are frequently kept hidden."[128] As with anti-pornography campaigns, the primary method of revealing sexual exploitation entails collecting accounts of individual women's experiences and placing them within a radical feminist context.[129] As Javarte de Dios explains:

> A turning point on the issue of prostitution and trafficking are the voices of former prostitutes and victims of trafficking who are providing us with the most authoritative account of trafficking operations, as well as the devastating impact of prostitution and trafficking on the lives of women and children.[130]

Javarte de Dios's use of the word "authoritative" is significant—recall that not all voices of prostitutes, former or current, are granted such authority. Abolitionists argue that many prostituted women cannot recognize the objective condition of their oppression, whether because

---

[125] Doezema, "Ouch! Western Feminists' 'Wounded Attachment' to the 'Third World Prostitute'," 26.

[126] Ibid., 29.

[127] Durbar Mahila Samanwaya Committee (DMSC), "Sex Workers' Manifesto" (paper presented at the First National Conference of Sex Workers in India, Calcutta, November 14–16, 1997).

[128] Bunch, "Network Strategies and Organizing against Female Sexual Slavery," 54.

[129] Hughes, "Introduction."

[130] Aurora Javarte de Dios, "Confronting Trafficking, Prostitution and Sexual Exploitation in Asia—the Struggle for Survival and Dignity," ibid.

they've become demoralized and no longer expect any better, because they have come to identify with their abusers, or because they wish to preserve the illusion of having agency. Leidholdt likens prostituted women to battered women, who "have been known to enter abusive situations voluntarily, to choose to stay in or return to abusive situations voluntarily, to deny that they are being subjected to abuse, and to defend their abusers."[131]

From the abolitionist perspective, self-described "sex workers"[132] and their political allies are, at best, victims or dupes of male supremacy:

> For some, the 'sex work' model is a misguided attempt to bestow dignity on a stigmatized and marginalized population; what in fact it does, however, is to confer legitimacy on the systems of sexual exploitation that devastates the lives of prostituted women and children.[133]

Abolitionists point to the dangers in recognizing prostitution as work, arguing that this position supports those who sexually exploit women for profit, and makes it more difficult for governments to end human trafficking. In Raymond's words, "the term, sex work, doesn't dignify the worker; all it dignifies is the sex industry—the pimps, procurers, and traffickers. And coming from human rights activists and feminists, it gives the sex industry more dignity than it has ever had, or could anyplace else."[134] Sex workers and human rights organizations that prioritize harm reduction, workers' rights, and improving the quality of life of prostituted women rather than ending prostitution entirely are seen as taking the easy road rather than the high road. Raymond continues:

> Such NGO groups talk about women's empowerment *in* prostitution and primarily teach women how to be better prostitutes, how to negotiate with customers, and how to get men to use condoms and make it part of the sex, but they don't offer women a way out. Why? Because it's easier to

---

[131] Leidholdt, "Presentation to UN Special Seminar on Trafficking, Prostitution and the Global Sex Industry-Postion Paper for CATW."

[132] I alternate references to "prostituted women" and "sex workers" in accordance with the preferred usage of the individuals or groups I am currently discussing.

[133] Leidholdt, "Presentation to UN Special Seminar on Trafficking, Prostitution and the Global Sex Industry-Postion Paper for CATW."

[134] Janice G. Raymond, "Prostitution as Violence against Women: NGO Stonewalling in Beijing and Elsewhere," *Women's Studies International Forum* 21, no. 1 (1998): 2.

believe that prostitution is a choice for these women. And talking about women's empowerment in prostitution means you don't have to confront the controversial issue of the customer.[135]

Raymond's "controversial issue of the customer" alludes, of course, to the ultimate culprits: men.

If sex workers and sex workers' right activists are misguided at best, inadvertently providing dignity and political cover for pimping and pornography, abolitionists further present them as distracting and, at worst, mere fronts for the (male supremacist) sex industry. Leidholdt characterizes an early coalition of sex workers' rights activists, Wages for Housework, as "glib," "media-savvy," and "aggressive" women who "took over our protest and drowned out our message."[136] She likewise dismisses COYOTE (Call Off Your Old Tired Ethics), an organization of sex workers and their supporters, as "a mix of libertarian activists and sex industry profiteers,"[137] while Raymond criticizes those in the sex industry for deploying the language of civil liberties in defense of their business interests.[138] Barry further describes the witting defenders of the sex industry as selfish, arguing that "to 'embrace' prostitution sex as one's self-chosen identity is to be actively engaged in promoting women's oppression on behalf of oneself."[139] The result, as seen in the period interrogated in Chapter 3 of this book, is that sex workers are denied not only the right to speak but any presumption of ethical impulses animating their activism.

Rather than validating the testimony of sex workers arguing in support of prostitution, Raymond suggests privileging the voices of "survivors" of prostitution "who oppose prostitution per se as a human rights violation, who are not linked with the sex industry, and who work primarily to help women out of prostitution and create sustainable alternatives to prostitution in women's lives."[140] Examples of survivors-turned

---

[135] Ibid., 4. Emphasis in the original.

[136] Leidholdt, "Demand and the Debate," 2.

[137] Ibid.

[138] Raymond and Hughes, 19.

[139] Barry, *The Prostitution of Sexuality*, 71.

[140] Raymond, "Prostitution as Violence against Women: NGO Stonewalling in Beijing and Elsewhere," 3.

anti-prostitution and anti-trafficking activists include the late Norma Hotaling, cofounder of Standing Against Global Exploitation (SAGE), a counseling and advocacy organization for sexually exploited women and men in San Francisco, California, and Vednita Carter, founder of Breaking Free in St. Paul, Minneapolis. That said, credibility is not limited only to survivors—recall my earlier argument that feminist abolitionists also establish their standing to speak on this issue through their assertion of prostitution's universal harm to all women.

"Authoritative" accounts of trafficking and prostitution typically employ a rhetorical strategy described by Aradau as "the politics of pity,"[141] highlighting the violence and trauma that abolitionists take to be characteristic of prostitution in order to establish the prostituted or trafficked woman as a victim worthy of help. In books, articles, speeches, and testimony before local, state, and federal legislative bodies, feminist abolitionists describe acts of violence frequently accompanying prostitution, documenting recurrent "beatings, rapes, torture, and homicides."[142]

> Women in prostitution describe the sex they must endure from customers as unwanted bodily invasions—painful, disgusting, humiliating, dangerous, and rape-like. They also report that male customers often subject them to abusive and dehumanizing sexual practices that non-prostituted women refuse to engage in.[143]

Abolitionists' emphasis on the violence purportedly inherent to prostitution marginalizes the position of self-identified sex workers in two ways. First, experiences of sex in prostitution are universalized as harmful, suggesting that those who either enjoy or are indifferent to performing commercial sex acts are established as deviant or suffering from false consciousness—as lacking credibility, even concerning their own situations. Second, the portrayal of prostitution as inherently brutal and coercive, akin to slavery, renders demands for workers' rights unspeakable and

---

[141] Claudia Aradau, "The Perverse Politics of Four-Letter Words: Risk and Pity in the Securitization of Human Trafficking," *Millennium Journal of International Studies* 33, no. 2 (2004).

[142] Leidholdt, "Presentation to UN Special Seminar on Trafficking, Prostitution and the Global Sex Industry-Postion Paper for CATW."

[143] Ibid.; See also Barry, *Female Sexual Slavery*, 136.

programs for harm reduction abhorrent.[144] As CATW ally, religious abolitionist, and eventual director of the Office to Combat and Monitor Trafficking in Persons (G/TIP) John Miller wrote to *The New York Times*, "Apologists for the trans-Atlantic slave trade of yesteryear advocated for better ventilation and mattresses on ships for slaves, but all the regulation in the world would not have changed the fact that people used as slaves deserved freedom."[145] Statements of feminist abolitionists quoted above and in the previous chapter depict the same rhetorical tactic as used by Miller, narrowing the universe of acceptable—even utterable—statements in the arena of anti-trafficking politics by equating opponents with apologists for slavery.

The explicit depiction of the "enormous harm, violence and human rights abuses"[146] suffered by trafficked women and children follows in the tradition of other successful appeals to the public conscience; as Keck and Sikkink observe, the most effective issues for advocacy networks involve "bodily harm to vulnerable individuals."[147] Yet neither feminist abolitionists nor the liberal constructivist account of TANs in *Activists Beyond Borders* treat the reproduction of this subject position—"vulnerable" individuals primarily identified with violations of bodily integrity—as problematic. At the same time, the compulsory power of rapists and johns is emphasized, the productive power in which anti-trafficking activism is implicated is ignored. Rights activists are applauded for speaking truth to power; the power to silence counterdiscourses, constitute subjects as deserving or deserving, and deny actors the authority to understand and interpret their own experiences is elided.

Women and Children as Chattel

Abolitionists follow in another tradition, of course, by virtue of their chosen name. While recognizing the symbolic weight and thus strategic implications of equating trafficking and slavery, feminist abolitionists

---

[144] Julia O'Connell Davidson, *Prostitution, Power and Freedom* (Ann Arbor: University of Michigan Press, 1998), 15.

[145] John R. Miller, "The Slavery of Prostitution," *New York Times*, December, 20, 2005.

[146] Janice G. Raymond, *Legitimating Prostitution as Sex Work: UN Labor Organization (ILO) Calls for Recognition of the Sex Industry* (The Coalition Against Trafficking in Women, 1999).

[147] Keck and Sikkink, 27.

maintain that the latter term should be taken as description rather than metaphor. In Barry's words, "female sexual slavery is not an illusive condition; the word "slavery" is not merely rhetorical. [...] Slavery is an objective social condition of sexual exploitation and violence."[148] Leidholdt explained the logic behind this position in a presentation to the UN Working Group on Contemporary Slavery:

> [CATW defines] slavery as the domination and control by an individual or group over other individuals or groups through violence, the threat of violence, or a history of violence. Slavers are motivated by a desire for sexual gratification, economic gain, or power and domination, or a combination of these factors. We reference the definition of slavery in the Convention on Slavery, Forced Labor, and Similar Institutions and Practices: "Slavery is the status or condition of a person over whom any or all of the powers attaching to the right of ownership are exercised." All of the practices addressed by the Coalition emerge from the historical reality of the chattel status of women and children and represent an attempt to revive and maintain it.[149]

Leidholdt's argument specifically refers to chattel slavery, echoing the conclusion that feminist philosopher Carole Pateman draws from Gerda Lerner: "the first slaves were *women*."[150]

Vednita Carter likewise refers to chattel slavery, but to emphasize another aspect of sex trafficking. Carter, the founder of Breaking Free, a service and advocacy organization in St. Paul, Minnesota intended primarily for African-American survivors of prostitution, perceives the same underlying racism at work in historical black slavery and contemporary prostitution of black women. She contends that "the system of prostitution functions now as slavery did then."[151] Carter characterizes a typical customer's search for commercial sex evocatively:

---

[148] Barry, *Female Sexual Slavery*, 40.

[149] Leidholdt, "Prostitution: A Modern Form of Slavery."

[150] Carole Pateman, *The Sexual Contract* (Stanford: Stanford University Press, 1988), 65. Emphasis in original.

[151] Vednita Carter, "Providing Services to African American Prostituted Women," in *Prostitution, Trafficking, and Traumatic Stress*, ed. Melissa Farley (New York: Routledge, 2004), 275.

Middle-class men, predominantly of European descent, drive through these [poor, urban] neighborhoods for the purpose of finding a girl or woman to buy and use for sexual gratification. Like slave women on the auction block, African-American women are displayed on the streets or in strip clubs, surveyed like cattle, and selected to perform at the orders of a stranger [...] It is not difficult for thoughtful people to see the connection between slavery and prostitution."[152]

For Carter, prostitution and slavery share the same function of promoting racial and sexual domination of white men over women of color within a racist and sexist order spanning centuries. Lederer, in contrast, compares sex trafficking to traditional slavery in kind and degree but not necessarily in terms of the affected population. Setting aside racial analyses, she asserts that "trafficking of women and children for the purposes of prostitution has become a contemporary form of slavery, and the numbers may soon be on par with the African slave trade of the 1700s."[153]

Both the presence and the absence of analyses linking historical slavery of African women and their descendants to modern-day sex trafficking of African-American women are notable in relation to abolitionists' frequent invocation of historical "white slavery." Lederer, for example, goes on to note in her testimony before Congress that "almost every country in the world has some law that could be used to prosecute traffickers. Some of them are very old. Some of them go back to the turn of the century with the white slave trade and are related to that."[154] As Lederer suggests, the pairing of prostitution and slavery originates not with contemporary abolitionists but with their nineteenth-century predecessors such as Josephine Butler. She joins other radical feminist and feminist abolitionists, however, in persistently neglecting the manner in which fin-de-siècle concerns surrounding "the white slave trade" legitimated the contemporaneous rapes of black women by white men and the historical legacy of rape associated with antebellum slavery.[155]

[152] Ibid., 274.

[153] Subcommittee on International Operations and Human Rights of the Committee on International Relations, *Hearing on Trafficking of Women and Children in the International Sex Trade*, 106th Cong. 1st session, September 14, 1999, 39.

[154] Ibid., 46.

[155] See Doezema, "Loose Women or Lost Women? The Re-emergence of the Myth of 'White Slavery' in Contemporary Discourses of 'Trafficking in Women'"; Gretchen Soderlund, "Running from the Rescuers: New U.S. Crusades against Sex Trafficking and the Rhetoric of Abolition," *NWSA Journal* 17, no. 3 (2005).

The Villains Are the Same

For all of the criticism feminist abolitionists direct at feminists with con-flicting viewpoints on sexuality, prostitution, and trafficking, the root of the problem remains that which was first identified by radical femi-nists: male supremacist sexuality. Returning to Leidholdt's comparison between domestic and international prostitution, she continues:

> The customers are the same—men with disposable income who achieve sex-ual gratification by purchasing and invading the body of a woman or child.[156]

Here Leidholdt underscores abolitionists' identification of male demand for sex and sexual dominance as the principal cause of prostitution and trafficking. As Donna Hughes states, "It is men who create the demand, and women and children who are the supply."[157] Johns—men who buy sexual services—are remarkable for being unremarkable:

> There is one and only one explanation for the stunning and devastating escalation over the past two decades of sex trafficking: the demand created by men with the means to purchase the body of a woman or child. These men are our fathers, brothers, husbands, and sons. They live in our com-munities. They attend our churches, synagogues, temples, and mosques. Most consider themselves to be good family men. Indeed research shows that the typical sex exploiter is a married, employed man with children. Few consider themselves serial sexual predators—although that, in fact, is what they are. Even fewer regard what they inflict on the women and chil-dren they use as casually as spittoons or urinals as rape—although that is precisely how their victims experience it.[158]

Hughes's indictment of men who use prostitutes logically follows from the feminist abolitionist position, as does her contention that such men likely consider themselves to be "good family men," even religiously observant. The omnipresence of male supremacist sexuality—recognition

---

[156]Leidholdt, "Prostitution: A Modern Form of Slavery."

[157]Donna M. Hughes, "The Demand: Where Sex Trafficking Begins" (paper presented at the US Embassy to the Holy See 20th Anniversary Conference—A Call to Action: Joining the Fight Against Trafficking in Persons, The Pontifical Gregorian University, June 17, 2004), 32.

[158]Ibid.

of which is an integral principle of radical feminism—suggests that male sexual predation is common, and, most crucially, that all men benefit from predation insofar as male sexual power "is first and foremost the basis for power and authority in society."[159]

CONCLUSION

This chapter opened with Dorchen Leidholdt's criticism of New York police officers for not knowing an "obvious" victim of trafficking when they saw one. The notion that victimization is self-evident rests upon ground prepared by radical feminists and tilled by feminist abolitionists whose discourse populates the world with two kinds of subjects: victims and victimizers. In the case of human trafficking, the immediate victims are prostituted women and children, but their victimhood is shared by all women, universally oppressed by male supremacist sexuality.

Feminist abolitionism is vulnerable, however, on at least three counts. The first tension appears in their use of radical feminist epistemological grounds to justify the position that all female prostitutes are victims. Support for this conclusion is provided by appeal to the lived experiences of prostitution survivors, yet only the testimony that fits abolitionist conclusions is admitted in the first place.

The second issue lies with abolitionists' abandonment of the conceptual framework of "female sexual slavery," which connected all forms of women's sexual exploitation, in favor of "trafficking in women" and "human trafficking." Focusing exclusively on prostitution flies in the face of Barry's reasoning in 1995 that she approached trafficking and prostitution "by understanding prostitute women not as a group set apart, which is a misogynist construction, but as women whose sexual exploitation is consonant with that of all women's experience of sexual exploitation."[160] Relying primarily on the framework of trafficking means that feminist abolitionists do, in fact, single out prostitutes, and in so doing they de-emphasize related forms of sexual exploitation. The shift from female sexual slavery to trafficking further increases the difficulty

---

[159] Barry, *Female Sexual Slavery*, 194.
[160] *The Prostitution of Sexuality*, 9.

of addressing domestic prostitution in addition to international prostitution due to the still-pervasive conflation of trafficking and migration. Leidholdt complained in 2004 that she "had just received a program for a conference on 'Human Trafficking' that will soon take place in New York City. You would never know that trafficking has anything to do with gender, sex, or women."[161] I suggest that one of the reasons is that feminist abolitionists unwittingly diluted their own message. The rhetorical movement back to "slavery" on the part of other anti-trafficking advocates may help to mitigate this problem, but it may also lead non-feminist audiences to question whether all instances of prostitution can properly be considered "slavery," a term that in the US more frequently calls to mind historical forms of chattel slavery.

The third tension for feminist abolitionism also relates to diluting the radical feminist position, this time through their close association with religious abolitionists. Kathleen Barry's contention that "religious moralists" had co-opted Josephine Butler's feminist campaign against sexual slavery reads, more than thirty years later, as a prescient yet unheeded warning. In *Female Sexual Slavery*, she writes:

> Looking back from historical perspective, Josephine's work, because it was in part motivated by religious beliefs, now appears to have been part of the social purity movement. Yet the goals of the social purity movement were in direct opposition to those of Butler's feminist work no matter how much they both appealed to religious sentiment. What in fact happened was that *the social purity movement by attaching itself to women's causes was able to build a mass movement and to undermine the goals of feminist leaders like Josephine Butler*.[162]

Indeed, Barry's condemnation of men engaged in the spectacle of rescue work[163] appears particularly relevant given recent criticisms of similar rescue missions undertaken by journalist Nicholas Kristof and religious

---

[161] Leidholdt, "Demand and the Debate."

[162] *Female Sexual Slavery*, 29. Emphasis added.

[163] Barry writes, "When men entered the campaign against regulated prostitution, particularly in rescue work and investigations, one notes that consistently their behavior was dominated by righteous heroics in which the fate of the victim is secondary to the escapade they are performing." Ibid., 23.

abolitionist NGOs such as the IJM.[164] Yet even as the predominantly evangelical Christian anti-trafficking network in the United States is largely directed by men and women who have expressed public hostility towards feminists and feminist causes,[165] feminist abolitionists have still to engage in a sustained, public conversation about the potential pitfalls of this political alliance. Radical feminists such as Hughes and Lederer, moreover, retain the "feminist" label even while they have shifted their political loyalties to support candidates and causes explicitly opposed to radical principles.[166] As both the previous and subsequent chapters suggest, the anti-trafficking alliance has weakened the feminist aspects of abolitionism while empowering conservatives within the religious abolitionist network whose political stances on other issues are antithetical to those held by radical feminists. Dissent between feminist advocates for sex workers' rights and feminist abolitionists is frequently portrayed as a return to the feminist sex wars of the 1980s, but it may be the case that compared to religious abolitionists, both feminist sides are losing the battle.

[164]On the importance of rescue work, see Hughes, "Accommodation or Abolition? Solutions to the Problem of Sexual Trafficking and Slavery"; Dawn Herzog Jewell, "Red-Light Rescue," *Christianity Today*, January, 2007; Cheryl Noble, "Justice Seekers: Bringing Rescue and Healing to the Oppressed," *Journal of Student Ministries* (2007); Nicholas D. Kristof, "Raiding a Brothel in India," *The New York Times*, May 25, 2011; and Samantha Power, "The Enforcer: A Christian Lawyer's Global Crusade," *The New Yorker*, January 19, 2009. For criticism, see Laura María Agustín, *Sex at the Margins: Migration, Labor Markets, and the Rescue Industry* (London: Zed Books, 2007); Melissa Ditmore, "Kicking Down the Door: The Use of Raids to Fight Trafficking in Persons" (New York: The Sex Workers Project, 2009); Doezema, "Ouch! Western Feminists' 'Wounded Attachment' to the 'Third World Prostitute'"; Soderlund; and VAMP Collective and SANGRAM, "Resisting Raids and Rescue," *Research for Sex Work* 10 (2008).

[165]See, e.g., William J. Bennett and Charles W. Colson, "The Clintons Shrug at Sex Trafficking," *The Wall Street Journal*, January 10, 2000; Michael J. Horowitz, "Right Abolitionism," *The American Spectator*, December/January 2005/2006.

[166]See, e.g., Kathryn Jean Lopez, "The New Abolitionist Movement: Donna Hughes on Progress Fighting Sex Trafficking," accessed September 29, 2009, http://old.national-review.com/interrogatory/hughes200601260824.asp; Jacqueline Berman, "The Left, the Right, and the Prostitute: The Making of U.S. Anti-Trafficking in Persons Policy," *Tulane Journal of International and Comparative Law* 14 (2005–2006). I discuss Laura Lederer's conversion to Christianity in Chapter 5.

REFERENCES

Abusharaf, Rogaia Mustafa. "Virtuous Cuts: Female Genital Circumcision in an African Ontology." In *Going Public: Feminism and the Shifting Boundaries of the Private Sphere*, edited by Joan W. Scott and Debra Keates, 201–24. Urbana and Champaign: University of Illinois Press, 2004.

Agustín, Laura María. *Sex at the Margins: Migration, Labor Markets, and the Rescue Industry*. London: Zed Books, 2007.

Aradau, Claudia. "The Perverse Politics of Four-Letter Words: Risk and Pity in the Securitization of Human Trafficking." *Millennium Journal of International Studies* 33, no. 2 (2004): 251–77.

Bales, Kevin. *Understanding Global Slavery*. Berkeley: University of California Press, 2005.

Barry, Kathleen. *Female Sexual Slavery*. New York: New York University Press, 1979.

———. "The Network Defines Its Issues: Theory, Evidence and Analysis of Female Sexual Slavery." In *International Feminism: Networking against Female Sexual Slavery: Report of the Global Feminist Workshop to Organize against Traffic in Women*, edited by Kathleen Barry, Charlotte Bunch, and Shirley Castley. Rotterdam: International Women's Tribune Center, 1983.

———. "The Opening Paper: International Politics of Female Sexual Slavery." In *International Feminism: Networking against Female Sexual Slavery: Report of the Global Feminist Workshop to Organize against Traffic in Women*, edited by Kathleen Barry, Charlotte Bunch, and Shirley Castley. Rotterdam: International Women's Tribune Center, 1983.

———. *The Prostitution of Sexuality*. New York: New York University Press, 1995.

Barry, Kathleen, Charlotte Bunch, and Shirley Castley, eds. *International Feminism: Networking against Female Sexual Slavery: Report of the Global Feminist Workshop to Organize against Traffic in Women*. Rotterdam: International Women's Tribune Center, 1983.

Bell, Diane, and Renate Klein. "Beware: Radical Feminists Speak, Read, Write, Organize, Enjoy Life, and Never Forget." In *Radically Speaking: Feminism Reclaimed*, edited by Diane Bell and Renate Klein, xvii–xxx. North Melbourne: Spinifex Press, 1996.

Bell, Shannon. *Reading, Writing, and Rewriting the Prostitute Body*. Bloomington and Indianapolis: Indiana University Press, 1994.

Bennett, William J., and Charles W. Colson. "The Clintons Shrug at Sex Trafficking." *The Wall Street Journal*, January 10, 2000.

Berger, Joseph. "Sex Trafficking Arrests Are Few, Despite Laws." *The New York Times*, December 4, 2009, A32.

Berman, Jacqueline. "The Left, the Right, and the Prostitute: The Making of U.S. Anti-trafficking in Persons Policy." *Tulane Journal of International and Comparative Law* 14 (2005–2006): 269–93.

Brownmiller, Susan. *In Our Time: Memoir of a Revolution.* New York: Dial Press, 1999.

Bunch, Charlotte. "Network Strategies and Organizing against Female Sexual Slavery." In *International Feminism: Networking against Female Sexual Slavery: Report of the Global Feminist Workshop to Organize against Traffic in Women,* edited by Kathleen Barry, Charlotte Bunch, and Shirley Castley. Rotterdam: International Women's Tribune Center, 1983.

———. "Women's Rights as Human Rights: Toward a Re-vision of Human Rights." *Human Rights Quarterly* 12 (1990): 486–98.

Bunch, Charlotte, and Shirley Castley. "Introduction." In *International Feminism: Networking against Female Sexual Slavery: Report of the Global Feminist Workshop to Organize against Traffic in Women,* edited by Kathleen Barry, Charlotte Bunch, and Shirley Castley. Rotterdam: International Women's Tribune Center, 1983.

Butler, Judith. *Gender Trouble: Feminism and the Subversion of Identity.* New York: Routledge, 1999. doi: 99029349. 1990.

Carter, Vednita. "Providing Services to African American Prostituted Women." In *Prostitution, Trafficking, and Traumatic Stress,* edited by Melissa Farley. New York: Routledge, 2004.

CATW. "Biography of Dorchen A. Leidholdt." Coalition Against Trafficking in Women. Accessed September 29, 2009. http://www.catwinternational.org/bio_DorchenLeidholdt.php.

Chapkis, Wendy. *Live Sex Acts: Women Performing Erotic Labor.* New York: Routledge, 1997.

Ditmore, Melissa. *Kicking Down the Door: The Use of Raids to Fight Trafficking in Persons.* New York: The Sex Workers Project, 2009.

Doezema, Jo. "Loose Women or Lost Women? The Re-emergence of the Myth of 'White Slavery' in Contemporary Discourses of 'Trafficking in Women'." *Gender Issues* 18, no. 1 (2000): 23–50.

———. "Now You See Her, Now You Don't: Sex Workers at the UN Trafficking Protocol Negotiation." *Social & Legal Studies* 14, no. 1 (2005): 61–89.

———. "Ouch! Western Feminists' 'Wounded Attachment' to the 'Third World Prostitute'." *Feminist Review* 67, no. 1 (2001): 16–38.

Durbar Mahila Samanwaya Committee (DMSC). "Sex Workers' Manifesto." Paper presented at the First National Conference of Sex Workers in India, Calcutta, November 14–16, 1997.

Dworkin, Andrea. "Dworkin on Dworkin." In *Radically Speaking: Feminism Reclaimed,* edited by Diane Bell and Renate Klein, 203–17. North Melbourne: Spinifex Press, 1996.

———. *Letters from a War Zone: Writings, 1976–1989*. New York: E. P. Dutton, 1989.

———. "Prostitution and Male Supremacy." *Michigan Journal of Gender & Law* 1 (1993): 1.

———. "Woman-Hating Right and Left." In *The Sexual Liberals and the Attack on Feminism*, edited by Dorchen A. Leidholdt and Janice G. Raymond, 28–40. New York: Pergamon Press, 1990.

Ehrenreich, Barbara. "What Is Socialist Feminism?" *WIN*, June 3, 1976.

Ferguson, Ann. "Sex War: The Debate between Radical and Libertarian Feminists." *Signs: Journal of Women in Culture and Society* 10, no. 1 (1984): 106–12.

Giobbe, Evelina. "Confronting the Liberal Lies About Prostitution." In *The Sexual Liberals and the Attack on Feminism*, edited by Dorchen A. Leidholdt and Janice G. Raymond, 67–82. New York: Pergamon Press, 1990.

Grant, Judith. *Fundamental Feminism: Contesting the Core Concepts of Feminist Theory*. New York: Routledge, 1993.

Horowitz, Michael J. "Right Abolitionism." *The American Spectator*, December/January 2005/2006, 14–17.

Hosken, Fran P. "Toward a Definition of Women's Human Rights." *Human Rights Quarterly* 3, no. 2 (1981): 1–10.

Hughes, Donna M. "Accommodation or Abolition? Solutions to the Problem of Sexual Trafficking and Slavery." National Review Online. Accessed September 29, 2009. http://www.nationalreview.com/articles/206761/accommodation-or-abolition/donna-m-hughes.

———. "The Demand: Where Sex Trafficking Begins." Paper presented at the US Embassy to the Holy See 20th Anniversary Conference—A Call to Action: Joining the Fight against Trafficking in Persons, The Pontifical Gregorian University, June 17, 2004.

———. "Introduction." In *Making the Harm Visible: Global Sexual Exploitation of Women and Girls*, edited by Donna M. Hughes and Claire M. Roche. Kingston, RI: Coalition Against Trafficking in Women, 1999.

Irwin, Mary Ann. "'White Slavery' as Metaphor: Anatomy of a Moral Panic." *Ex Post Facto: The History Journal* 5 (1996). Accessed September 29, 2009. http://userwww.sfsu.edu/~epf/1996/wslavery.html.

Jackson, Patrick Thaddeus, and Daniel H. Nexon. "Relations before States." *European Journal of International Relations* 5, no. 3 (1999): 291.

Jaggar, Alison M. *Feminist Politics and Human Nature*. Totowa, NJ: Rowman & Allanheld, 1983.

Javarte de Dios, Aurora. "Confronting Trafficking, Prostitution and Sexual Exploitation in Asia—The Struggle for Survival and Dignity." In *Making the Harm Visible: Global Sexual Exploitation of Women and Girls*, edited by

Donna M. Hughes and Claire M. Roche. Kingston, RI: Coalition Against Trafficking in Women, 1999.

Jeffreys, Sheila. "Eroticizing Women's Subordination." In *The Sexual Liberals and the Attack on Feminism*, edited by Dorchen A. Leidholdt and Janice G. Raymond, 132–35. New York: Pergamon Press, 1990.

———. "Sexology and Antifeminism." In *The Sexual Liberals and the Attack on Feminism*, edited by Dorchen A. Leidholdt and Janice G. Raymond, 14–27. New York: Pergamon Press, 1990.

Jewell, Dawn Herzog. "Red-Light Rescue." *Christianity Today*, January, 2007.

Johnson, Sonia. "Taking Our Eyes Off the Guys." In *The Sexual Liberals and the Attack on Feminism*, edited by Dorchen A. Leidholdt and Janice G. Raymond. New York: Pergamon Press, 1990.

Jordan, Ann D. *The Annotated Guide to the Complete UN Trafficking Protocol*. Washington, DC: International Human Rights Law Group, 2002.

Keck, Margaret E., and Kathryn Sikkink. *Activists Beyond Borders: Advocacy Networks in International Politics*. Ithaca, NY: Cornell University Press, 1998.

Kristof, Nicholas D. "Raiding a Brothel in India." *The New York Times*, May 25, 2011.

Lederer, Laura. *Take Back the Night: Women on Pornography*. New York: Harper Perennial, 1980.

Leidholdt, Dorchen A. "A Call to Action: Joining the Fight against Trafficking in Persons." Paper presented at the U.S. Embassy to the Holy See 20th Anniversary Conference—A Call to Action: Joining the Fight against Trafficking in Persons, The Pontifical Gregorian University, June 17, 2004.

———. "Demand and the Debate." Coalition Against Trafficking in Women. Accessed September 29, 2009. http://www.childtrafficking.com/Docs/leidholdt_2003_demand_and_the_debate.pdf.

———. "Presentation to UN Special Seminar on Trafficking, Prostitution and the Global Sex Industry—Postion Paper for CATW." Coalition against the Trafficking of Women. Accessed September 29, 2009. http://action.web.ca/home/catw/readingroom.shtml.

———. "Prostitution: A Modern Form of Slavery." In *Making the Harm Visible: Global Sexual Exploitation of Women and Girls*, edited by Donna M. Hughes and Claire M. Roche. Kingston, RI: Coalition Against Trafficking in Women, 1999.

———. "When Women Defend Pornography." In *The Sexual Liberals and the Attack on Feminism*, edited by Dorchen A. Leidholdt and Janice G. Raymond, 125–31. New York: Pergamon Press, 1990.

Limoncelli, Stephanie A. *The Politics of Trafficking: The First International Movement to Combat the Sexual Exploitation of Women*. Palo Alto: Stanford University Press, 2010.

Lopez, Kathryn Jean. "The New Abolitionist Movement: Donna Hughes on Progress Fighting Sex Trafficking." Accessed September 29, 2009. http://old.nationalreview.com/interrogatory/hughes200601260824.asp.

Lugones, María C., and Elizabeth V. Spelman. "Have We Got a Theory for You! Feminist Theory, Cultural Imperialism, and the Demand for 'the Woman's Voice'." *Women's Studies International Forum* 6, no. 6 (1983): 573–81.

MacKinnon, Catharine. "Feminism, Marxism, Method, and the State: An Agenda for Theory." In *Feminist Social Thought: A Reader*, edited by Diana Tietjens Meyers, 64–91. New York: Routledge, 1997.

———. *Toward a Feminist Theory of the State*. Cambridge: Harvard University Press, 1989.

———. "Liberalism and the Death of Feminism." In *The Sexual Liberals and the Attack on Feminism*, edited by Dorchen A. Leidholdt and Janice G. Raymond. New York: Pergamon Press, 1990.

Miller, John R. "The Slavery of Prostitution." *New York Times*, December 20, 2005, A30.

Mohanty, Chandra Talpade. *Feminism without Borders: Decolonizing Theory, Practicing Solidarity*. Durham: Duke University Press, 2003.

Moon, Katharine H. S. *Sex among Allies: Military Prostitution in U.S.-Korea Relations*. New York: Columbia University Press, 1997.

Morgan, Robin. "Light Bulbs, Radishes, and the Politics of the 21st Century." In *Radically Speaking: Feminism Reclaimed*, edited by Diane Bell and Renate Klein, 5–8. North Melbourne: Spinifex Press, 1996.

———. "Theory and Practice: Pornography and Rape." In *Take Back the Night: Women on Pornography*, edited by Laura Lederer. New York: William Morrow, 1980.

Noble, Cheryl. "Justice Seekers: Bringing Rescue and Healing to the Oppressed." *Journal of Student Ministries* (May/June 2007): 40–43.

O'Connell Davidson, Julia. *Prostitution, Power and Freedom*. Ann Arbor: University of Michigan Press, 1998.

Pateman, Carole. *The Sexual Contract*. Stanford: Stanford University Press, 1988.

Power, Samantha. "The Enforcer: A Christian Lawyer's Global Crusade." *The New Yorker*, January 19, 2009, 52.

Raymond, Janice G. "Guide to the New UN Trafficking Protocol." North Amherst, MA: Coalition Against Trafficking in Women, 2001.

———. *Legitimating Prostitution as Sex Work: UN Labor Organization (ILO) Calls for Recognition of the Sex Industry*. North Amherst, MA: The Coalition Against Trafficking in Women, 1999.

———. "Prostitution as Violence against Women: NGO Stonewalling in Beijing and Elsewhere." *Women's Studies International Forum* 21, no. 1 (1998): 1–9.

Raymond, Janice G., and Donna M. Hughes. *Sex Trafficking of Women in the United States: International and Domestic Trends*. New York: Coalition Against Trafficking in Women, 2001.

Rich, Adrienne. "Compulsory Heterosexuality and Lesbian Existence." *Signs: Journal of Women in Culture & Society* 5, no. 4 (1980): 631–60.

Roof, Judith, and Robyn Wiegman, eds. *Who Can Speak? Authority and Critical Identity*. Urbana and Champaign: University of Illinois Press, 1995.

Rowland, Robin. "Politics of Intimacy: Heterosexuality, Love and Power." In *Radically Speaking: Feminism Reclaimed*, edited by Diane Bell and Renate Klein, 77–86. North Melbourne: Spinifex Press, 1996.

Rowland, Robin, and Renate Klein. "Radical Feminism: History, Politics, Action." In *Radically Speaking: Feminism Reclaimed*, edited by Diane Bell and Renate Klein, 9–36. North Melbourne: Spinifex Press, 1996.

Sarachild, Kathie. "Consciousness-Raising: A Radical Weapon." *Feminist Revolution* (1978): 144–50. Accessed September 29, 2009. http://scriptorium.lib.duke.edu/wlm/fem/sarachild.html.

Saunders, Penelope. "Traffic Violations: Determining the Meaning of Violence in Sexual Trafficking Versus Sex Work." *Journal of Interpersonal Violence* 20, no. 3 (2005): 343.

Soderlund, Gretchen. "Running from the Rescuers: New U.S. Crusades against Sex Trafficking and the Rhetoric of Abolition." *NWSA Journal* 17, no. 3 (Fall 2005): 64–87.

Subcommittee on International Operations and Human Rights of the Committee on International Relations. *Hearing on Trafficking of Women and Children in the International Sex Trade*, 106th Cong. 1st session, September 14, 1999.

UNHCHR. "Committee on the Elimination of Discrimination against Women." Office of the United Nations High Commisioner for Human Rights. Accessed September 29, 2009. http://www2.ohchr.org/english/bodies/cedaw/index.htm.

United Nations. "Report of the World Conference of the United Nations Decade for Women, Equality, Development, and Peace." Copenhagen, 1980.

VAMP Collective and SANGRAM. "Resisting Raids and Rescue." *Research for Sex Work* 10 (2008): 3–5.

Vance, Carol S., and Ann Barr Snitow. "Toward a Conversation about Sex in Feminism: A Modest Proposal." *Signs: Journal of Women in Culture and Society* 10, no. 1 (1984): 106–12.

Vanwesenbeeck, Ine. "Another Decade of Social Scientific Work on Sex Work: A Review of Research 1990–2000." *Annual Review of Sex Research* 12 (2001): 242–89.

CHAPTER 5

Who's to Bless and Who's to Blame

The anti-trafficking advocacy network that I refer to as religious abolitionism is formally ecumenical, including the Religious Action Center of Reformed Judaism and the United States Conference of Catholic Bishops (USCCB) as well as evangelical Christian organizations such as the Southern Baptist Convention (SBC) and the National Association of Evangelicals (NAE). Yet despite the inclusion of activists and policymakers from various religions and denominations, religious abolitionist discourse is chiefly reflective of evangelical Christianity, drawing its analyses of trafficking and justifications for political action from evangelical interpretations of the Bible.[1] Evangelical styles of rhetoric, which I discuss more fully later in this chapter, are frequently employed by non-evangelical religious abolitionists, and shared religious texts such as the scriptures referred to as the Old Testament (Christian) and the Hebrew Bible (Jewish)[2] are invoked by Protestant, Roman Catholic, and Jewish abolitionists alike.

---

[1] Allen D. Hertzke, *Freeing God's Children: The Unlikely Alliance for Global Human Rights* (Rowman and Littlefield, 2004), 3.

[2] The scriptures are shared but not identical. The seven "deuterocanonical" books of the Catholic Old Testament are included in neither the Protestant Old Testament nor the Hebrew Bible, while the order of books in the Hebrew Bible differs significantly from both Christian versions. See William Safire, "The New Old Testament," *The New York Times Magazine*, May 25, 1997.

© The Author(s) 2019   163
J. K. Lobasz, *Constructing Human Trafficking*, Human Rights
Interventions, https://doi.org/10.1007/978-3-319-91737-5_5

In this chapter, I investigate the construction of human trafficking as a problem by asking how subjects are made intelligible and practices made possible through the predominantly evangelical Christian religious abolitionist discourse. The chapter begins with an overview of evangelical Christianity in the United States. I discuss the core tenets of the religious movement and consider its recent connections to US political life. Next, I assess the evangelical influences on anti-trafficking advocacy. I find that religious abolitionism is deeply shaped by (1) evangelical Christian styles of rhetoric and justification, (2) evangelicals' emphasis on the struggle between good and evil, (3) the principle of *imago Dei*, and (4) evangelical beliefs regarding sexuality.

Turning to the religious abolitionist advocacy network based in the United States, I introduce prominent figures and organizations, considering how they have constructed human trafficking as an urgent issue to address. I compare the approach of abolitionists such as US Representative Chris Smith and neoconservative political strategist Michael Horowitz, both of whom see trafficking as a problem revolving around the international prostitution of women and children, with that of organizations such as the Salvation Army, which grounds its comparatively broader understanding of human trafficking in its history of fighting against multiple forms of slavery. I contend that the articulation of human trafficking to slavery, and the connection that contemporary religious abolitionists draw between themselves and Christian anti-slavery activists of centuries past, creates space within abolitionist discourse for reconceptualizing human trafficking.

The chapter concludes by bringing analysis to bear on the relationship between religious abolitionism and two additional evangelical themes: testimony, and redemption. Both abolitionist advocacy networks make strategic use of the testimony of trafficked persons to garner interest in and support for the anti-trafficking cause. In contrast to feminist abolitionism, however, in which testimony is used to establish the truth of women's oppression, religious abolitionists use the testimony of trafficked persons and of abolitionists themselves to convey messages about their faith. One of the primary messages is that not only victims but traffickers and abolitionists, too, can find restoration and redemption through Jesus Christ.

EVANGELICALISM IN AMERICA

Given the influence of evangelical Christianity in constructing the problem of human trafficking as well as the basis for US anti-trafficking policy, it is worthwhile to establish some general parameters for categorizing what is in fact a politically, ethnically, and sometimes theologically diverse set of Christians.[3] Joel Nichols identifies the following tenets as central to evangelical theology:

> a very strong belief in the authority and primacy of scripture, an emphasis on sin and the fallenness of all humans (although grace is increasingly part of the discussion), a highlighting of the redemptive and salvific power of Christ alone, and a strong emphasis on individual—as opposed to communal—interpretation and individual salvation.[4]

Evangelicalism is not itself a denomination, and many who identify themselves as evangelical also describe themselves as "non-denominational," "Christian," or "followers of Christ," as opposed to adherents of a particular sect of Christians.[5] While evangelicals are frequently described as a subset of Protestants, El-Faizy contends that "there are many denominations that are primarily evangelical, particularly in Protestantism, but evangelicals can be found everywhere. There is, for example, a robust movement of evangelicals in the Catholic and Episcopalian churches."[6] In fact, two of the most influential evangelical voices within religious abolitionism belong to conservative Catholics: Representative Chris Smith (R-NJ) and Sam Brownback, a Republican former senator and governor, now ambassador, from Kansas. Notably, both Smith and Brownback are also prominent proponents of "the sanctity of life"

---

[3] In this book, I capitalize "evangelical" only when used as a proper noun. I use "evangelicalism" to refer to a religious movement, and "evangelism" to refer to the practice of spreading the message of Christianity in the pursuit of religious conversion.

[4] Joel A. Nichols, "Evangelicals and Human Rights: The Continuing Ambivalence of Evangelical Christians' Support for Human Rights," *Journal of Law and Religion* 7 (2009): 106. For a similar, widely-accepted definition of evangelicalism, see David Bebbington, *Evangelicalism in Modern Britain: A History from the 1730s to the 1980s* (London: Unwin Hyman, 1989), 2–19.

[5] Monique El-Faizy, *God and Country: How Evangelicals Have Become America's New Mainstream* (New York: Bloomsbury USA, 2006), 10. See also Institute for the Study of American Evangelicals (ISAE), "Defining Evangelicalism," Wheaton College, accessed September 29, 2009, http://isae.wheaton.edu/defining-evangelicalism/.

[6] El-Faizy, 9–10.

movement in Congress that has fought to restrict abortion rights, access to certain forms of contraception, embryonic stem cell research, and physician-assisted suicide.[7]

Evangelicals' predominance within religious abolitionism mirrors their leadership in the broader return of conservative religious influence within American politics. According to Martin Medhurst:

> What is going on—and has been going on for at least the last 25 years—is the reemergence of one segment of the electorate to full participation in the rhetorical barnyard that constitutes the 'public square' in America. This segment is American Evangelicalism. Having abandoned the public square in the 1920s, the Evangelicals, along with their Fundamentalist allies, returned in full force in the 1970s.[8]

Medhurst distinguishes here between evangelicals and fundamentalists, who are frequently conflated in secular American discourse with one another and with the "Religious Right." The distinction between evangelicalism and fundamentalism is amorphous, and often more indicative of the person drawing the distinction than the religious groups themselves. One common practice is to identify fundamentalists as the most politically, socially, and theologically conservative subset of a broader category of evangelicals.[9] That is, all fundamentalists are evangelicals, but

---

[7] "A devout Catholic, Smith traces his political convictions to his upbringing in the faith. As former director of New Jersey Right-to-Life, Smith entered Congress as a fierce opponent of abortion, which led some in the press to lump him into the new Christian Right movement. But throughout his career Smith has been supportive of labor unions, spending on poor children, international relief programs, and human rights, with a notably liberal voting record on a number of issues. In a sense he represents the distinct Roman Catholic political witness that combines more progressive economic ideas with traditional moral teachings." Hertzke, 137.

[8] Martin J. Medhurst, "Forging a Civil-Religious Construct for the Twenty-First Century," in *The Political Pulpit Revisited*, ed. Roderick P. Hart and John L. Pauley (West Lafayette: Purdue University Press, 2005), 157. See also Nicholas D. Kristof, "Learning from the Sin of Sodom," *The New York Times*, February 28, 2010.

[9] El-Faizy, 62. The Institute for the Study of American Evangelicals specifies: "Most self-described fundamentalist churches today are conservative, separatist Baptist (though often calling themselves "Bible Baptist" or simply "Bible" churches) congregations such as the churches of the General Association of Regular Baptist Churches (GARBC), or the Independent Fundamental Churches of America (IFCA). Institutions associated with this movement would include Bob Jones University (Greenville, SC) and Tennessee Temple

not all evangelicals are fundamentalists. The same is true of the political movement dubbed the Religious Right, which primarily consists of fundamentalists and some politically conservative but non-fundamentalist evangelicals, but is hardly representative of evangelicals as a whole.[10] In this book, I follow the standard practice of using "evangelical" to refer to the broader group except for the cases in which I distinguish between "evangelicals" and "fundamentalists," at which point I am emphasizing an intra-group debate.[11]

EVANGELICAL INFLUENCES ON ANTI-TRAFFICKING ADVOCACY

The evangelical influence within religious abolitionism is evident not only in the religious affiliations of its membership but more importantly, in the broader philosophical grounds upon which religious abolitionist analyses of trafficking and identification of appropriate policy interventions and political struggles are constructed. In this section, I identify the theological themes that I take to be most significant in shaping the content and structure of American religious abolitionist trafficking discourse. As with the previous chapter, my purpose is both descriptive and analytic; my primary task in mapping the rhetorical topography[12] is to accurately reflect abolitionists' *self*-narration of the moral principles guiding or even mandating anti-trafficking efforts.

Among the prominent evangelical influences within religious abolitionism, I identify the following as most significant: (1) biblical rhetoric and justification, (2) emphasis on the struggle between good and evil, (3) the principle of *imago Dei*, and (4) beliefs regarding sexuality. As with the imposition of any set of categories, this discussion runs the risk of essentializing the subjects made visible through my analytical

---

(Chattanooga, TN); representative publications would be *The Sword of the Lord* and *The Biblical Evangelist*." Institute for the Study of American Evangelicals (ISAE), "Defining Evangelicalism: Fundamentalism," Wheaton College, accessed September 29, 2009, http://isae.wheaton.edu/defining-evangelicalism/fundamentalism/.

[10] D. Michael Lindsay, "Evangelicals in the Power Elite: Elite Cohesion Advancing a Movement," *American Sociological Review* 73 (2008); Hertzke, 116.

[11] El-Faizy, 10.

[12] Patrick Thaddeus Jackson, *Civilizing the Enemy: German Reconstruction and the Invention of the West* (Ann Arbor: University of Michigan, 2006), 46.

schema, and so I strive throughout this research to balance identification of prominent themes with the acknowledgment that their selection, meaning, significance, and rhetorical deployment may be contested both within and without the community of religious abolitionists.

Biblical Rhetoric and Justification

The most immediately recognizable evangelical influence on religious abolitionism appears in the movement's rhetoric, which is saturated with references to the Bible and its teachings. The following excerpt from the Evangelical Covenant Church's "Resolution on Global Slavery and Human Trafficking" is indicative of this mode of argumentation in which each element of the argument is supported by specific scripture passages:

> Actively seeking justice on behalf of the weak and victims of oppression is one of God's highest priorities and commands. The Hebrew prophets tell us that God requires us "to do justice" (Micah 6:8) and to "seek justice, rescue the oppressed" (Isaiah 1:17). Jesus calls "justice" one of "the more important matters of the law" (Matthew 23:23) and says that "proclaiming freedom for prisoners and releasing the oppressed" is central to God's mission (Luke 4:18–19). God calls all of us as co-laborers to accomplish God's bold purposes on earth. Therefore, as we face the reality of global slavery and human trafficking, we should not ask, "Where is God?" (Malachi 2:17), but rather, "Where are God's people—where are we?" (Isaiah 59:15–16; Ezekiel 22:25–30). And instead of despairing, we should find hope in the God of justice who has overcome the world (John 16:33).[13]

The significance of this type of statement is not limited to rhetoric or strategy, although the rhetorical force of successfully yoking one's position to divine commandment is undeniably strong. That said, evangelicals' frequent deployment of scriptural references—sometimes referred to as "proof texting"[14]—more importantly, reflects a theology and

---

[13] Evangelical Covenant Church, "2008 Resolution on Global Slavery and Human Trafficking," Evangelical Covenant Church, accessed September 29, 2009, http://www. covchurch.org/2008-slavery-human-trafficking/.

[14] The term "proof texting" can be used as both a neutral reference to the skillful use of individual Bible verses for the purpose of establishing the scriptural validity of one's argument (i.e., a form of Biblical exegesis), and as a pejorative reference to the opportunistic selection of verses taken out of their historical and literary context for the purpose of supporting a position that is either absent from or actually contradicts scripture.

epistemology predicated on understanding the Bible as the inerrant word of God, accessible and intelligible to all who seek it.[15] I introduce the most significant theological issues now and return to the question of epistemology later in the chapter.

Good and Evil

Religious abolitionism, like evangelicalism more generally, rests upon a foundational belief in "a vast spiritual conflict we can only barely perceive, but which affects everything that happens on this planet."[16] Hertzke, for example, characterizes Horowitz as one who "sees the world in stark moral terms, of clear good and evil," and contends that "this trait resonated with his evangelical allies."[17] From an evangelical perspective, the continual struggle between good and evil is but one front in "the age-old conflict between God and Satan."[18] Evil established its foothold in the world when Adam and Eve were tempted by Satan in the Garden of Eden, "a preview of what happens to us every day."[19] Adam and Eve's defiance of God's law and their consequent fall from grace both introduced sin into the world and established it as a constitutive element of human nature. Billy Graham explains:

> Theologians have called this primeval tragedy at the dawn of the human race "the Fall" and rightly so. From the heights of the honor and glory they had once known, Adam and Eve now fell into a pit of disgrace and shame. They became fallen creatures, living in a fallen world. In an instant they lost their innocence and came under sin's domination.[20]

Sin's domination is encouraged at every turn by Satan, the incarnation of evil. Drawing a contrast to popular characterization of the devil as a

---

[15] See National Association of Evangelicals (NAE), "Statement of Faith," accessed September 29, 2009, http://www.nae.net/about-us/statement-of-faith.

[16] Billy Graham, *The Journey: How to Live by Faith in an Uncertain World* (Nashville: W Publishing Group, 2006), 98.

[17] Hertzke, 164.

[18] Hertzke, 98. On the significance off evil in U.S. evangelical politics, see Ronald R. Krebs and Jennifer K. Lobasz, "Fixing the Meaning of 9/11: Hegemony, Coercion, and the Road to War in Iraq," *Security Studies* 16, no. 3 (2007): 425–29.

[19] Graham, 36.

[20] Ibid.

pitchfork-wielding cartoon villain with horns, Graham plainly asserts, "Satan is real, and the most important truth you need to remember about him is that he is absolutely and implacably opposed to God and His people [...] his unchanging purpose is to defeat God's plans at every turn."[21]

Given the recurrent effects of Adam and Eve's sin and Satan's unending promotion of evil, Haugen maintains that Christians motivated to work for justice must first recognize that "the Bible declares that our world is fallen, sinful."[22] Therefore, "preparing our mind for action means coming to grips with the true nature of the world into which Christ has cast us, his disciples. It means coming to grips with how the Fall is playing itself out around the world in the present day."[23] For those who see few signs of evil lurking in their own vicinity, this might entail looking beyond one's community in order to reveal and oppose Satan's influence at play in situations such as political persecution and slave labor.[24] Even as Haugen and his colleagues emphasize the need for those who fight injustice to recognize Satan's hand in "the rank evil of naked injustice,"[25] they return to the more hopeful message central to Christianity: that evil can and will be overcome, but only through the power of the son of God, Jesus Christ. In Graham's words, "the final battle has not yet been fought—but the outcome is certain. Satan has been defeated and Christ is the victor!"[26] Despite this reassurance, those who stand against evil may still be challenged to keep their faith, as evangelicals interpret the Book of Revelation

---

[21] Ibid., 35.

[22] Gary A. Haugen, *Good News About Injustice* (Downers Grove, IL: InterVarsity Press, 1999), 46.

[23] Ibid., 47. I thank Janel Kragt Bakker for drawing my attention to an additional dynamic at work in Haugen's argument—"the more recent efforts on behalf of socially conscious evangelicals to convince the rest of the evangelical fold that sin is not just individual but systemic—and that as God's good though fallen creation, the world is valuable and therefore worth redeeming. Haugen is part of a segment of evangelicals countering a purely otherworldly spirituality." Janel Kragt Bakker, Personal Communication, E-Mail, April 26, 2011.

[24] Haugen, *Good News About Injustice: A Witness of Courage in a Hurting World*, 54–60.

[25] Ibid., 83.

[26] Graham, 50.

to mean that the "final battle" will not occur until Christ's return to Earth and the end of time.[27] Further in this chapter, I will show how religious abolitionists attempt to balance between these two poles: recognition of Satan's influence in the evil of trafficking, and belief that justice will ultimately be served, albeit on a divine rather than a human timeline.

Imago Dei and Human Rights

Many Christians read the Gospel of Matthew as an exhortation to work for social justice.[28] Hertzke recounts an interview with Chris Smith, in which Smith "sees his work flowing from Gospel injunctions, describing himself as a Matthew 25 Christian."[29] Smith tells Hertzke:

> The Gospel message has a very strong social justice component, especially Matthew 25 where Christ asked, "When I was hungry, did you give me food to eat? Visit me in prison?" And you know the bottom line to that is he says, "Whatsoever you do to the least of my brethren, you do to me." And that has been the core, the absolute bedrock of all right-to-life and human rights work that I've done.[30]

---

[27] Christians strongly disagree among themselves regarding the imminence of this event and the specific chronology of episodes said to be foretold such as Christ's expected 1000 year reign over the earth, the rapture, and the final battle between the armies of Christ and of Satan. See ibid., 306; Institute for the Study of American Evangelicals (ISAE), "Evangelicals and the End Times," Wheaton College, accessed September 29, 2009, http://www.wheaton.edu/ISAE/Defining-Evangelicalism/End-Times.

[28] Haugen, in contrast, refers more frequently to the Christian obligation to care for the oppressed and less fortunate as established in Isaiah 1:17. He explains, "Isaiah 1:17 says, 'Seek justice, rescue the oppressed, defend the orphan, plead for the widow' [IJM exists] as an organization to help Christians understand that deeply but also act upon it with obedience." Quoted in Francis Helguero, "Recovering God's Justice: Interview with International Justice Mission President Gary Haugen," *The Christian Post*, March 7, 2005; See also Haugen, *Good News About Injustice: A Witness of Courage in a Hurting World*, 17, 22, 27, 46, 76, 178, 212, 16, 41; and Samantha Power, "The Enforcer: A Christian Lawyer's Global Crusade," *The New Yorker*, January 19, 2009.

[29] , 137.

[30] Smith quoted in ibid. See also Shirley Love Rayburn and Danielle Paxton, "Set the Captives Free: A Bible Study Accompaniment to Not for Sale," (Montara, CA: Not for Sale Campaign, 2009), Week 2, Encounter 3.

The belief that service to "the least of my brethren" is the equivalent of service to God accords with the principle most strongly linked to Christian defenses of human rights: *imago Dei*, or the belief in "the dignity of each person deriving from his or her creation in the image of God."[31] Graham explains:

> Our souls make us uniquely human, and they give dignity and value to every human life. The Bible says, "You made him a little lower than the heavenly beings and crowned him with glory and honor" (Psalm 8:5). That is why human life should never be scorned or abused or wantonly destroyed, for every person was created in God's image, no matter how young or old.[32]

Neither this belief nor its application to contemporary abolitionism is limited to Christianity. Horowitz, for example, presents his political alliance and feelings of kinship towards Christians as rooted in the shared "powerful, radical political message" of Judaism and Christianity: "the equality of all in the eyes of God."[33] Similarly, an article in the Christian periodical *World Magazine* characterizes the religious impetus driving former Congressman John Miller (R-WA) and his work as head of the State Department's Office to Monitor and Combat Trafficking in Persons:

> That passion for human rights arises in part from Mr. Miller's Conservative Jewish roots. "I don't generally go around quoting Scripture," he says, but then points to Exodus 7, where the Lord tells Moses to say to Pharaoh, "Let My people go that they may serve Me." The message, he believes, "is pretty clear: You cannot be a slave to man if you want to develop a full and wholesome relationship with God." As well, he argues, the values of the Judeo-Christian ethical tradition "tell us that God has told us that slavery is wrong and that we have a moral mission" to stop it.[34]

As unequivocal as Miller's account of biblical foundations for Judeo-Christian opposition to slavery appears, his articulation of the Exodus

---

[31] Nichols, 121.

[32] Graham, 26.

[33] "How to Win Friends and Influence Culture," *Christianity Today*, September 2005, 75.

[34] Anne Morse, "The Abolitionist," *World Magazine*, March 1, 2003.

narrative to other instances of slavery is not uncontested. There are competing interpretations of whether the Bible supports or opposes slavery, and some Christian denominations and churches explicitly condoned the slavery of peoples deemed outside of a covenant relationship with God, such as Africans enslaved in the United States.[35] Contemporary evangelicals, however, generally consider slavery to be anti-Christian. As the organization Free the Slaves notes, although "Jesus was silent on the issue of slavery the epistles of his disciple, St. Paul, condemned slave traders and called for slaves to be treated as 'brethren.'"[36]

Sexuality

The final biblical foundation I identify as central to religious abolitionism concerns the proper role of sexuality. As with feminist abolitionists, religious abolitionists are philosophically opposed to all forms on prostitution.[37] In "The New Abolitionists," journalist Nina Shapiro quotes Ron Sider:

> "[Trafficking] certainly fits with an evangelical concern for sexual integrity," says Ron Sider, founder of the Pennsylvania-based Evangelicals for Social Action, which challenges his peers to work for economic and racial justice. By sexual integrity, he means that "sex is to be reserved for a marriage relationship where there is a lifelong covenant between a man and a woman"—a tenet clearly abridged by prostitution.[38]

Evangelicals hold that the institution of heterosexual marriage, with its attendant sexual monogamy, is a foundational part of God's plan for

[35] Charles F. Irons, *The Origins of Proslavery Christianity: White and Black Evangelicals in Colonial and Antebellum Virginia* (Chapel Hill: The University of North Carolina Press, 2008), 25; See also Peter J. Thuesen, "The Logic of Mainline Churchliness: Historical Background since the Reformation," in *The Quiet Hand of God: Faith-Based Activism and the Public Role of Mainline Protestantism*, ed. Robert Wuthnow and John Hyde Evans (Berkeley: University of California Press, 2002), 36–37; and Ronald C. Potter, "Good Question: Was Slavery God's Will?," *Christianity Today*, May 22, 2000.

[36] Free the Slaves, "Faith in Action: Christianity," Free the Slaves, accessed September 29, 2009, http://www.freetheslaves.net/take-action/faith-in-action-ending-slavery/.

[37] Initiative Against Sexual Trafficking, "What Is the Initiative against Sexual Trafficking," The Salvation Army, accessed September 29, 2009, http://www.iast.net.

[38] Nina Shapiro, "The New Abolitionists," *Seattle Weekly*, August 25, 2004.

humanity.[39] In Sider's words, "The very first institutions to appear in the biblical story are marriage and family. The Creator made persons male and female designed for the divinely ordained institutions of marriage and family. Only when Eve arrives is Adam's heart satisfied."[40]

RELIGIOUS ABOLITIONISM

Speaking at a 2004 National Training Conference on Human Trafficking in Tampa, Florida, President George W. Bush condemned human trafficking as an affront not only to its victims but to God. According to Bush:

> Human life is the gift of our Creator, and it should never be for sale. It takes a special kind of depravity to exploit and hurt the most vulnerable members of society. Human traffickers rob children of their innocence; they expose them to the worst of life before they have seen much of life. Traffickers tear families apart. They treat their victims as nothing more than goods and commodities for sale to the highest bidder.[41]

The religious strand of argumentation was hardly unusual for Bush, a professed evangelical Christian who made frequent use of religious allusions and imagery in his public speeches, piquing an increase in scholarly and media attention to the role of religious discourse in the construction and justification of contemporary American public policy.[42] Bush's Christian rhetoric was perhaps most notable in his discussions of the "War on Terror,"[43] but as we see above it likewise pervaded his administration's response to human trafficking.

---

[39] Amy DeRogatis, "'Born Again Is a Sexual Term': Demons, STDs, and God's Healing Sperm," *Journal of the American Academy of Religion* (2009): 281.

[40] Ronald J. Sider, "Justice, Human Rights, and Government," in *Toward an Evangelical Public Policy*, ed. Ronald J. Sider and Diane Knippers (Grand Rapids: BakerBooks, 2005), 185. See also Tom Minnery and Glenn T. Stanton, "Family Integrity," ibid.

[41] George W. Bush, "Remarks at the National Training Conference on Human Trafficking in Tampa, Fl," in *Presidential Documents Online* (Washington, DC: Government Printing Office, 2004).

[42] Krebs and Lobasz; Roderick P. Hart and John L. Pauley, *The Political Pulpit Revisited* (West Lafayette: Purdue University Press, 2005); and Garry Wills, *Head and Heart: American Christianities* (New York: Penguin Press, 2007), 498.

[43] Krebs and Lobasz.

The faith-based human rights movement that largely set Bush's anti-trafficking agenda, however, predates Bush's own presidency, originating instead with a mid-1990s political mobilization on behalf of persecuted Christians worldwide. Perhaps surprisingly, this campaign was largely initiated not by prominent Christians, but by Jewish attorney and neoconservative Michael Horowitz, a former Reagan administration appointee.[44] Political scientist Allen Hertzke argues that Jews such as Horowitz "have been among the most aggressive and effective advocates of persecuted Christians abroad."[45] Horowitz himself draws a parallel between the historical discrimination against Jews and contemporary discrimination against Christians, writing in *Christianity Today*, an evangelical magazine, "As the battle for the soul of the 21st century is fought, too many of my people have been killed for us to be fully useful scapegoats. Thus, my evangelical friends, you have become the Jews of the 21st century."[46] Horowitz's leadership on the issue even led the SBC to name him one of the "Top Ten Christians" of 1997.[47]

Following his successful advocacy on behalf of the International Religious Freedom Act of 1998, Horowitz turned his attention to the issue of human trafficking, focusing in particular on the trafficking of women and children for sex. He traces his interest in the subject to a 1998 front-page story in the *New York Times* about the traffic in

[44] Hertzke, 42; See also Mark R Amstutz, "Faith-Based NGOs and U.S. Foreign Policy," in *The Influence of Faith: Religious Groups and U.S. Foreign Policy*, ed. Elliott Abrams (Lanham: Rowman and Littlefied Publishers, Inc., 2001). Horowitz, a neoconservative now at the Hudson Institute, had formerly been President Ronald Reagan's general counsel for the Office of Management and Budget (OMB).

[45] Hertzke, 76. Marshall J. Breger elaborates: "Horowitz is a unique person in this story. While not connected with the organized Jewish community, he comes from a strong Jewish background [...] He threw himself into the cause of persecuted Christians with zeal and was both a moral catalyst and a political advisor to the effort. He alternatively bullied and shamed the evangelicals into greater efforts, while seeking coalitions with unlikely suspects and particularly with the Jewish community." "Evangelicals and Jews in Common Cause," *Journal of Ecumenical Studies* 44, no. 1 (2009).

[46] Horowitz, 75.

[47] E. Benjamin Skinner, *A Crime So Monstrous: Face-to-Face with Modern-Day Slavery* (New York: Free Press, 2009), 50. Morse implies that the Baptists had not realized Horowitz was Jewish. Anne Morse, "Screaming People Awake," *World Magazine*, February 3, 2001.

women from the former Soviet Union to Israel.[48] Horowitz claims that the *Times* story inspired him to recruit his political allies from the religious freedom campaign to support a new faith-based movement against human trafficking.[49]

Whatever their religious identification, religious abolitionists credit their initial awareness of human trafficking to a variety of sources: media coverage, encounters with trafficked persons, and hearing trafficking narratives through intermediaries. The same year that Horowitz was moved to action by *New York Times* reportage, Representative Linda Smith, a Republican congresswoman from Washington State, was invited to tour a brothel district in Mumbai by David Grant, a missions director for the Assemblies of God churches.[50] Grant's intention to enlist Smith as an advocate for "little girls in cages"[51] was soon fulfilled, and Smith writes that upon seeing these girls she felt called by God to finish her work in Congress and dedicate her life to ending human trafficking and rehabilitating trafficked women and girls.[52] Like Smith, Gary Haugen, a prominent religious abolitionist, explains his move from the US federal government to the faith-based NGO sector as a response to personally witnessing suffering abroad. Haugen, initially a civil rights attorney for the US Department of Justice, founded an evangelical Christian human rights organization after his experiences as the Officer in Charge of the UN's genocide investigation in Rwanda.[53] Since Haugen established the International Justice Mission (IJM) in 1997, "three hundred Christian lawyers, criminal investigators, social workers, and advocates at Haugen's

[48] Michael Specter, "Traffickers' New Cargo: Naïve Slavic Women," *The New York Times*, January 11, 1998.

[49] Hertzke, 150, 321; Ori Nir, "US Official Does 'God's Work': Eradicating Slavery," *Forward: The Jewish Daily*, May 7, 2004; and Skinner, 51.

[50] At the time, Smith described herself as an active member of an Assemblies of God Church. Linda Smith, *From Congress to the Brothel: A Journey of Hope, Healing, and Restoration* (Vancouver, WA: Shared Hope International, 2007), 13–14. According to Shapiro, Smith now attends a nondenominational Christian church.

[51] Shapiro; Smith, 13–14.

[52] Ibid., 16–17. She has since founded Shared Hope International, a network of safe houses and rehabilitation programs for victims of sexual exploitation, and the War Against Trafficking Alliance.

[53] International Justice Mission, "Speaker—Gary Haugen, President and CEO," accessed September 29, 2009, http://www.ijm.org/resources/garyhaugen. For a discussion of Haugen's political influence, see Power.

mission now work with local law-enforcement officials in twelve countries on behalf of individuals in need," including people who have been trafficked and enslaved.[54]

As stated above, faith-based opposition to human trafficking initially drew its membership from Horowitz's earlier campaign against global religious persecution. Hertzke suggests that the movement's lineage was clearly evident

> at a strategy meeting that occurred on May 11, 1999, in a hideaway room in the US Capitol with a dozen or so in attendance. Charles Colson thanked Michael Horowitz for convening the meeting, then opened it with an ecumenical prayer (to the "God of Abraham, Isaac, and Jacob"). Colson set the tone by declaring that the nation must use its economic power and moral authority to protect the vulnerable and that for him abolition of trafficking is a Christian mandate.[55]

Others who attended included feminist abolitionist attorney Laura Lederer, Congressman Chris Smith, House Majority Leader Dick Armey, Richard Cizik of the NAE, William Bennett, Richard Land of the SBC, and Rabbi David Saperstein of the Religious Action Center of Reform Judaism.[56] Hertzke continues:

> After the meeting, the top leadership of the evangelical world swiftly mobilized their networks in support of the legislation. The SBC and NAE passed resolutions; Colson and Land went on the air; the Salvation Army made trafficking a key priority; and religious presses featured victims of modern slavery.[57]

The potential audience for this mobilization was vast, benefiting from connections to "the thriving grassroots reach of evangelical networks in the United States."[58]

---

[54] Power.

[55] Hertzke, 324.

[56] The politically liberal Saperstein became associated with the cause after having already been successfully courted by Horowitz to support the cause of international religious freedom. Hertzke quotes Horowitz as describing Saperstein "as a man whom I love and with whom I agree on almost nothing." Ibid., 153.

[57] Ibid., 325.

[58] Ibid., 116.

Defining the Problem

Despite the religious press's broad coverage of many forms of what they termed "modern slavery," the first wave of religious abolitionist political efforts exclusively targeted sex trafficking. Chris Smith, for example, argued for such an approach because "forcible and fraudulent trafficking of women and children for the commercial sex trade is a uniquely brutal practice."[59] Smith goes on to note that sex trafficking constitutes "mass rape," "a crime against humanity," and should therefore take a higher priority over trafficking that does not include rape.[60] Comparing his proposed legislation on sex trafficking to competing bills that addressed labor trafficking as well, Smith stated, "I support the other bills, but this bill is designed to go after the most egregious type of involuntary servitude, which is rape. This is rape."[61] Likewise, Haugen testified at Smith's hearing that sex trafficking needed to be addressed separately, and chided representatives from the State Department for failing to use the phrase "sexual trafficking" during their presentations. He elaborated, "We have in criminal law the notion of assault, but we don't consider it sufficient that we don't also have a notion of sexual assault. We have a notion of child abuse, but we also have a notion of child sexual abuse. There is trafficking, but there is also trafficking for sexual purposes."[62] In other words, trafficking for sexual exploitation must be differentiated from other forms of trafficking, and prioritized as an issue.

Horowitz fought hard to limit the TVPA to sex trafficking. Like Smith and Haugen, Horowitz presented sex trafficking as unquestionably more egregious a crime than labor trafficking. Horowitz also, however, asserts a strategic rationale for prioritizing sex, arguing that demonstrable success against sex trafficking by the federal government would generate political momentum that could then be harnessed against other forms of exploitative labor:

---

[59] Subcommittee on International Operations and Human Rights of the Committee on International Relations, *Hearing on Trafficking of Women and Children in the International Sex Trade*, 106th Cong. 1st session, September 14, 1999, 4.

[60] Ibid., 43.

[61] J. Scott Orr, "House Panel Moves to Stem Sex-Slave Trade and Aid Victims," *The Star-Ledger*, August 5, 1999.

[62] *Hearing on Trafficking of Women and Children in the International Sex Trade*, 41.

If you want to end enslavement of those in debt bondage in the brick factories in India, the best thing you can do is put all of the sex traffickers
in jail, and just drive a stake right through the heart of that system. The
connection is these ripple effects, where if you succeed in taking out some
people, you send a message to everybody else saying: 'You're next.'[63]

The underlying assumption is that sex trafficking is itself a more clearly
bounded and hence identifiable and actionable set of criminal activities
as compared to labor trafficking. While the decades-long intra-feminist
dispute regarding prostitution mentioned in the previous chapter might
suggest that the conceptual boundaries of sex trafficking and related
practices are not so easily defined, religious abolitionists simplify the issue
in a manner similar to that of feminist abolitionists and seek to abolish all
forms of prostitution.

It is hardly a surprise that the rationales for the two abolitionist
approaches differ, though it is perhaps more curious that the proposed
policy responses are the same. Religious abolitionist discourse does not
maintain that all prostitution amounts to sex trafficking, but it does hold
that all prostitution is sin and should be opposed on that ground alone.[64]
From an evangelical perspective, sex trafficking—like prostitution and
any other sexual act occurring outside the bounds of heterosexual marriage—is a perversion of the proper role of sexuality. In the words of Tim
Gardner, the author of an evangelical Christian sex manual, "Christians
acknowledge that God connects sex with oneness and reserves it for mar-
ried couples only."[65] As I discuss later in this chapter, sex trafficking is
distinguished from the more common sins of non-marital sex by its associated brutality and lack of consent. *Set the Captives Free*, the Bible study
accompaniment to David Batstone's *Not For Sale*,[66] explains, "Sex trafficking is heart-breaking because it takes sex, a beautiful gift of God, and
turns it into a self-serving instrument of bondage and torture."[67]

---

[63] Skinner, 53.

[64] Notably, when Linda Smith compares the biblical story of Judah and Tamar (Genesis
38) to the experience of a trafficking survivor named Charity, Smith singles out Judah and
Charity's abusive stepfather for condemnation. Smith, 75–80.

[65] Tim Alan Gardner, *Sacred Sex: A Spiritual Celebration of Oneness in Marriage*
(Colorado Springs: Waterbrook Press, 2002), 1.

[66] David B. Batstone, *Not for Sale: The Return of the Global Slave Trade—And How We
Can Fight It* (San Francisco: HarperCollins, 2007).

[67] Rayburn and Paxton, Week 5, Encounter 1.

A Different Approach

Even as religious abolitionists' political focus centered on sex trafficking, a small number of associated organizations, most notably the Salvation Army and the USCCB, have taken a broader approach by addressing their anti-trafficking efforts to both the sex trade and forced labor. For the National Anti-trafficking Council of the Salvation Army:

> All forms of trafficking are horrific and unacceptable, and all its victims are equally worthy of rescue and assistance. The Council will, in as much as possible, endeavor to promote and support services for all victims of trafficking in the US irrespective of the victim's country of origin, gender, age or form of exploitation.[68]

The Council justifies its inclusive mission on the basis that "trafficking in persons denies the innate and infinite value of human beings as beloved children made in the image of God by destroying their personhood and reducing them to an economic and service value."[69]

The principle of *imago Dei* is likewise drawn upon by Catholic organizations dedicated to serving victims of trafficking, broadly defined. Sister Mary Ellen Doughtery, Program Administrator for Human Trafficking in the Department of Migration and Refugee Services of the USCCB, connects her organization's campaign against all forms of trafficking in persons with related Catholic social teachings:

> For example, the themes prominent in the social teaching of the Catholic Church–human dignity, human rights and responsibilities, the call to family and community, option for the poor, the dignity of work and the rights of workers, solidarity and care for creation–all address evils inherent in human trafficking.[70]

This is not to suggest that these groups never prioritize one form of trafficking over another—the Salvation Army, for example, maintains a

---

[68] The Salvation Army, "National Anti-trafficking Council," accessed September 29, 2009, http://www.salvationarmyusa.org/usn/www_usn_2.nsf/vw-dynamic-index/FBC65EB916B7547F852574400063B682?Opendocument.

[69] Ibid.

[70] Mary Ellen Dougherty, "The Role of Faith-Based Organizations in the Fight against Trafficking in Persons" (paper presented at the A Call to Action: Joining the Fight Against Trafficking in Persons, The Pontifical Gregorian University, June 17, 2004), 27.

separate Initiative Against Sexual Trafficking (IAST) in addition to its National Anti-Trafficking Council.[71] Nonetheless, their efforts to paint trafficking for sex and trafficking for labor as two manifestations of the same kind of crime represent a marked departure from the dominant religious abolitionist political interventions of the time.

Modern-Day Slavery

Further complicating the issue of how to differentiate between and comparatively assess various forms of exploitative labor, abolitionists' application of the historically and emotionally charged term "slavery" to instances of trafficking in persons is inconsistent, as is the basis for designation of activities as such. The most common usage establishes slavery as an umbrella concept encompassing situations such as trafficking in persons and chattel slavery, but conceptual distinctions are neither finely drawn nor internally policed within the movement. The Salvation Army provides a case in point of how "slavery" is conceptualized unevenly even by individual actors. In the following passage, for example, trafficking in persons is presented as both analogous to or like historical forms of slavery and also as a contemporary manifestation or type of slavery:

> Trafficking in persons is frequently referred to as modern-day slavery. Slavery is an apt analogy that shocks and challenges us. Americans in particular are moved by this comparison. To us, slavery is a sordid, indelible stain on our national heritage, but nevertheless it is an evil most believe we conquered and relegated to the history books. However, news media accounts, on-the-ground intelligence from nongovernmental organizations, and reports from agencies the U.S. Department of State and the United Nations Office on Drugs and Crime, create a different picture. They reveal the inescapable truth that trafficking is one of the principle means by which slavery survives.[72]

---

[71] The IAST, a coalition of Christian churches and parachurch organizations launched by the NAE in 1999, moved its home base to the Salvation Army in 2001. See Mark R. Elliott, "Faith-Based Responses to Trafficking in Women from Eastern Europe," in *Lilly Fellows Program National Research Conference on Christianity and Human Rights* (Birmingham, AL: Samford University, 2004), 9.

[72] The Salvation Army, "What Is Human Trafficking?" The Salvation Army, accessed September 29, 2009, http://www.salvationarmyusa.org/usn/combating-human-trafficking.

In a similar way, the Evangelical Covenant Church treats trafficking and debt bondage as conceptually distinct, in contrast to those who would classify the latter as an instance of the former, but considers both to be forms of slavery.[73] This type of distinction between trafficking in persons and debt bondage typically rests on the belief that "trafficking" requires the affected individual to be transported either domestically or internationally.

The above statement from the Salvation Army showcases a second frequently asserted thematic link between trafficking and slavery. Both religious and feminist abolitionists argue that trafficking, as a form of slavery, represents a shameful legacy of the past that has shockingly reappeared in the present.[74] At the same time, trafficking is established as the return of evils once defeated, religious abolitionists portray themselves as the natural heirs to the nineteenth-century abolitionists responsible for the cessation of slavery in that era. In some cases, continuity of struggle can be established for an individual organization. The Salvation Army, for instance, founded in 1865 London as an evangelical and charitable organization by Methodist minister William Booth and his wife Catherine, soon added anti-slavery activism to its portfolio. As the Web site of the IAST states:

> This is not the first time society has been called on to confront such evils. There were those like Amy Carmichael, missionary to India, who fought tirelessly to save children from wretched lives of temple prostitution. Likewise, there was the great Abolitionist struggle of 18th and 19th century England, led by heroes such as William Wilberforce, Granville Sharp, and Henry Thorton. Without the burning zeal of these great leaders, the British Empire's African slave trade may have continued indefinitely. And, too, in the late 1800s there was The Salvation Army's campaign to halt the trafficking of women and girls in Great Britain. Under the leadership of Bramwell and Florence Booth and many others the horrid trade was exposed and Parliament was forced to take action.[75]

---

[73] Evangelical Covenant Church.

[74] John R. Miller, "Call It Slavery," *Wilson Quarterly* 32, no. 3 (2008).

[75] Initiative Against Sexual Trafficking; See also Thompson quoted in Kathryn Jean Lopez, "Sexual Gulags: Facing and Fighting Sex Trafficking," *National Review Online*. One might also note the mingling here of prostitution, the enslavement of black Africans, and "white slavery."

In short, the Salvation Army can demonstrate both experience and success in fighting slavery. This includes the fight to end "sexual slavery," a term of art shared by religious and feminist abolitionists alike. The Salvation Army's reference to their earlier campaign against trafficking of women and girls in Great Britain is particularly notable for another reason. Their narrative of Josephine Butler, the nineteenth-century British heroine to contemporary feminist abolitionists, is markedly different from Barry's narrative, which I recounted in the previous chapter. In the Salvation Army's version of events, Butler's motivation to "rescue and restore 'fallen women'"[76] arose from her beliefs as an evangelical Christian. IAST coordinator Lisa I. Thompson likewise provides a triumphal reading of the investigative work of famous journalist W.T. Stead,[77] whose practices were decried by Barry in *Female Sexual Slavery* as exploitative and paternalistic.[78] As Thompson recounts the story:

> In one of the most fascinating chapters its history, the Salvation Army participated in the execution of an undercover investigation into the trafficking of young girls for prostitution—a detailed account of which was published in July 1885 by the Pall Mall Gazette in a series of articles called, "The Maiden Tribute of Modern Babylon." At the heart of the series was the report of how W. T. Stead, Pall Mall Gazette editor, arranged for the purchase of a young girl, Elizabeth Armstrong, from her mother, with the mother's knowledge that the girl would ostensibly meet with an illicit and immoral fate.[79]

While recognizing that both Stead and Rebecca Jarrett, an associate of Butler, were jailed for their purchase of Armstrong, Thompson goes on to describe their short sentences as a setback for the abolitionist cause, but not through any fault of Stead or the Salvation Army.[80] The ability of the Salvation Army to reclaim and represent a historical figure that Barry had invoked in 1979 as the guiding spirit of feminist abolitionism

---

[76] Thompson quoted in Barry recognizes Butler's religious motivation, but notes that Butler's feminist leanings led her to different conclusions than those made by the Salvation Army and other "religious moralists." Kathleen Barry, *Female Sexual Slavery* (New York: New York University Press, 1979), 29.

[77] See also Thompson quoted in Lopez.

[78] Barry, 24–28.

[79] Thompson quoted in Lopez.

[80] Ibid.

provides another clue that the abolitionist alliance has come at a cost to radical feminist principles.

A second, more prominent figure invoked by the Salvation Army, evangelical Christian William Wilberforce, is paramount as a hero and figure for emulation.[81] John Miller, for example, credits Wilberforce in part as the inspiration for his own abolitionist efforts, lauding the "great British reformer who led the 20-year campaign in Parliament to abolish the slave trade in the British Atlantic."[82] Marshall J. Breger writes in the *Journal of Ecumenical Studies* that former congressman Frank Wolf (R-VA),[83] who had been the primary sponsor of the Horowitz-driven Freedom from Religious Persecution Act in 1997, kept in his private office "a ceiling-to-floor poster of William Wilberforce."[84] Breger adds that as a result of Wilberforce's activism, "he may well have lost the chance to be Prime Minister, but he succeeded in ending this moral scourge on the British polity. Wilberforce's political stance is the lodestar that drives evangelicals in foreign policy [...]."[85]

Brownback, too, draws upon Wilberforce's example as a Christian dedicated to the noble cause of ending slavery, linking the work of Wilberforce to Christian abolitionists in the antebellum United States. Brownback traces his own anti-slavery zeal "to his roots in Pottawatomie County, the hotbed of evangelically inspired abolitionist agitation in the Kansas territory of the 1850s [He sees his work] as flowing from that same antislavery impulse that animated his for bearers."[86] In his introduction to a Senate Committee on Foreign Relations hearing "on worldwide slavery," Brownback noted that slavery "is an issue with historic significance to me growing up in Kansas, a state that was born in the battle in our country over whether it would be a free state or a

---

[81] See Nichols, 108; Haugen, *Good News About Injustice*; and Michael J. Horowitz, "Right Abolitionism," *The American Spectator*, December/January 2005/2006.

[82] Miller.

[83] Wolf, "a devout Presbyterian," is a friend and Christian prayer partner of fellow members of Congress Chris Smith and Tony Hall (D-OH) Hertzke, 134. Hertzke describes the trio as leaders in the faith-based international human rights community on Capitol Hill. Ibid., 134–40.

[84] Breger.

[85] Ibid.

[86] Hertzke, 142.

slave state."[87] Among those testifying, Brownback argued, were "people who have dedicated their lives [to] revealing the truth about modern day slavery. These are abolitionists in the great tradition of William Wilberforce."[88]

Haugen provides another example of the role that historical abolitionists play within the religious abolitionist imaginary. In an extensive 2009 *New Yorker* profile of the evangelical Christian human rights advocate, Samantha Power writes that Haugen "had wanted to be a lawyer ever since elementary school, where he read about Abraham Lincoln's emancipation of the slaves."[89] Similarly, in *Good News about Injustice* Haugen recounts the stories of "three courageous Christians"[90] he identifies as Sister K., Brother E., and Sister J., all of whom fought against "strongholds of injustice."[91] After describing the situations each one faced, Haugen reveals their identities: Dr. Kate Bushnell, "a devout Christian [...] heartbroken by the plight of girls victimized by forced prostitution in America [in the 1880s];"[92] Alabama minister Edgar Gardner Murphy, who at the turn of the twentieth century "was particularly burdened by the oppression suffered by the tens of thousands of children under age fourteen who toiled in the textile mills of his native American South;"[93] and Jessie Daniel Ames, who in 1930, "with only twelve compatriots [...] created the Association of Southern Women for the Prevention of Lynching (ASWPL)."[94]

In representing trafficked persons—especially women and girls trafficked for sex—as survivors of *slavery*, religious abolitionists are able to evoke compassion for those who have engaged in what otherwise might be considered sexual sin. The following excerpt from the IAST Web site is representative of movement efforts to establish sex trafficking as a fate no woman would choose:

---

[87] Committee on Foreign Relations, *Hearing on Slavery Throughout the World*, 106th Congress, Second Session, September 28, 2000, 3–4.

[88] Ibid.

[89] Power.

[90] Haugen, *Good News About Injustice: A Witness of Courage in a Hurting World*, 66.

[91] Ibid.

[92] Ibid.

[93] Ibid., 70.

[94] Ibid., 72.

> In their daily lives victims of trafficking endure unspeakable acts of physical brutality, violence and degradation including rape by so-called customers and pimps; undergo forced abortions; acquire drug and alcohol dependencies; live in fear of their lives and in fear for the lives of their family and friends; suffer acute psychological reactions as a result of their extreme physical and emotional trauma; and contract sexually transmitted diseases which all too often bring life-long illness or hasten death. If they survive, the physical, psychological and spiritual impacts of these experiences on victims are devastating and enduring.[95]

In the same way that feminist abolitionists highlight trafficked women's accounts of violence and degradation to establish sympathy for a marginalized group, religious abolitionists rely on the force of victims' personal testimonies as a call to action for evangelical churchgoers and the broader public to support abolitionist policies and social services. As Hertzke summarizes this approach:

> The [religious abolitionist] lobbying campaign also featured victims themselves—trafficked women—who provided the most dramatic moments in the process, riveting hushed audiences with the brutality of their accounts and the dignity of their mien. Their testimony, which received wide play in religious magazines, palpably affected members of Congress, energized the coalition, and fortified provisions of the legislation dealing with treatment of victims—who often suffer further victimization by host countries when free from traffickers.[96]

As I discussed in the preceding chapter, for feminist abolitionists this kind of personal testimony can be understood as both the strategic use of rhetoric and the logical extension of an epistemology that privileges women's lived experiences. For those responsible for setting the evangelical tone of religious abolitionism, the use of individual testimony reflects the same strategic ends but a markedly different epistemological standpoint.

Individual's accounts of one's personal relationship with Jesus Christ, which most often emphasize the moment of conversion but can also include evidence of God's influence throughout one's life, command a long-established respect within the evangelical tradition.

---

[95] Initiative Against Sexual Trafficking.

[96] Hertzke, 322.

El-Faizy documents the role such statements played in the "First Great Awakening" of the eighteenth century, and goes on to note:

> Indeed, giving one's testimony, the story of how one became a Christian, remains a popular tool in evangelical outreach today. It is common in Christian forums for people to talk about the journey that led them to Christ, much in the same way that alcoholics and drug users tell the stories of their sobriety in support groups.[97]

As with all argument from experience, testimonies of faith require some standard for establishing truth. The specific practices through which veracity is established differ according to local context, but must generally achieve the perceived status of fidelity to God's message.

Trafficking testimonies themselves have religious significance insofar as they serve to spread the message of Christianity. Delivered by trafficked persons, testimonies affirm God's grace and power and, in the case of converts to Christianity, represent the success of evangelism. Delivered by anti-trafficking experts, they can do the same thing. Laura Lederer, an attorney at the forefront of radical feminist anti-pornography and anti-trafficking campaigns, provides an unexpected and compelling example.

Although most feminist abolitionists disagree with the religious abolitionist beliefs regarding sexuality, they find common ground in the prioritization of sex trafficking above labor trafficking, and in their shared opposition to all forms of prostitution. Lederer herself played a critical role in bringing the two groups together.[98] In the beginning, religious activist Mariam Bell suggested that Lederer, who had worked with Bell on child pornography issues, join forces with Michael Horowitz to work against trafficking. As Hertzke characterizes the alliance, "this partnership between Horowitz and Lederer turned out to be pivotal in helping to set the agenda on international trafficking. Lederer brought to bear her voluminous documentation of the problem, and Horowitz connected her to the advocacy community in Washington."[99] The daughter of a Christian mother and Jewish father who was raised in a Unitarian

---

[97] El-Faizy, 14.

[98] Gretchen Soderlund, "Running from the Rescuers: New U.S. Crusades against Sex Trafficking and the Rhetoric of Abolition," *NWSA Journal* 17, no. 3 (2005): 68.

[99] Hertzke, 321.

Universalist church, Lederer explains how her fight against trafficking eventually led her to Christianity:

> After confronting the palpable evil of human trafficking every day for years, I felt as though I was looking into a black hole. Around that time, a Christian friend who worked in the Justice Department said to me, "You need the Lord guiding you. You need the reassurance he's right there beside you. You can't do this work by yourself." I began to go to church with him, and attended weekend retreats. I also began reading the Bible again, this time to hear what God had to say.

> [...] Working to stop the buying and selling of human beings is what led me to God [...] After I became a Christian, I realized God had been right there by my side all along, even in the darkest of days, and after that I didn't experience the same fear or pessimism; I know I'm not facing this evil alone.[100]

Lederer's narrative is not rare in religious abolitionist discussions of trafficking. Both *Good News About Injustice*, and *Set the Captives Free*, among others, emphasize the despair that those fighting against trafficking naturally feel in the face of evil and suffering, and the necessity of trusting in God's ability to steel his followers in their quest against injustice, and to ultimately provide justice to the trafficked and the traffickers.

Redemption: The Cross Is the Answer

Divine justice, however, is not the only gift that religious abolitionists believe is available to those ensnared in trafficking; so too is rehabilitation, and eventually, redemption. Lederer points to the centrality of Christian churches and organizations in "rescuing and restoring" women and children trafficked for sex. She asks the rhetorical question:

> Why is a victim-centered approach important? Unlike drug or arms trafficking, sex trafficking involves a human being who needs to be rescued and restored [...] I'm convinced faith-based communities all around the world are the only ones qualified to provide long-term care for trafficking survivors.

---

[100]Camerin Courtney, "TCW Talks to... Laura Lederer," *Today's Christian Woman*, January/February 2008.

It's the area of biggest need concerning sex trafficking, and I think it's a perfect area for the church to take leadership.[101]

The belief that redemption from sin and salvation are available solely through Christ underlies Lederer's contention that "faith-based communities [...] are the only ones qualified to provide long-term care for trafficking survivors." Lederer's comments to *Today's Christian Woman* echo the counsel in popular evangelical sex manuals and personal memoirs: "The cross is the answer, the solution, and the healing for those who have been victimized by sexual abuse."[102]

Though all anti-traffickers are committed to the notion that victims of trafficking can be rehabilitated, given appropriate resources, religious abolitionists profess a unique explanation for how and why trafficked persons can be, in their words, redeemed from the physical and emotional trauma of being trafficked. Ultimately, trafficked persons' spiritual needs must be attended to as much as their physical needs, and victims can find spiritual healing and cleansing through Christ alone. When evangelicals speak of the new life that they can offer trafficking survivors they are speaking of much more than relocation and job training. In *From Congress to the Brothel: A Journey of Hope, Healing, and Restoration*, Linda Smith echoes this position, telling "of what God has done through us *to give life* to the girls we get to serve."[103] The "new life" that Smith's organization, Shared Hope, provides is most significantly a new spiritual life; one that can take, for example, a "lovely, once hopeless, once utterly destroyed young woman" "full circle," resulting in marriage to a "wonderful young man."[104]

Redemption is not only for trafficked persons; religious abolitionists hold it as a possibility even for the traffickers themselves. Smith, for example, points to a young woman in India named Shobona, who was "once a brothel manager, before coming to know the Christian God's unconditional love for her and the girls she once brutalized."[105]

---

[101] Ibid.

[102] Gardner, 183; see also Joyce Meyer, *Beauty for Ashes* (Tulsa, OK: Harrison House, 1994).

[103] Smith, 5. Emphasis in the original. See also Dawn Herzog Jewell, "Red-Light Rescue," *Christianity Today*, January 2007.

[104] Smith, 100.

[105] Ibid., 16.

Traffickers who do not repent of their ways and accept God's saving grace, however, remain on Satan's side in the battle between good and evil. So too do the purportedly neutral, who the USCCB's Dougherty strikingly places among the culpable:

> In *The Divine Comedy*, in the third circle of the Inferno, Dante places at the gates of hell those influential people who, in the face of great moral debate, remained neutral. Fortunately, among faith-based organizations there are not many whose members are neutral about the moral issue of human trafficking.[106]

In rejecting neutrality to wholeheartedly join in the fight against trafficking and slavery, religious abolitionists are buoyed by a sense of fighting on God's side in a war of cosmic proportions.[107] Further in Lederer's testimony of her movement from feminist to religious abolitionism, she recalls how God renewed her strength to continue fighting in what had seemed to be an impossible battle:

> This battle was a David-and-Goliath one—the trans-national traffickers in the sex industry were Goliath—and suddenly the Lord seemed to speak directly to me. I love the passage in Ephesians 6:12–18: "For our struggle is not against flesh and blood, but against the rulers, against the authorities, against the powers of this dark world and against the spiritual forces of evil in the heavenly realms." That passage goes on to instruct us what to do: "Stand firm then, with the belt of truth buckled around your waist, with the breastplate of righteousness in place, and with your feet fitted with the readiness that comes from the gospel of peace. In addition to all this, take up the shield of faith." It's God's battle plan for living in the world.[108]

Lederer's words underscore the folly of seeking to understand religious abolitionism divorced from its larger context and relation to evangelical Christianity. Even as religious abolitionists grapple with seemingly technical questions regarding the precise wording of trafficking legislation or

---

[106] Dougherty, 29.

[107] See Cheryl Noble, "Justice Seekers: Bringing Rescue and Healing to the Oppressed," *Journal of Student Ministries* (2007): 42; Haugen, *Good News About Injustice: A Witness of Courage in a Hurting World*, 60–65; and Rayburn and Paxton, Week 1, Encounter 1.

[108] Courtney.

best practices in survivor care, this chapter has attempted to show how each element of abolitionist anti-trafficking efforts participates in a larger moral war in which trafficking in persons is but a single front.

CONCLUSION

The world of religious abolitionism is a world populated with heroes, predators, and the defenseless. Historical figures such as William Wilberforce and Amy Carmichael are represented as heroes not for their accomplishments alone, but also for the role that their Christian faith had played in giving them the strength to work for justice against great odds.[109] Such heroes are taken as role models in the most literal sense; contemporary abolitionists portray themselves as following directly in the footsteps of historical abolitionists, led by God to continue the work of their predecessors.[110] Abolitionists will not become millionaires, Brownback noted as he opened the Senate's second hearing on human trafficking, "but they will have riches in other places."[111]

And then there are those who will find "other places" less congenial.[112] If abolitionists are doing heroes' work on behalf of God, human predators[113] are doing the work of the devil.[114] *Set the Captives Free: A Bible Study Accompaniment to* Not for Sale, instructs those who cannot

[109] "Ordinary people can do extraordinary things when they make themselves available for God's purposes." Rayburn and Paxton, Week 1, Encounter 2.

[110] The religious abolitionist advocacy network also includes children, who speak of their mission in the same way. See, e.g., Zach Hunter, *Be the Change: Your Guide to Freeing Slaves and Changing the World* (Grand Rapids, MI: Zondervan, 1997); Noble; *Hearing on Slavery Throughout the World*.

[111] Subcommittee on Near Eastern and South Asian Affairs of the Committee on Foreign Relations, *Hearings on International Trafficking in Women and Children: Prosecution, Testimonies, and Prevention,* 106th Cong. 2nd session, February 22 and April 4, 2000, 76.

[112] *Set the Captives Free* reminds its readers that God will ultimately punish traffickers: "Just because we may not see God's judgment in our purview does not mean the wicked are not in God's line of sight." Rayburn and Paxton, Week 2, Encounter 4.

[113] See Linda Smith's discussion of the Predator Project: Smith, 71–72.

[114] As Cheryl Noble, the head of IJM's student ministry programming, declares, "I believe Satan trembles each time a student understands [Micah 6:8]'s call to 'do justice, love mercy, and walk humbly with your God' because he knows they have the courage and power to be effective—and I also believe Satan will do anything in his power to thwart the good works 'God prepared in advance for them to do' (Ephesians 2:10)," 43.

understand how God could countenance human trafficking to look beyond physical reality into the realm of the spiritual:

> No one is suggesting that those who exploit have no choice because of the 'devil-made-me-do-it' syndrome. However, the spiritual reality is that the devil is the ultimate evil, and behind all humankind's evil is the devil [...] The battle against human trafficking cannot solely be to stop the perpetrators but also to stop Satan's spread of evil. Christians must pray against the devil and his work of evil. *In other words, both exploited and exploiter need to be rescued from their sin, by Christ's sacrifice on the cross.*[115]

The final sentence in the passage above hearkens back to the theme of redemption, available for the repentant trafficker as well as for the trafficking victim.

It is thus to the victim subjects—the defenseless—that I turn. Religious abolitionists are agreed that trafficking victims are slaves, but divided as to the expanse of the category and whether subsets of slaves merit higher priority than others. Constituted as slaves, trafficked persons are further represented as passive,[116] needing rescue from their captors in most cases, and needing restoration and renewal from their physical and spiritual wounds in all cases. Once the victim has finally healed—and accepted baptism as a Christian—she can then go forth as a hero, following in the footsteps of a particularly powerful set of abolitionists: freed slaves.[117] Those who resist the earthly salvation of rescuers or the heavenly salvation of God are doomed to tread a different path.

REFERENCES

Amstutz, Mark R. "Faith-Based NGOs and U.S. Foreign Policy." In *The Influence of Faith: Religious Groups and U.S. Foreign Policy*, edited by Elliott Abrams, 175–87. Lanham: Rowman and Littlefied Publishers, Inc., 2001.

Bakker, Janel Kragt. Personal Communication, E-Mail, April 26, 2011.

---

[115] Rayburn and Paxton, Week 3, Encounter 4. Emphasis added.

[116] Victims are typically represented as having initially resisted their captors, particularly in narratives of sex trafficking, but eventually acquiescing once their spirits (and often, bodies) have been broken.

[117] Contemporary examples of trafficked persons who have gone on to become religious abolitionists include Given Kachepa and Francis Bok. See Hunter; *Hearing on Slavery Throughout the World*.

Barry, Kathleen. *Female Sexual Slavery*. New York: New York University Press, 1979.

Batstone, David B. *Not for Sale: The Return of the Global Slave Trade—And How We Can Fight It*. San Francisco: HarperCollins, 2007.

Bebbington, David. *Evangelicalism in Modern Britain: A History from the 1730s to the 1980s*. London: Unwin Hyman, 1989.

Breger, Marshall J. "Evangelicals and Jews in Common Cause." *Journal of Ecumenical Studies* 44, no. 1 (2009): 95–106.

Bush, George W. "Remarks at the National Training Conference on Human Trafficking in Tampa, Fl." In *Presidential Documents Online*, 1309–12. Washington, DC: Government Printing Office, 2004.

Courtney, Camerin. "TCW Talks to... Laura Lederer." *Today's Christian Woman*, January/February 2008.

Committee on Foreign Relations. *Hearing on Slavery Throughout the World*, 106th Congress, Second Session, September 28, 2000.

DeRogatis, Amy. "'Born Again Is a Sexual Term': Demons, STDs, and God's Healing Sperm." *Journal of the American Academy of Religion* 77, no. 2 (2009): 275–302.

Dougherty, Mary Ellen. "The Role of Faith-Based Organizations in the Fight against Trafficking in Persons." Paper presented at the A Call to Action: Joining the Fight Against Trafficking in Persons, The Pontifical Gregorian University, June 17, 2004.

El-Faizy, Monique. *God and Country: How Evangelicals Have Become America's New Mainstream*. New York: Bloomsbury USA, 2006.

Elliott, Mark R. "Faith-Based Responses to Trafficking in Women from Eastern Europe." In *Lilly Fellows Program National Research Conference on Christianity and Human Rights*, Samford University, Birmingham, AL, 2004.

Evangelical Covenant Church. "2008 Resolution on Global Slavery and Human Trafficking." Evangelical Covenant Church. Accessed September 29, 2009. http://www.covchurch.org/2008-slavery-human-trafficking/.

Free the Slaves. "Faith in Action: Christianity." Free the Slaves. Accessed September 29, 2009. http://www.freetheslaves.net/take-action/faith-in-action-ending-slavery/.

Gardner, Tim Alan. *Sacred Sex: A Spiritual Celebration of Oneness in Marriage*. Colorado Springs: Waterbrook Press, 2002.

Graham, Billy. *The Journey: How to Live by Faith in an Uncertain World*. Nashville: W Publishing Group, 2006.

Hart, Roderick P., and John L. Pauley. *The Political Pulpit Revisited*. West Lafayette: Purdue University Press, 2005.

Haugen, Gary A. *Good News About Injustice*. Downers Grove, IL: InterVarsity Press, 1999.

————. *Good News About Injustice: A Witness of Courage in a Hurting World*. Tenth Anniversary ed. Downer's Grove, IL: InterVarsity Press Books, 2009.

Helguero, Francis. "Recovering God's Justice: Interview with International Justice Mission President Gary Haugen." *The Christian Post*, March 7, 2005.

Hertzke, Allen D. *Freeing God's Children: The Unlikely Alliance for Global Human Rights*. Lanham, MD: Rowman & Littlefield, 2004.

Horowitz, Michael J. "How to Win Friends and Influence Culture." *Christianity Today*, September 2005, 70–78.

————. "Right Abolitionism." *The American Spectator*, December/January 2005/2006, 14–17.

Hunter, Zach. *Be the Change: Your Guide to Freeing Slaves and Changing the World*. Grand Rapids, MI: Zondervan, 1997.

Initiative Against Sexual Trafficking. "What Is the Initiative against Sexual Trafficking." The Salvation Army. Accessed September 29, 2009. http://www.iast.net.

Institute for the Study of American Evangelicals (ISAE). "Defining Evangelicalism." Wheaton College. Accessed September 29, 2009. http://isae.wheaton.edu/defining-evangelicalism/.

————. "Defining Evangelicalism: Fundamentalism." Wheaton College. Accessed September 29, 2009. http://isae.wheaton.edu/defining-evangelicalism/fundamentalism/.

————. "Evangelicals and the End Times." Wheaton College. Accessed September 29, 2009. http://www.wheaton.edu/ISAE/Defining-Evangelicalism/End-Times.

International Justice Mission. "Speaker—Gary Haugen, President and CEO." Accessed September 29, 2009. http://www.ijm.org/resources/garyhaugen.

Irons, Charles F. *The Origins of Proslavery Christianity: White and Black Evangelicals in Colonial and Antebellum Virginia*. Chapel Hill: The University of North Carolina Press, 2008.

Jackson, Patrick Thaddeus. *Civilizing the Enemy: German Reconstruction and the Invention of the West*. Ann Arbor: University of Michigan, 2006.

Jewell, Dawn Herzog. "Red-Light Rescue." *Christianity Today*, January 2007.

Krebs, Ronald R., and Jennifer K. Lobasz. "Fixing the Meaning of 9/11: Hegemony, Coercion, and the Road to War in Iraq." *Security Studies* 16, no. 3 (July–September 2007): 409–51.

Kristof, Nicholas D. "Learning from the Sin of Sodom." *The New York Times*, February 28, 2010.

Lindsay, D. Michael. "Evangelicals in the Power Elite: Elite Cohesion Advancing a Movement." *American Sociological Review* 73 (February 2008): 60–82.

Lopez, Kathryn Jean. "Sexual Gulags: Facing and Fighting Sex Trafficking." *National Review Online*.

Medhurst, Martin J. "Forging a Civil-Religious Construct for the Twenty-First Century." In *The Political Pulpit Revisited*, edited by Roderick P. Hart and John L. Pauley, 109–16. West Lafayette: Purdue University Press, 2005.

Meyer, Joyce. *Beauty for Ashes*. Tulsa, OK: Harrison House, 1994.

Miller, John R. "Call It Slavery." *Wilson Quarterly* 32, no. 3 (Summer 2008): 52–56.

Minnery, Tom, and Glenn T. Stanton. "Family Integrity." In *Toward an Evangelical Public Policy*, edited by Ronald J. Sider and Diane Knippers, 245–64. Grand Rapids: BakerBooks, 2005.

Morse, Anne. "The Abolitionist." *World Magazine*, March 1, 2003.

———. "Screaming People Awake." *World Magazine*, February 3, 2001.

National Association of Evangelicals (NAE). "Statement of Faith." Accessed September 29, 2009. http://www.nae.net/about-us/statement-of-faith.

Nichols, Joel A. "Evangelicals and Human Rights: The Continuing Ambivalence of Evangelical Christians' Support for Human Rights." *Journal of Law and Religion* 7 (2009): 629–62.

Nir, Ori. "US Official Does 'God's Work': Eradicating Slavery." *Forward: The Jewish Daily*, May 7, 2004.

Noble, Cheryl. "Justice Seekers: Bringing Rescue and Healing to the Oppressed." *Journal of Student Ministries* (May/June 2007): 40–43.

Orr, J. Scott. "House Panel Moves to Stem Sex-Slave Trade and Aid Victims." *The Star-Ledger*, August 5, 1999, 4.

Potter, Ronald C. "Good Question: Was Slavery God's Will?" *Christianity Today*, May 22, 2000.

Power, Samantha. "The Enforcer: A Christian Lawyer's Global Crusade." *The New Yorker*, January 19, 2009, 52.

Rayburn, Shirley Love, and Danielle Paxton. "Set the Captives Free: A Bible Study Accompaniment to Not for Sale." Montara, CA: Not for Sale Campaign, 2009.

Safire, William. "The New Old Testament." *The New York Times Magazine*, May 25, 1997.

Shapiro, Nina. "The New Abolitionists." *Seattle Weekly*, August 25, 2004.

Sider, Ronald J. "Justice, Human Rights, and Government." In *Toward an Evangelical Public Policy*, edited by Ronald J. Sider and Diane Knippers, 163–93. Grand Rapids: Baker Books, 2005.

Skinner, E. Benjamin. *A Crime So Monstrous: Face-to-Face with Modern-Day Slavery*. New York: Free Press, 2009.

Smith, Linda. *From Congress to the Brothel: A Journey of Hope, Healing, and Restoration*. Vancouver, WA: Shared Hope International, 2007.

Soderlund, Gretchen. "Running from the Rescuers: New U.S. Crusades against Sex Trafficking and the Rhetoric of Abolition." *NWSA Journal* 17, no. 3 (Fall 2005): 64–87.

Specter, Michael. "Traffickers' New Cargo: Naïve Slavic Women." *The New York Times*, January 11, 1998.

The Salvation Army. "National Anti-trafficking Council." Accessed September 29, 2009. http://www.salvationarmyusa.org/usn/www_usn_2.nsf/vw-dynamic-index/FBC65EB916B7547F852574400063B682?Opendocument.

———. "What Is Human Trafficking?" The Salvation Army. Accessed September 29, 2009. http://www.salvationarmyusa.org/usn/combating-human-trafficking.

Subcommittee on International Operations and Human Rights of the Committee on International Relations. *Hearing on Trafficking of Women and Children in the International Sex Trade*, 106th Cong. 1st session, September 14, 1999.

Subcommittee on Near Eastern and South Asian Affairs of the Committee on Foreign Relations. *Hearings on International Trafficking in Women and Children: Prosecution, Testimonies, and Prevention*, 106th Cong. 2nd session, February 22 and April 4, 2000.

Thuesen, Peter J. "The Logic of Mainline Churchliness: Historical Background Since the Reformation." In *The Quiet Hand of God: Faith-Based Activism and the Public Role of Mainline Protestantism*, edited by Robert Wuthnow and John Hyde Evans, 27–53. Berkeley: University of California Press, 2002.

Wills, Garry. *Head and Heart: American Christianities*. New York: Penguin Press, 2007.

CHAPTER 6

Victims, Villains, and the Virtuous

In *Rethinking Trafficking in Women*, Claudia Aradau points to a widespread lack of recognition "that debates about who is trafficked, what type of migrant, prostitute, etc. they are, are not just technical but deeply political."[1] In this book I have argued that the "problem of human trafficking" is itself inescapably political. Research that approvingly portrays the global proliferation of anti-trafficking initiatives as unproblematic instances of the triumph of an emancipatory liberalism fails to recognize the play of power relations *internal* to norm construction. In contrast, this book serves as a call to appreciate the continual, power-laden process of shaping and renegotiating meaning that is entailed in the production of political "problems." The anti-trafficking discourses I have examined further illustrate the many ways in which TANs and the state are mutually implicated in governance and its attendant relations of power. Both sets of actors have played a key role in establishing trafficking as a problem necessitating governmental intervention, constituting traffickers and trafficking victims as subjects, and reproducing as well as reshaping conceptualizations of migrants, slaves, gender, race, religion, and the United States.

I have also shown that anti-trafficking discourses, even when dominant or when specific elements are widely shared, are never fully stable or successful. Discourses necessarily contain gaps, fissures, and

[1]Claudia Aradau, *Rethinking Trafficking in Women: Politics out of Security* (New York: Palgrave Macmillan, 2008), 14.

J. K. Lobasz, *Constructing Human Trafficking*, Human Rights Interventions, https://doi.org/10.1007/978-3-319-91737-5_6

instabilities—the differences in interpretation and emphasis, internal and external criticism, and other signs of the impossibility of total conceptual closure.[2] I argue that existing cleavages provide multiple possibilities for different perspectives and policies concerning the practices currently associated with human trafficking.

CONTRIBUTIONS OF A CRITICAL CONSTRUCTIVISM

Anti-trafficking as an Anti-politics

> Mr. Speaker, our legislation, H.R. 3244, has attracted such broad support not only because it is pro-women, pro-child, pro-human rights, pro-family values, and anti-crime, but because it addresses a problem that absolutely cries out for a solution.
>
> —Representative Chris Smith[3]

Within the discipline of international relations, some of the most noteworthy scholarship regarding human trafficking has been undertaken by liberal constructivists[4] interested in explaining the success of an international norm against trafficking. In the liberal constructivist tradition, individuals such as Kathleen Barry, Laura Lederer, Paul Wellstone, and Chris Smith can be seen as *norm entrepreneurs* whose role is to

> mobilize popular opinion and political support both within their host country and abroad; they stimulate and assist in the creation of like-minded organizations in other countries; and they play a significant role in elevating their objective beyond its identification with the national interests of their governments.[5]

[2] Jutta Weldes, "Bureaucratic Politics: A Critical Constructivist Assessment," *Mershon International Studies Review* 42, no. 2 (1998): 219.

[3] Christopher H. Smith, *Remarks on Trafficking Victims Protection Act of 2000* (Washington, DC: U.S. House of Representatives, 2000), H2683.

[4] E.g., Andrea M. Bertone, "Transnational Activism to Combat Trafficking in Persons," *Brown Journal of World Affairs* 10, no. 2 (2004); Birgit Locher, *Trafficking in Women in the European Union: Norms, Advocacy-Networks and Policy-Change* 1. Aufl. ed. (Wiesbaden: VS Verlag für Sozialwissenschaften, 2007), Thesis (doctoral)—Universität Bremen, 2002; and Alison Brysk, "Sex as Slavery? Understanding Private Wrongs," *Human Rights Review* 12, no. 3 (2011).

[5] Ethan A. Nadelmann, "Global Prohibition Regimes: The Evolution of Norms in International Society," *International Organization* 44, no. 4 (1990): 489.

Likewise, Smith's statement on behalf of H.R. 3244 is easily identified as an instance of framing a commodity-like norm.[6] An underlying entity—the Trafficking Victims Protection Act of 2000—is packaged and presented in an attractive manner by its sponsor in the hopes that audiences buy the product.[7]

I suggest, however, that there is more to be gleaned from Smith's above remarks, and that a critical constructivist perspective helps to capture these additional facets. Take, for instance, the congressman's identification of human trafficking as "a problem that absolutely cries out for a solution." This book represents a call for scholars of international norms and transnational advocacy networks to pay greater attention to the politics of norm constitution, including the production of "problems" to be addressed and subjects to govern and be governed. In Chapters 3 and 5, I showed that the problem with which Smith is concerned pertains to the cross-border migration of women and girls forced into prostitution. That problem, as constructed by Smith and his fellow religious abolitionists, is one of "mass rape," of a uniquely brutal practice in which "millions of women and children who are forced every day to submit to the most atrocious offenses against their persons and against their dignity as human beings."[8] In contrast, Senator Paul Wellstone, many of his Democratic colleagues in Congress, and senior Clinton administration officials were concerned with a different problem, albeit one with some overlapping features. The problem was not only "sexual slavery," but one

[6]On framing, see Margaret E. Keck and Kathryn Sikkink, *Activists Beyond Borders: Advocacy Networks in International Politics* (Ithaca, NY: Cornell University Press, 1998), 17. Jutta Joachim, "Framing Issues and Seizing Opportunities: The UN, NGOs, and Women's Rights," *International Studies Quarterly* 47 (2003); Joshua William Busby, "Bono Made Jesse Helms Cry: Jubilee 2000, Debt Relief, and Moral Action in International Politics," ibid. 51, no. 2 (2007).

[7]My language here is meant to emphasize Laffey and Weldes' reference to norms scholars' reliance on "the commodity metaphor." In their words, "In order to be causally effective, 'ideas require 'political entrepreneurs' whose role is to 'select' and then to 'market,' 'sell' or 'peddle' them." "Beyond Belief: Ideas and Symbolic Technologies in the Study of International Relations," *European Journal of International Relations* 3, no. 2 (1997): 207. Nadelmann employs another suggestive metaphor, that of proselytizing, 482. As generations of "religious entrepreneurs" have demonstrated, the two metaphors are not mutually exclusive.

[8]Subcommittee on International Operations and Human Rights of the Committee on International Relations, *Hearing on Trafficking of Women and Children in the International Sex Trade*, 106th Cong. 1st session, September 14, 1999, 4.

in which individuals "are brought to this country as employees, often, legally and illegally, and are then worked beyond all reasonable length of time in completely abhorrent conditions."[9] The feminist abolitionists surveyed in Chapter 4, meanwhile, saw a problem of worldwide sexual oppression of women, drawing connections

> between the private violence of incest, rape, and spousal abuse and the public violence of commercial sexual exploitation; between local prostitution businesses and the global sex industry; between the condition of prostituted women and the status of all women.[10]

As these examples make clear, a great deal of work was required to shoehorn these various practices into a single problem, and even then relevant actors argued (and have, in the subsequent eleven years, continued to argue) about the nature of the problem.

Liberal constructivists have not been wholly inattentive to these issues. Keck and Sikkink, for example, explain that the term "violence against women" emerged as the result of a process

> through which the [international women's human rights] network helped 'create' the issue, in part through naming, renaming, and working out definitions, whereby the concept 'violence against women' eventually unified many practices that in the early 1970s were not understood to be connected.[11]

What is omitted from such accounts, particularly those concerned with "values or principled ideas"[12] is recognition of the politics—the power relations—intimately woven into the unification of formerly disarticulated practices as a single issue. Smith's description of the TVPA as

---

[9] Sam Gejdenson, *Remarks on Trafficking Victims Protection Act of 2000* (Washington, DC: U.S. House of Representatives, 2000), H2684. See also Subcommittee on International Operations and Human Rights of the Committee on International Relations, *H.R. 1356, the Freedom from Sexual Trafficking Act of 1999, Markup*, 1st session, 106th Congress, August 4, 1999, 5.

[10] Dorchen A. Leidholdt, "Demand and the Debate," Coalition against Trafficking in Women, accessed September 29, 2009, http://www.childtrafficking.com/Docs/leidholdt_2003_demand_and_the_debate.pdf.

[11] Keck and Sikkink, 171.

[12] Ibid., 2.

"pro-family values," for example, is not merely an instance of strategic framing, or of signaling directed toward a conservative Christian political constituency. Rather, the articulation of "family values" rhetoric to anti-trafficking brings with it a set of beliefs about sexuality and gender relations that shape and suffuse the constitution of subjects[13] and the creation of policy.[14] The exercise of power is veiled, however, by assertions of broad or universal support, stipulations that the "moral question" of opposition to trafficking has been settled, the taking for granted of the value of a norm against trafficking, and even by accounts of dueling definitions that presume a "correct" definition is somehow attainable.[15]

Alison Brysk's liberal constructivist analyses of anti-trafficking norms demonstrate a related problem. On the one hand, Brysk's efforts in her later work to highlight some of the harmful consequences of dominant constructions of trafficking are both laudable and rare in this strand of the literature, and I do not wish to minimize the importance of this contribution. On the other hand, these efforts repeat a limitation of similar feminist critiques of anti-trafficking discourses highlighted in Chapter 2. Brysk draws on the work of Agustín and Doezema and Kempadoo[16] to argue, for example, that "anti-trafficking policies are systematically distorted by uninformed or biased analyses of sex work and the wider spectrum of forced labor."[17] This reading of the aforementioned scholar-activists is plausible yet limited in important and revealing ways suggested by Brysk's use of the words "distorted" and "biased." Recall my earlier arguments concerning not the likelihood but the impossibility of

---

[13] The frequent references to fathers and daughters in Chapter 3, for example, relates to evangelical Christian beliefs about fathers' responsibilities for guarding their daughters' sexual purity. See Amy DeRogatis, "'Born Again Is a Sexual Term': Demons, STDs, and God's Healing Sperm," *Journal of the American Academy of Religion* (2009): 279.

[14] Post-TVPA policy is outside the scope of the present work, but see Jacqueline Berman, "The Left, the Right, and the Prostitute: The Making of U.S. Anti-trafficking in Persons Policy," *Tulane Journal of International and Comparative Law* 14 (2005–2006); Elizabeth Bernstein, "The Sexual Politics of the 'New Abolitionism'," *Differences* 18, no. 3 (2007).

[15] See also Wendy Brown, *States of Injury: Power and Freedom in Late Modernity* (Princeton: Princeton University Press, 1995), 40.

[16] Specifically Laura María Agustín, *Sex at the Margins: Migration, Labor Markets, and the Rescue Industry* (London: Zed Books, 2007); Kamala Kempadoo and Jo Doezema, eds., *Global Sex Workers: Rights, Resistance, and Redefinition* (New York: Routledge, 1998).

[17] Brysk, 259.

apolitical or objective conceptualizations of human trafficking, and the consequences of transforming trafficking from a political problem into a technical challenge. At the same time Brysk refers to the social construction of human trafficking—again, in a manner that departs in important ways from, e.g., Keck and Sikkink's account of the violence against women frame and Locher's explanation for the success of the anti-trafficking norm in the EU—the specter of a discrete problem whose true nature states and transnational civil society have yet to adequately capture remains.[18]

CONDITIONS OF POSSIBILITY AND POSSIBILITIES FOR CHANGE

The U.S. Trafficking Victims Protection Act of 2000 represented the first and most influential comprehensive anti-trafficking legislation passed by an individual state. Legislators and civil servants in the U.S. joined abolitionists and NGO representatives in deploying narratives of sexually violated feminine innocence, a racialized opposition between "trafficking victims" and "illegal immigrants," human rights rhetoric, and parallels to the African slave trade throughout the legislative process. The campaign against human trafficking was soon rendered politically and morally unassailable as a campaign on behalf of quintessentially American values.

At the same time, the latter chapters of this book remind us that discourses resist closure. In contrast to structural accounts of totalizing systems such as that offered by radical feminists, my analysis of the production of human trafficking emphasizes the ability to uncover space for contestation even within putatively hegemonic systems of meaning. Feminist political philosopher Judith Butler famously argues that even something as seemingly impervious to change as gender can be called into question: "That there is a need for repetition at all is a sign that identity is not self-identical. It requires to be instituted again and again, which is to say that it runs the risk of becoming de-instituted at every interval."[19] Following Butler, one might view the ritualized recitations of trafficking's perils as evidence that the case for intervention requires renewal.[20]

---

[18] One might say that human trafficking's "turtles," to borrow a phrase, only go so far down. Chris Brown, "'Turtles All the Way Down': Anti-foundationalism, Critical Theory and International Relations," *Millennium*, no. 23 (1994).

[19] Judith Butler, "Imitation and Gender Insubordination," in *Inside/Out*, ed. Diana Fuss (New York: Routledge, 1991), 309.

[20] Quite literally insofar as the TVPA required reauthorization in 2003, 2005, 2008, and 2013.

The possibility that such times offer opportunities for change is not only speculative. My genealogy of feminist and religious abolitionism points to inconsistencies as well as regularities, and discursively linkages that are open to rearticulation. The specific substance of a future rearticulation, or even a rejection, of the subject categories of human trafficking cannot be predicted with any certainty. I refrain from advocating a particular position in this book as well for the reasons given in Chapter 1. My goal has been neither to establish a "better" definition of human trafficking, nor to resolve disputes within anti-trafficking policy and advocacy spheres, but rather to understand how the US anti-trafficking debate has been shaped and what it reveals about the role of norms and productive power in the study of global governance more generally.

REFERENCES

Agustín, Laura María. *Sex at the Margins: Migration, Labor Markets, and the Rescue Industry*. London: Zed Books, 2007.

Aradau, Claudia. *Rethinking Trafficking in Women: Politics out of Security*. New York: Palgrave Macmillan, 2008.

Berman, Jacqueline. "The Left, the Right, and the Prostitute: The Making of U.S. Anti-trafficking in Persons Policy." *Tulane Journal of International and Comparative Law* 14 (2005–2006): 269–93.

Bernstein, Elizabeth. "The Sexual Politics of the 'New Abolitionism'." *Differences* 18, no. 3 (2007): 128.

Bertone, Andrea M. "Transnational Activism to Combat Trafficking in Persons." *Brown Journal of World Affairs* 10, no. 2 (Winter/Spring 2004): 9–22.

Brown, Chris. "'Turtles All the Way Down': Anti-foundationalism, Critical Theory and International Relations." *Millennium*, no. 23 (June 1994): 213–36.

Brown, Wendy. *States of Injury: Power and Freedom in Late Modernity*. Princeton: Princeton University Press, 1995.

Brysk, Alison. "Sex as Slavery? Understanding Private Wrongs." *Human Rights Review* 12, no. 3 (2011): 259–70.

Busby, Joshua William. "Bono Made Jesse Helms Cry: Jubilee 2000, Debt Relief, and Moral Action in International Politics." *International Studies Quarterly* 51, no. 2 (2007): 247–75.

Butler, Judith. "Imitation and Gender Insubordination." In *Inside/Out*, edited by Diana Fuss. New York: Routledge, 1991.

DeRogatis, Amy. "'Born Again Is a Sexual Term': Demons, STDs, and God's Healing Sperm." *Journal of the American Academy of Religion* 77, no. 2 (2009): 275–302.

Finnemore, Martha, and Kathryn Sikkink. "International Norm Dynamics and Political Change." *International Organization* 52, no. 4 (1998): 887–917.

Gejdenson, Sam. *Remarks on Trafficking Victims Protection Act of 2000.* Washington, DC: U.S. House of Representatives, 2000.

Joachim, Jutta. "Framing Issues and Seizing Opportunities: The UN, NGOs, and Women's Rights." *International Studies Quarterly* 47 (2003): 247–74.

Keck, Margaret E., and Kathryn Sikkink. *Activists Beyond Borders: Advocacy Networks in International Politics.* Ithaca, NY: Cornell University Press, 1998.

Kempadoo, Kamala, and Jo Doezema, eds. *Global Sex Workers: Rights, Resistance, and Redefinition.* New York: Routledge, 1998.

Laffey, Mark, and Jutta Weldes. "Beyond Belief: Ideas and Symbolic Technologies in the Study of International Relations." *European Journal of International Relations* 3, no. 2 (1997): 193.

Leidholdt, Dorchen A. "Demand and the Debate." Coalition against Trafficking in Women. Accessed September 29, 2009. http://www.childtrafficking.com/Docs/leidholdt_2003_demand_and_the_debate.pdf.

Locher, Birgit. *Trafficking in Women in the European Union: Norms, Advocacy-Networks and Policy-Change* 1. Aufl. ed. Wiesbaden: VS Verlag für Sozialwissenschaften, 2007. Thesis (doctoral)—Universität Bremen, 2002.

Nadelmann, Ethan A. "Global Prohibition Regimes: The Evolution of Norms in International Society." *International Organization* 44, no. 4 (Autumn 1990): 479–526.

Scott, Joan Wallach. "Deconstructing Equality Versus Difference, or, the Uses of Poststructuralist Theory for Feminism." In *Feminist Social Thought: A Reader*, edited by Diana Tietjens Meyers, 758–70. New York: Routledge, 1988.

Smith, Christopher H. *Remarks on Trafficking Victims Protection Act of 2000.* Washington, DC: U.S. House of Representatives, 2000.

Subcommittee on International Operations and Human Rights of the Committee on International Relations. *H.R. 1356, the Freedom from Sexual Trafficking Act of 1999, Markup*, 1st session, 106th Congress, August 4, 1999.

Subcommittee on International Operations and Human Rights of the Committee on International Relations. *Hearing on Trafficking of Women and Children in the International Sex Trade*, 106th Cong. 1st session, September 14, 1999.

Weldes, Jutta. "Bureaucratic Politics: A Critical Constructivist Assessment." *Mershon International Studies Review* 42, no. 2 (November 1998): 216–25.

INDEX

© The Editor(s) (if applicable) and The Author(s), under exclusive license to Springer International Publishing AG, part of Springer Nature 2019
J. K. Lobasz, *Constructing Human Trafficking*, Human Rights Interventions, https://doi.org/10.1007/978-3-319-91737-5